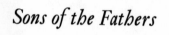

Sons of the Fathers

Sons of the Fathers

THE CIVIL RELIGION OF THE
AMERICAN REVOLUTION

CATHERINE L.
ALBANESE

Temple University Press
PHILADELPHIA

To my parents,

   Louis and Theresa

Temple University Press, Philadelphia 19122
© 1976 by Temple University. All rights reserved
Published 1976
Printed in the United States of America
International Standard Book Number: 0-87722-073-5
Library of Congress Catalog Card Number: 76-17712

Contents

Foreword

Two ages come together in this book. The first is the author's own. She intends to throw light on a major controversy of the late twentieth century. Rather than write a tract for the times, an argument without grounding, she traces its origins in the outlines of debate in the late eighteenth century. Catherine Albanese makes clear, on the first few pages and in her subtitle, that the period of Enlightenment, Revolution, and nation-building set many of the terms for the "civil religion" controversy in today's world.

The men and women of the late eighteenth century did not use the term "civil religion." It derives, says its modern proponent, from the thought of Jean-Jacques Rousseau. As such, it would be a questionable and alien import. Yet the name is not important. The idea of a civic faith that would somehow unite disparate and differing populations was already articulated in the Roman Empire, when *Romanitas* and the religiously sanctioned "Roman Way of Life" served as a substructure for coexistent faiths in the known world.

The nation-builders of America had a similar problem: how to find the cement for social bonding, the lubrication for cultural process, the common terms for public discourse. Already by then it was clear that people had come to these shores with too many and too diverse opinions to mesh and to meld with ease. How could they settle disputes about morality and virtue? How would they find themselves drawn together over against foreign powers?

It was unthinkable that they could do so without something like a common religion, but this common faith did not dare to appear to be opposed to the differing views about ultimate reality held by Deists and Congregationalists, Episcopalians and nonbelievers, Presbyterians and Nothingarians.

In that climate, it was Benjamin Franklin who first stepped forward with a plea. In 1749 he wrote "Proposals Relating to the Education of Youth in Pennsylvania." His fellow-citizens should note that

History will . . . afford frequent Opportunities of showing the Necessity of a *Publick Religion*, from its Usefulness to the Publick; the Advantage of a Religious Character among private Persons; the Mischiefs of Superstition, &c. and the Excellency of the CHRISTIAN RELIGION above all others antient or modern.

Traces of concern for religious character and the excellency of the inherited Christianity show up on these pages, but for the most part it is Franklin's *Publick Religion* that is the subject.

Debate over its necessity, its possibility, its existence, and its character course through subsequent American history. But so long as the old Protestant majority retained enough power, the argument was not urgent. In the middle of the twentieth century a new understanding of pluralism, one that saw Protestantism, Catholicism, Judaism, and none of the above vying for place and tolerating each other, inspired fresh statements about the nation's bonding. In 1955 Will Herberg blasted a civic faith that he saw to be necessary, not all evil, but all to be judged by canons and norms of biblical prophetic traditions. Shortly before, another sociologist, Robin Williams, had reminded his readers of what the European traditions in sociology of religion as propounded by Emile Durkheim and Max Weber knew, that a complex society would need and would generate a common faith.

If Herberg helped set the terms for the recent debate in a negative framework, the historian Sidney E. Mead was to come on the scene with a very positive affirmation of this civic faith, whose roots he traced to the period Professor Albanese is discussing, the late eighteenth century. That was the hinge period in American religion (and, indirectly, politics), averred Mead, a contention with which Professor Albanese and I would agree. Mead spoke of "the religion of the Republic." It was Robert N. Bellah, another sociologist, who in an essay printed in 1967 spoke of an institutionalized civil religion in America's past and present. Debate over it has ensued.

So much for background, for light on why there is fuss and fury about the topic. I have just mentioned that the late eighteenth century is a hinge period, the pivot or turning point for the spiritual side of American history. If that is so, it deserves careful examination, since an understanding of it will illumine much of what follows. It may also explain why Americans have been able to tolerate so much toleration, experiment with so much experiment, and endure so much change while feeling that they are in continuity with their past. They have *had* their revolution. Their past seems to come to them as a package deal from the generations of the "founding fathers." The French visitor Alexis de Tocqueville pondered this feature of American life (*Oeuvre complètes*, ed. J. P. Mayer, 1(2): 262, 264):

Two things are astonishing about America, the great changeableness of most human behavior and the singular fixity of certain principles. . . . Men living in democratic societies . . . are forever varying, altering, and restoring secondary matters, but they are very careful not to touch fundamentals. They love change, but they dread revolutions.

They dread all revolutions but one. That one had made them the first modern power to free itself from colonial dominion, to win independence. "The King is Dead = God is Dead!" New assumptions about the divine right of monarchs and people came to operate. *Novus ordo saeclorum*, a new order of ages was here. They had passed over the hump of transition, carrying their ideology with them, to their new approved social contract or covenant. Ever after, they would have to add to or lighten the burden of that original package and baggage, to transform its contents. But basically the contents had been determined. They were aware of the "singular fixity of certain principles" even if they had come to these as the result of a process marked by great fluidity, flux, and subtlety in understanding change.

The reader of *Sons of the Fathers*—the maleness and patriarchalism of metaphors in the documents of the period are simply plunked onto the table for purposes of pondering by an author who cannot be content with all the terms—will have considerable difficulty seeing just how and why the debate emerged in the form it did late in the eighteenth century. Yes, as Albanese shows time and again, there are continuities with colonial and especially New England religion. The biblical metaphors are consistent and constant. But the proponents of the new faith have also moved into a new mental condominium. They are no longer living out a plot that had been simply prescripted in the Hebrew Scriptures. They might still be on errands and missions, but they now mark their days less by the story of a historical exodus or exile or trip toward the land of promise and the eternal city than by what an immediate nature and reason make available to them in what Franklin called "the age of experiments."

If what preceded this period seems to show up only as shadow, reflection, or raw material for new production, what follows also can hardly be anticipated. Given the new celebrations of reason and the Enlightenment myths, who could have foreseen that in the subsequent century revivalists and evangelists would reinvoke and intensify the language that had been forged in the First Great Awakening of the 1730s? Who would have envisioned that "the affections" and the emotion stirred by promulgators of particular visions, agents of sub-communities, would so dominate the Protestant scene? And who could have envisioned the extent to which continental immigrants, Catholic, Lutheran, Orthodox, and Jewish, would come to embody what to the civil religionists of Washington's time would have looked like the "mischiefs of superstition" and less than excellent versions of the Christian religion?

Yet those who followed in the faith of the "sons of the fathers" rarely saw much clash between the public and the private, the common and the particular, the national and the sectarian faiths. Tocqueville's traveling companion, Gustave de Beaumont, observed that "this extreme tolerance on the one hand towards religion in general—on the other this considerable zeal of each individual for his own religion, is a phenomenon I can't yet explain to myself." He noted that he would "gladly know how a lively and sincere faith can get on with such a perfect toleration; how one can have equal respect for religions whose dogmas differ." His tentative conclusion, that Americans could live with both because their faiths were broad but not deep, had enough truth to it to obscure the deeper reasons. These had to do with the character of the common faith.

Sons of the Fathers examines that character in detail and with an encompassing curiosity rare in works of this sort. Those of us who do not specialize in eighteenth-century materials but who must have access to them in order to deal with subsequent periods of American history usually work with secondary sources. That secondary literature, one soon notes, cites the same texts with such regularity that one soon grows weary and loses a sense of expectation. A few canonical texts by a number of clerics and statesmen are repeated with great frequency. In the present book, however, everything seems fresh and new. I chanced to meet Catherine Albanese as she entered the library for a period of research into new sources. Some months later she emerged after what must have been an orgy of Faustian pushing and probing into long-neglected texts. But her findings are not from arcane corners of forgotten civilizations. She found something different because she looked for something different. Not content only with billboard-sized emblazonings of civil faith in election day sermons, she examined the fine print, the hidden assumptions, the often overlooked traces.

What equipped the author to find so much that is fresh is her rather delicate sense of how consciousness is structured, how symbols generate societies and how societies generate symbols, how a myth comes to be a myth and how it is transformed even as it transforms. Without a great amount of comment about structuralism and hermeneutics she deals with considerable sophistication with techniques that those families of inquiry inspired. History, she is saying, is not made only at Lexingtons and Bunker Hills and Yorktowns, at Paris peace tables and in Independence Halls. It is made when there are subtle shifts in consciousness and sensibility, when populations show the need for altered myths and the capacity to respond to them. Such shifts are as much the stuff of history as are cannon and treaties, and deserve telling in the form of a story. But, now, let her tell it.

MARTIN E. MARTY
The University of Chicago

Acknowledgments

My debts are extensive. Martin E. Marty sparked in me an interest in both civil religion and the transformation of symbols in classes at the University of Chicago. In turn, in his classes Charles H. Long introduced me to Mircea Eliade and Claude Lévi-Strauss, to history-makers and the "others." Further conversations with Professor Long have greatly aided me in developing the thesis of this study, and Professor Marty has suggested bibliographic sources.

An honors course on Religion and the American Revolution, which I taught through the Honors Program at Wright State University in the spring of 1975, provided interaction in research and discussion at a formative stage in my thinking. Questions, comments, and bibliographical suggestions were forthcoming from the class, and all were helpful. Later, a grant from the National Endowment for the Humanities enabled me to spend the summer in further research and writing.

Martin Marty and Charles Long read early drafts of the manuscript and offered helpful general suggestions. A close line-by-line reading by Charles H. Lippy led to many constructive criticisms and subsequent revisions on my part. The book reflects the good offices of these readers, but its remaining errors and misinterpretations are my own.

Librarians at the Regenstein Library of the University of Chicago, the Wright State University Library, and the Center for Research Libraries aided me in my expedition through eighteenth-

and nineteenth-century sources. Joy Iddings of Interlibrary Loan at Wright State was especially facilitative in the early stages of the project. Margaret Roach, also of the Wright State University Library, has contributed many hours in indexing the study.

Finally, Lois Walker typed the index and interminable endnotes and proofread, and William Walker also aided in the task of proofreading.

Numerous thanks are due to all of these persons and to many others who have encouraged me and cheered me on, my parents the first among them. My hope is that they will be pleased with the results on the following pages.

Sons of the Fathers

Introduction
In Illo Tempore

In August 1974 newscasters from the television networks stood outside the modest suburban home of Gerald Ford in Alexandria, Virginia, and queried individuals in a large crowd gathered there. "What is it you came out to the suburbs to see?" was the substance of their question. Invariably, the answer came that the interviewee had a sense of history in the making and that he or she wanted to be in the place in which a central act in the great drama was unfolding. Already as Richard Nixon read his resignation speech in the Oval Office, he had been relegated by some to the past. They stood in the suburbs because it was there that the newness would reveal itself.

By the following spring, it was clear that the Republic would survive. Millard E. Crane of Fonda, New York, wrote to the editors of *Time* to ask them and *Time*'s readers, as the governments of Cambodia and Vietnam fell: "Where is the spirit of '76? . . . Are we to celebrate with fireworks while rockets are crushing freedom in other parts of the world? What a time for us to deserve a Congress like this. We need a Patrick Henry to stir our blood, a George Washington to stiffen our backbone." Jewish and German-born, neither stirring nor stiff, Secretary of State Henry Kissinger nonetheless reaffirmed the national purpose in the midst of the Bicentennial year.

Americans have always made history rather than let history chart our course. We, the present generation of Americans, will do no less. . . . Let us usher in an era of national reconciliation and rededication by all Americans to their common destiny. Let us have a clear vision of what is before us—glory and danger alike.[1]

Most Americans would probably agree that the three items are typical of innumerable others in the popular media. These same Americans would be surprised and even shocked, however, if the three items were described as religious. Yet all three of the communications were making religious statements, participating in a common understanding about the "real," the "true," the underlying character of events. The crowd at the home of Gerald Ford, the author of the letter to the editor, the secretary of state, all were structuring their world in terms of a preconceived vision of the meaning of life and the significance of human endeavor.

The hiddenness of the religion we are noticing is itself not exceptional. The Judaeo-Christian and Graeco-Roman heritage of our culture has led us to define religion in terms of clearly articulated institutions (churches/synagogues) and ideas (theology), and often the religiousness of those objects, events, and attitudes which do not fall under such a rubric is largely invisible. J. Paul Williams, in *What Americans Believe and How They Worship*, caught a glimpse of the problem.

The careless assumption of the past has too often been that religion is what goes on in and around the churches. Theorizing about religion has too consistently been left to clergymen and theologians. As a result the role of denominational religion has been overstressed; indeed a frequent assumption has been that this is the only kind of religion which exists. This view is parochial.[2]

Williams saw religion functioning in society in private, denominational, and societal realms, and he understood societal religion in sociological terms as a "common religion."[3] This kind of understanding does not go unsupported beyond the Williams book. The data of comparative religion suggest that religion is the way one orients oneself in the world, with reference to both the transcendent and the ordinary; that symbols, which are the records of human experience, may be condensed or they may be diffused; that institutions and ideas are symbols among other symbols; and that in order to understand religious experience fully, we must place ecclesiastical and theological symbols in the matrix from which they emerge and look at the other symbolic forms which emerge with them.

Part of that life-orientation system which is societal religion in America is civil religion. The term itself became au courant with Robert N. Bellah's celebrated essay in 1967,[4] but the reality has been with Americans a long time, in fact since the Puritans and Pilgrims set about founding theocratic states in the American wilderness where citizens would be visible saints and the bond of their union a figure or type of their prior union with the great Jehovah. As Puritans became Yankees and grew more and more aware of their brethren to the south, it was clear that all through the colonial enterprise ran a current of participatory understanding which made of civil duty a major mode of being in the world. Writing in the midst of the Revolution, Joseph Galloway, who had become a Loyalist, was astute enough to recognize the shape of events.

The fundamental and general laws of every society are the lessons of instruction by which the subject is daily taught his duty and obedience to the State. It is the uniformity of these lessons, flowing from the same system of consistent polity, which forms the same habits, manners, and political opinions throughout the society, fixes the national attachment, and leads the people to look up to one system of government for their safety and happiness, and to act in concert on all occasions to maintain and defend it.[5]

Galloway was describing civil religion, and he rightly perceived that the American Revolution was effecting a fundamental change in the civic faith of the thirteen colonies which had declared themselves American states.

Other students of the American historical and religious scene in the twentieth century have analyzed the phenomenon which later wore the label of civil religion in their own terms, sometimes stressing the transcendence of the reality and sometimes its everydayishness. Sidney Mead and Will Herberg, William Lloyd

Warner and Martin E. Marty, among others, have called attention
to a religion which lay outside the churches and synagogues of the
land.[6] These studies have in general focused on the contemporary
manifestations of civil religion, and they have been characterized
by an intense ethical concern.

At the same time, relatively little attention has been paid to the
origins of civil religion in the era of the American Revolution.
Sidney Mead has contributed several notable essays on the strands
of pietism and rationalism which intertwined in the revolutionary
era and on the Jeffersonian heritage of religious freedom. The
work of Alan Heimert has explored the bond between the Great
Awakening and the Revolution, and that of Carl Bridenbaugh has
probed the complexities of the struggle over a New World Anglican episcopate as one cause of the war. Winthrop Hudson has
pursued an interest in the days of fast and thanksgiving appropriated from the Puritan past by the Continental Congress and
American presidents. Similarly, Conrad Cherry has looked to the
religious roots of nationalism in its documentary sources and
hinted provocatively of what lay waiting in the texts from America's past. Cushing Strout's intellectual history of "political religion" in America has provided welcome insights from one perspective, while in a recent work, Robert Bellah has devoted a
chapter to sounding the revolutionary waters toward the discovery of a myth of origins.[7]

It is in the same direction as this last that the present endeavor
attempts to move, for rather than seeing the relationship between
religion and the American Revolution as causal or connective
("religion and . . ."), it suggests that the American Revolution
was *in itself* a religious experience, a hierophany collectively
manifested and received, which provided the fundamental basis
for American civil religion as we know it. The study seeks to
explore the roots of this civil religion in order to deepen a historical understanding of the phenomenon, necessary to an eluci-
dation of its meaning and value in the present. With the Bicentennial upon us, such an undertaking seems timely and useful, for

the myth of the American Revolution, while it may not captivate all of the people all of the time, has certainly succeeded in attracting many of the media much of the time. If the records of popular culture are any indication, it has succeeded in keeping a hold on the imaginations and hearts of mainstream America.

The scholarly "language" found most useful for this attempt is derived largely from the history of religions. Although this discipline was originally developed in the context of the study of primitive and archaic peoples, it is surprisingly adaptable to the concerns and expressions of the more sophisticated culture of the United States. It has already been applied in high cultural contexts to traditional religions such as Islam, Hinduism, and Buddhism with a success which suggests that the primitive-archaic "problem" may not be so problematic. Structuralists such as Claude Lévi-Strauss have demonstrated in a number of instances that the "savage mind" is not so different from our own as we sometimes like to think.[8] Finally, as traditional religions in the United States become simply one center among others for the life-orientation of the populace, more and more a state of affairs exists which might be described as a "re-primitivization" of religion in the United States. That is, as the religion which is perceived as religion occupies a smaller compartment in the heads and lives of its practitioners (some things they do and think some of the time), the "real religion" of the American people lies to a greater degree outside the confines of traditional definitions. To state the matter baldly, the American penchant for teeth-brushing or flag-waving may have as much or more to do with religious orientation than church and synagogue attendance.

This work should be understood as an attempt to demonstrate how history of religions categories, among others, can illuminate the American religious experience. For by means of its form-comparative approach, history of religions presents an opportunity to view native realities which might not otherwise disclose their religion visibly. The concern of the work, in dealing with the material out of which civil religion comes, has been to search for the structures of consciousness which informed it. Here we are referring to various perceptions of the world, to the conceptual and emotional concomitants of these perceptions, to their expression in language and behavior, and finally their reinternalization as objective realities after they have been projected onto the world as word and action. Reading the language and watching the extraordinarily heightened ritual behavior of the American Revolution suggest that the inner drum to which the patriots marched was a general mythic consciousness. This fundamental orientation led them to appropriate their past as a sacred tale of origins and amalgamate it to their present, thereby creating a new sacral myth of origins out of the very events of the Revolution.

One gets a hint of the process in Benjamin Rush's letter to his son James, who was away at school. "Your letter diffused pleasure through all our family," the elder Rush wrote. "It is correctly written. . . . In the use of capitals remember to use them only in the beginning of sentences and for the names of persons, cities, countries, and important words such as Religion, Revolution, Reformation, and the like."[9] Rush needed only to add the words "liberty," "union," and "Washington," which unfortunately did not begin with R.

What is suggested here is that the structures of consciousness which sparked patriot thought and action created for these Americans their own truth to live by. It was an inner myth out of which they lived and operated, and it was *not* based on a cool assessment of external and "objective" conditions. The surest evidence of this is their collective near-blindness to the incongruity of the story of "liberty, not slavery" in the context of their own enslavement of blacks. In other words, in the myth of the Revolution the patriots had at hand a story which was true in that it explained the underlying meaningful structure of reality: it narrated those sacred events from which they were even then taking their origin and identity, and it empowered them through contact and involvement with these great and creative events.[10] While

the patriots began as "sons of the fathers," holding to the grand
model which the past had provided as its own sacred center and
myth for their future, somehow in the process of rallying around
their past, they discovered the sacrality of the present. And the
result was so powerful a hierophany that it became a new mythic
center for themselves and for those who would come after.
Perhaps because thirteen colonies could not rely on a mutual
past for their common center or perhaps because, with John
Adams, thirteen clocks had struck as one, the patriots, almost before they were aware of it, found that their myth of origins was
centering on the act of revolution. So in the newness itself, in the
establishment of a new center of power, the patriots discovered
their commonality. For those who would follow, the remembrance of the new thing the founders had done would unify and
identify the citizen-heirs. This would be evident in the regard for
sacred times and places such as the Fourth of July and Independence Hall, in the role of the Supreme Court as collective
exegete for the Constitution, in the pervading sense in American
life of a "winding-down" of patriotism with accompanying exhortation to draw strength from mythic remembrance.

In tune with their own character and consciousness, the patriots' myth was different from many another in the history of
religions: it was a myth for a history-making people, and so its
strong and sacred time (*illud tempus*) lay not outside time but
within it. The historicization of myth had been an aspect of the
Judaeo-Christian understanding from its inception, and it is obvious that historicized myth had precedent in the heritage of
Americans. Yet, to say this is not to say all; for Americans quickly
surpassed their forbears in the self-conscious energy with which
they developed their story, so much so that there arises the question of the relationship between the intentional construction of a
myth and the authenticity of the religious experience the myth
mediates. This self-consciousness had existed even in the early
years of the revolutionary era, roughly from 1763 to 1775, when
the patriots appropriated a myth of origins from the glorious

deeds of their fathers to which they believed they must prove faithful. But it became even more significant with the dawning realization among Americans that they were doing something new and hence, by their act of positive foundation, were in a time of their own creation.

Perhaps the chief facilitator for this self-consciousness was the literary quality of the myth. From the first, it was written as well as spoken and celebrated; it appealed to reason as well as imagination; it tied emotion and enthusiasm to concrete data and written record. "Men must be *convinced* before they become *converted*," wrote the *Pennsylvania Packet* early in 1776,[11] and in their conviction of this truth, the patriots left a fascinating written record of the development of their story. Broad avenues into the popular experience are present in both the productions of the leaders and the response of those who joined their cause. Orations, sermons, political essays, official public documents, and contemporary histories detail the story as enunciated by those who led—and also hint by their success at the agreement of a large block of the population. Diaries and letters uncover more fully the hidden perceptions of leaders as well as those who remained relatively obscure. Meanwhile, newspapers, songs, and broadsides give us some insights into popular appropriation of the myth and the nature of collective understandings of its meaning. Political satires, popular lyric poetry, humorous writing, and even drama can be means of tracing its evolution.

With a high rate of literacy in the colonies and a relatively large reading public,[12] printed matter achieved even wider circulation because it was rarely perused by just one person and was often read aloud. The historian David Ramsay noted that "the reading of those colonists who were inclined to books, generally favoured the cause of liberty."[13] By 1755, we are told, there were twenty-four presses in ten colonies which published about twelve hundred book titles a year, the number of which meant one book title for every one thousand Americans.[14]

But the newspaper was most effective in bringing converts to patriotism and the new order of things. With perhaps as many as forty-two separate sheets in the colonies by 1775, averaging in circulation between three hundred and six hundred copies per week, newspapers were already important sources of public opinion. Distribution figures, which soared higher and higher after the Stamp Act and during the climactic years before the Revolution, made the role of newspeople ever more powerful.[15] One patriot acknowledged that "more attention is paid by many to the *News Paper* than to Sermons," and few of the news organs were Tory in orientation.[16] Magazines, in the meantime, also turned to the events which were reconstituting the inner and outer world of Americans and, during the second half of the eighteenth century, made these events their chief subject. Political pamphlets and, later, official communications from Congress were readily at hand to interpret each new crisis. Even the almanacs became the bearers of revolutionary mythology with illustrated covers of allegorical subjects or pictures of Whig heroes and accompanying copy to rouse patriotic fervor. Anonymously printed broadsides were tacked up and handed out everywhere and read by ubiquitous good neighbors to the illiterate.

Enough work has already been done to underline the power of that "black regiment" which was the clergy as molder and shaper of the collective tale. For although church membership was minimal in the revolutionary era, there were still thirty-two hundred churches in 1775 with presumably nearly as many ministers to serve them.[17] Furthermore, churchmen did not gain an audience merely among their members: those who went unchurched were often still believers and might be thought to hear with respect either first-hand or second-hand reports of what the preacher had held forth. In New England, there had been a long tradition of artillery and general election sermons, fast and thanksgiving orations, and political addresses from meeting-house pulpits. While preachers in the southern colonies seemed far less active in the

patriot cause, the New Englanders more than made up for it, and
the middle colonists held their own, despite the presence of sizable Tory representation in New York and Pennsylvania. The
grumbling reminiscences of the Loyalist Anglican priest Jonathan
Boucher summarized the situation.

In America, as in the Grand Rebellion in England, much execution
was done by sermons. Those persons who have read any out of the
great number of Puritan sermons that were then printed as well as
preached, will cease to wonder that so many people were worked up
into such a state of frenzy; and I who either heard, or heard of, many
similar discourses from the pulpits in America, felt the effects of them
no less than they had before been felt here.[18]

And while ministers enjoyed both the immediate power of their
spoken word and its authoritative remembrance in print, town
meetings, committees of correspondence, and informal popular
meetings preached their own sermons to the newness and helped
to spread the spirit of 1776.

A casual reading of these accounts of the period may obscure
the central reality that, in keeping with the values of the patriots,
the story was above all acted out and played upon the public
stage either in the real-life spectacles of battles and political debates or in the plethora of rituals which grew up around these.
Orations and processions, liberty songs and "new" ballads, tolling
bells and mock funerals, standardized toasts, huzzas and feus de
joie, all provide a taste of the heady wine of living myth which
mere words can no longer supply. This book has tried to reflect
the high theater which the sources recount as the story of Revolution unfolds. Later, as ritual becomes focused on the sacred
objects which are the sacraments of the new dispensation, a new
kind of religious experience appears to be involved, and an attempt to describe and understand it occupies the final chapter at
the risk perhaps of taking the essay beyond the time limits otherwise observed.

Although historians of the phenomenon have been quick to
label this literary and dramatic mythology "propaganda" and

have recognized the "extraordinary skill in manipulating public opinion" it represented on the part of a "fairly well-to-do element in colonial society,"[19] and although we have already noticed the high degree of mythic *self*-consciousness among the patriots, this study will argue that the alteration of the qualities of "pure" myth which such activity effected was not sufficient to make the category of myth inoperative. For the first to be convinced by the story were usually the storytellers. The innocence of Americans in the midst of the manipulativeness seemed largely the naive belief in their own innocence.

With the curious kind of double vision which the inner certainty that living out of one's myth produces, the "self-conscious" myth was almost unconsciously so for many. That is, most if not all of the patriots seemed to know but not know what they were about. There was a background awareness; there was a foreground involvement in events and activity which precluded too reflective consideration of the degree of contrivance in what they themselves were creating. Hence it is through an analysis of the language and ritual in which these Americans engaged that we may begin to make the unconscious conscious and identify it further as religion.

This does not deny the obvious propagandistic value of the myth. There is no quarrel here with the conclusion of Philip Davidson that

the fears the propagandists aroused and the hopes they enkindled became the national fears and national hopes. The national ideals of American life, slowly maturing through the colonial period, thus came clearly into the consciousness of the American people through the effects of war propaganda.[20]

Indeed, that the myth was good propaganda becomes even more apparent when we recall that active patriots in America were probably at best a large minority. While Loyalist Jonathan Boucher complained that "nine out of ten of the people of America, properly so called, were adverse to the revolt," patriot James

Wilson found the number difficult to guess since "those of the particular circle in which one moved were commonly mistaken for the general voice" and the redoubtable John Adams, coming closest to the contemporary assessment, estimated that fully one-third of the colonial population opposed the patriot cause.[21] Moreover, there was decided arm-twisting involved in convincing people to jump on the revolutionary bandwagon. Committees of safety advertised the names of Loyalist "sinners" in the newspaper, and anyone who had drunk a British health in a tavern, ignored a Continental Fast Day, talked against enlistments, avoided taking the new currency, or sent food to the enemy might find himself or herself included in their number. One preacher shared with his flock the righteous conclusion that "God requires a people, struggling for their liberties, to treat such of the community who will not join them, as open enemies, and to reject them as unworthy the privileges which others enjoy."[22] Tarring and feathering was a popular instrument of persuasion for the recalcitrant, and the freedom-loving patriots seemed in general not free to quit the holy cause.

Yet, with all of this taken into account, it seems fair to say that the reason the cause succeeded was bound up with the essential *power* of the myth as a compelling center for identification and orientation as well as action. With one-third of the colonists probably nostalgic for British ties, the inability of these Loyalists to wage an effective counter-propaganda campaign is a telling argument, not only for the political expertise of the patriots, but also for the vitality of the myth out of which they lived and commanded the allegiance of others. The Loyalists failed, in the final analysis, not because they were poorer, less astute politically, less well educated, less shrewd, less situated in positions of communal responsibility, but because they had no story to match in cogency and inner truth the sacred story which the patriot leaders were noising abroad among the masses. Most of the themes which the patriots sounded had had precedent in earlier American understandings; now in the time of need, the various strands from the past came together and fused into a new tale generating an energy all its own as it functioned for a new purpose, in a new situation.

If it is the popular consciousness of the revolutionary era which requires examination in a search for the sources of American civil religion, it should be clear that a popular consciousness means here a dominant mainstream which controls the public language, becomes internalized in structures of consciousness, and celebrates its awareness in collective rituals. Its myth is anonymous and largely unconscious—invented by no one in particular and believed by everyone in general, autonomous and speaking with the voice of its own intrinsic authority. Founders and leaders give it succinct expression; everybody's people affirm and assent.

How the various minorities which comprised the population maintained their self-identity and yet participated in the national myth is altogether another question. The rising nationalistic myth was in some respects a threat to the continued existence of these groups in the form in which they had known themselves. In other respects it simply ignored their existence and rendered them almost unseeable as a people. Jews and Catholics, blacks and women, and distinctive ethnic minorities have been largely overlooked in the pursuit of a collective national consciousness. It is a highly significant question how these groups appropriated or failed to appropriate the myth and how they viewed their own participation therein, but it is a question that will not be answered here. Such a study must rest on prior monographic work on the mythic consciousness of each of these groups as a separate entity. Although it is beyond the purview of the essay, it is a necessary and vital piece of the puzzle if we are to understand the religion of the American Revolution as it has functioned in the American experience. On the other hand, it is hoped that this study, though tentative and far from exhaustive, will suggest a direction for further and future scholarship about the mainstream and become one step in a long and fruitful line of inquiry.

It has also been necessary to draw some limits in regard to time. Most central are the years of the revolutionary era from about 1763, when the French and Indian War ended, to 1789, when George Washington assumed office under the new Constitution as president of the young republic. Within that timespan, the clearest division for the development of the myth is between the early period ending in 1775, when the story of the ancestral fathers predominated in the consciousness of the patriots, and the events after 1775 which crystallized republican opinion around the symbol of independence and led to the transformation in which the patriotic sons discovered their own venerability and fatherhood. Yet an understanding of the story of the first fathers who had settled a bleak and "howling wilderness" has involved a backward glance into the seventeenth and early eighteenth centuries. Similarly, scrutiny of the developing story of the Revolution has meant expeditions into some part of the nineteenth century and even, on brief occasion, the twentieth. While the myth of Revolution *begins* during and in the events of the Revolution and the Constitution, it waxes with the succeeding generations, and a view of its future gives an indication of the vector along which the religious impulse was running.

The Civil War, on the other hand, lies outside the scope of the book because it represents a new and more intensive valorization of the theme of civil religion under the duress of events themselves highly dramatic and compelling. The question of how the Civil War changes the civil religion is in itself a subject for a study of this nature, and Ernest Lee Tuveson's *Redeemer Nation* is already an endeavor which provides a strong beginning for such work.[23]

Since the present study has attempted to be "structural" as well as "historical," it has perhaps focused more on the general pulse than its subtleties, elucidating the continuing shape of particular mythologems more than the precise moments at which individuals gave them utterance. Because this is so and because mythic materials resist the linear logic of classical exposition, the thread of

discourse sometimes runs in concentric circles, with earlier mythologems repeated in later chapters carrying additional nuances
and further meanings. For example, it has proved impossible to
treat millennialism adequately in any one discussion.

The closer one draws to primary sources and initial impressions
of the revolutionary era, the more confused and confusing, albeit
the more vital and challenging, the interpretation of events becomes. The intensity of the ritualization of the myth has by and
large been forgotten in popular and "schoolbook" histories of the
period which have come down to us. A reimmersion in sources
has meant in many instances a revelation about the intensity and
frequency of the celebratory and rebellious rituals the patriots
enacted.

In overview, the book begins with the inherited perceptions of
the colonists as they entered the era of Revolution, examines the
sources of these understandings, and investigates their utilization
as mythologems in a unifying tale of identity and purpose. But it
quickly finds that the story of the ancient fathers, around whose
memory the patriotic sons could rally, did not provide the only
spur for action. The present spun its own tale even as its critical
events unravelled, with the result that, out of a dialectic between
past and present, the new myth of Revolution took shape. The
book has tried to follow the course of the dialectic by treating
the early years from 1763 to 1775 in its terms, moving from a
consideration of the fathers to a treatment of the new world being
created by their revolutionary sons. Here the central symbol was
the sacred elm of Boston which became a kind of transcendent
cosmo-historical tree around which the other Liberty Trees and
liberty signs of the colonies took root.

With its subsequent discussion of Jehovah and the Great Governor, the study tries to pursue the advancing course of the dialectic and this time focuses mainly on the years when war was
imminent or had begun. The past had been transformed to new
intents as the God of Battles fought on the American side, while
the present found its own ally in the strands of tradition in which

a more passive deistic God lay hidden, one though who paradoxically supplied a ground with power enough to bear a new
foundation. As the war progressed, this God began to retain his
followers with an ever surer, if unmoving, hand.

Thus, still following the course of the dialectic, the essay moves
with it to the version of the myth which celebrates the new creation in the present of the Revolution. The deistic God, who was
Great Governor and Nature's God, provided a broad arena for
the action of patriots who involved themselves in the course of
human history without awaiting the arm of Jehovah. As representative Man among these men, George Washington summarized
their endeavor. In his apotheosis, which would increase as the
nineteenth century progressed, we discover sacred power in a
world from which the Governor was content to recede. Finally,
we see that, if Washington epitomized the emergent religious
identity of a new nation which would "flatten" transcendence
without obliterating it, he was pointing beyond himself to a new
covenant among Americans. It was a covenant symbolized in the
great twin sacraments of the Declaration of Independence and
the Constitution, linked as they were historically by the years in
which the hierarchy of the Continental Congress presided over a
"nation with the soul of a church." The two poles of the dialectic
did not preserve an equal strength as the youthful republic looked
with anticipation toward the nineteenth century. The energy of
the past had been grasped by a humanocentric present which centered itself on the act and institutionalization of its own Revolution. *In illlo tempore* had become 1776.

Chapter 1

Our Fathers Who Trod
the Wilderness

To live within a myth is to live within a subjective center of truth. To live outside it is to live within the sacred enclosure provided by another story. A person lives in one myth or lives in another, and there is no middle ground. It is an appreciation of the mythological dynamic which lies behind perceptions that "objective" history is impossible, and perhaps this kind of conclusion lay behind the letter of a skeptical John Adams to Jedidiah Morse. "When you apply to me to assist you in writing history, I know not whether I ought to laugh or cry. I have little faith in history, I read it as I do romance, believing what is probable and rejecting what I must."[1] Somehow though, for Adams and for the rest of us, our personal myth escapes this universal condemnation: what we perceive as true is normative, and we use it as our standard by which to measure other visions of the world.

In this respect, the patriots were little different from ourselves. What was different, however, was that for the men of the Revolution, the truth involved what Carl Bridenbaugh has called a species of "ancestor worship";[2] the memory of the fathers haunted the present from shadows of the past which were still alive. The ancestors were venerable men. More than that, they were virile men whose power dominated the lives of their sons as judge and jury of their condition. One catches a glimpse of the ancestral sway in the growing interest in history which preceded the American Revolution.

With the publication in 1764 of the first volume of Thomas Hutchinson's *History of the Province of Massachusetts Bay*, a Royalist was ironically providing grist for the patriot mill. Ezra Stiles observed that the book had "contributed more than anything else to reviving the ancestral Spirit of Liberty in New England."[3] Cheerfully ignoring the lectures on loyalty which Hutchinson furnished, the patriots read instead of the marvellous deeds of their fathers. When five years later Hutchinson published a documentary appendix, the influential few who read it included Samuel Adams, who regularly sent letters to the newspapers, and a number of pamphleteers. "History," Hutchinson had written in contemplation of the planting of Massachusetts Bay, "affords us no instance of so great movements in so short a time. The same passion still continues, and affords a prospect of the like happy effect for ages yet to come."[4]

Whether or not the action was prompted by Hutchinson's *History*, the year of his appendix was also the year when Plymouth first celebrated Forefathers' Day, an annual event thereafter remembering the Pilgrims' landing in the New World. The New Englanders of the Old Colony Club, which staged the demonstration, ate their way through a nine-course dinner and later marched to their hall. There, after a volley of small arms and a song, the evening continued with salutes to the "worthy ancestors" in twelve toasts, including one that "every enemy to civil or religious liberty meet the same or a worse fate than Arch-Bishop Laud."[5] The demise of the Old Colony Club brought official sponsorship by the town of Plymouth through 1780 and with it annual orations by clergymen as part of the Forefathers' Day celebrations.

New England was not alone in its desire to remember. In the middle colonies, where persecuted religious minorities had settled, there was a parallel development of interest in tradition, with William Penn already an almost legendary figure for Pennsylvanians. Meanwhile, Samuel Smith in 1765 offered New Jerseyites his *History of the Colony of Nova-Caesaria, or New-Jersey.*

During the same year, interest in history was spurred throughout the colonies by the publication of Blackstone's *Commentaries*, which traced the development of the English common law. In the south after 1780, David Ramsay was producing the *History of South Carolina*, while individuals in all the colonies were reading the first book of George Chalmers's *Political Annals of the Present United Colonies*. Chalmers, even more than Hutchinson, was an antihistorian for the kind of history the colonists wanted to read, and he had a special distaste for New England. Yet the inclusiveness of his work made it useful. His opening proposition concerning the origins of the colonies became a favorite for American orators.

Of these colonies, it cannot be asserted, as it is of European nations, that their origin is uncertain or unknown; that their ancient history is fabulous and dark; or that their original institutions have come down the current of time, loaded with the disputations of the antiquary. Here, there is as little room for the dreams of conjecture or the obscurities of tradition, as for the regret of the philosopher, that the establishment of nations, which is the most important and instructive part of their annals, is generally the most imperfect.[6]

That the truth of the colonists relied for its force upon an appeal to their past becomes even clearer in the records of their own consciousness which have come down to us. Taking themes which had been present in seventeenth- and early eighteenth-century election sermons, Americans shaped them to their own patriotic ends. Thus, Samuel Cooke in 1770 found it appropriate to preach before Royal Lieutenant-Governor Hutchinson that "our fathers supposed their purchase of the aboriginals gave them a just title to the land; that the produce of them, by their labor, was their property, which they had an exclusive right to dispose of; that a legislative power, respecting their internal polity, was ratified to them." To the query, "Our fathers—where are they?" Cooke could reply that they had "looked for another and better country, that is, an heavenly," and because they had found it, they heard no more "the voice of the oppressor."[7] The implication for

Hutchinson must have been unmistakable. Six years later, the election sermon was no longer preached before the royal representative. Now Samuel West declared that, when he considered "the dispensations of Providence towards this land ever since our fathers first settled in Plymouth," he found "abundant reason to conclude that the great Sovereign of the universe [had] planted a vine in this American wilderness which he [had] caused to take deep root."[8]

In like fashion, George Duffield, preaching to a Philadelphia congregation in 1776, told them that "our forefathers, who first inhabited yonder eastern shores, fled from the iron rod and heavy hand of tyranny." In the patriots' cause, a "DIVINE AFFLATUS" had breathed. It was the "same spirit that inspired our forefathers' breasts when first they left their native shores and embarked for this then howling desert."[9] Invariably, as the preachers told and retold the story, the fathers were memorable because they had suffered for the foundation of freedom, risking their lives to escape British tyranny, although it meant a liberty in the "howling wilderness." They pursued their goal and sought their freedom for the sake of the highest earthly reality—that of worshiping God in the manner the inner voice of conscience taught was most pleasing to him.

And invariably, as the preachers preached, there was a connection between the actions of the fathers and the present activity of their sons. Again, the spectre of British tyranny stood over them, and again they must face upheaval and the return to a state of nature, the "howling wilderness" of the war, in order to uphold the freedoms which the inner voice insisted belonged to them. Now, however, it was liberty itself which was the central issue and not, as in the past, liberty for the sake of religion. It was here that the analogy limped, and so it was here the preachers protested most vociferously. While some who lived out of a different myth might argue that British requests were reasonable, that the point was merely one of taxation and representation in Parliament, that there were complexities and subtleties in the dynamic of a political problem, the patriots brooked no response except the ringing truth of their myth. And perhaps here was the area of stress where the patriots knew but did not know, for it must have been liminally apparent to some of them that they had grown sleeker and fatter than their image of their religion-loving fathers whose purported asceticism they no longer imitated. In fact, as we shall see, they were indeed aware of the place of stress—and they dealt with it with the venerable seventeenth-century solution of the jeremiad, by mourning the declension of the present and beating their breasts in sorrow that the austerity and innocence of former ages was gone.

Moreover, private letters agreed with public sermons. One correspondent wrote back to England in 1775 that the Continentals were men "acting in defence of all those great and essential privileges which our forefathers ever held so dear." He added tellingly that "not a soldier dies of his wounds who does not believe he goes directly to heaven, notwithstanding all the anathemas of the general proclamation."[10] Benjamin Rush admitted that his passion for liberty had been "early cultivated by my ancestors. I am the great grandson of an officer John Rush who fell fighting against King Charles 1st under Oliver Cromwell."[11] Other correspondents who wrote to friends or relatives in England called the colonists "the descendants of Oliver Cromwell's army" and "the descendants of Cromwell's *elect*."[12] At the same time, a popular song of 1776 announced that "In story we're told/How our Fathers of old/Brav'd the rage of the wind and the waves,"[13] while John Dickinson's familiar "Liberty Song" began one stanza with a dedication to "Our worthy Forefathers."

In the public rituals in which the new religion of the Revolution was growing, both individual and collective consciousness were fused. Silas Downer, a Son of Liberty who spoke at the consecration of a Liberty Tree, evoked the well-worn theme at Providence in 1768.

Our fathers fought and found freedom in the wilderness; they cloathed themselves with the skins of wild beasts, and lodged under trees and among bushes; but in that state they were happy because they were free—Should these our noble ancestors arise from the dead, and find their posterity trucking away that liberty, which they purchased at so dear a rate, for the mean trifles and frivolous merchandize of *Great-Britain*, they would return to the grave with a holy indignation against us.[14]

In a Boston Massacre Oration for 1772, Joseph Warren told the populace that their "illustrious fathers" were the "zealous votaries" of freedom. They brought her "safe over the rough ocean and fixed her seat in this then dreary wilderness; they nursed her infant age with the most tender care; for her sake, they patiently bore the severest hardships; . . . neither the ravenous beasts that ranged the woods for prey, nor the more furious savages of the wilderness, could damp their ardor!" "No sacrifice," Warren underlined, "not even their own blood, was esteemed too rich a libation for her altar!"[15] Three years later, with British officers in the aisles and his life in danger, Warren sounded the theme again for the same anniversary, this time linking it to the old Puritan motif of the Israel of God.

Our fathers having nobly resolved never to wear the yoke of despotism, and seeing the European world, at that time, through indolence and cowardice, falling a prey to tyranny, bravely threw themselves upon the bosom of the ocean, determined to find a place in which they might enjoy their freedom, or perish in the glorious attempt. Approving heaven beheld the favorite ark dancing upon the waves, and graciously preserved it until the chosen families were brought in safety to these western regions.[16]

It was no surprise that the official publication of *Rules and Regulations for the Massachusetts Army* (1775) began with a celebration of the virtues of the "venerable Progenitors" and a reminder of the "indispensable Duty" of their descendants in the present.[17] A year earlier, the Continental Congress had passed the resolve which Massachusetts was echoing.

It is an indispensible duty which we owe to God, our country, ourselves and posterity, by all lawful ways and means in our power to maintain, defend and preserve those civil and religious rights and liberties, for which many of our fathers fought, bled and died, and to hand them down entire to future generations.[18]

If liberty was that highest good for which men died, it was in contrast with slavery that the colonists seemed to understand its meaning most forcefully. Songs enjoyed a propensity for being titled "Liberty Song," and not infrequently they contained verses similar to William Billings's "Hymn": "Let tyrants shake their iron rod,/And slavery clank her galling chains;/We fear them not; we trust in God—/New England's God for ever reigns."[19] Oratory dwelt on the horrors and miseries of being enslaved, while newspapers and broadsides carried written reminders of the terrors of a slave existence. Enunciating the popular resolve, the Boston Committee of Correspondence declared that "the right of freedom being *the gift of* GOD ALMIGHTY, it is not in the power of man to alienate this gift and voluntarily become a slave."[20] At the height of the frenzy, Congress petitioned King George III with a stern exhortation: "Had our Creator been pleased to give us existence in a land of slavery, the sense of our condition might have been mitigated by ignorance and habit. But, thanks to his adorable goodness, we were born the heirs of freedom."[21]

It is worth scrutinizing the incongruity of these slaveholding patriots who trembled at the peril of becoming British "slaves." Their fears might be dismissed as overreaction or condemned in a moralistic denunciation of the hypocrisy believed to stand behind them. But neither approach is particularly helpful in understanding how it came to be that the language of slavery operated with such power in the myth. At the center of their being, the patriots seemed to possess so graphic a sense of the meaning of slavery that it impelled them as a counterforce toward the fruits of liberty. One wonders if the memory of the sufferings of the fathers, though present, could have crystallized in such a sense.

One wonders, in fact, if the popular descriptions of clanking chains and iron bonds could by any stretch of the imagination be applied to the ancestors. Rather, the patriots knew what slavery was because they *owned* slaves, clamped irons on the limbs of these unfortunates, and saw and heard their chains. Guilty before their fathers because they had left the legendary asceticism for the fat of the land, the patriots were also guilty before their black slaves. Through all the distance which the mythology of ownership and possession had created, the slaves tormented their masters with the remnants of humanness which managed to filter through.

Yet as the patriots played out their inner drama on a public stage, it was England which became, instead of a nurturing mother, an enslaving demon, corrupt and rotten at the core. Of course, there were good reasons for separation from England, and the British did not on every occasion tread lightly and angelically on colonial minds and lands. However, the power which "screwed the colonists to the sticking place" in their fight for the kind of world they wanted emerged out of the dynamic of the play of hidden forces within them. So, with incredible ease and speed, the British became "our unnatural Enemies, who have in a hostile Manner been endeavouring to enslave the United Colonies."[22] Abroad in England in 1772, Benjamin Franklin declared, "Had I never been in the American Colonies, but was to form my Judgment of Civil Society by what I have lately seen, I should never advise a Nation of Savages to admit of Civilization."[23] As the Revolution progressed, a great outcry was raised over how the British looted and pillaged, burned the churches, horribly mistreated prisoners, raped the women, and tore sucking infants from their dying mothers' breasts. The forces of evil which England embodied were especially evident as a foil for the action of the God of Battles in the developing myth, and we shall have more to say about the demonization of the British when we confront Jehovah fighting for the American cause.

Particularly in New England, the fathers and sons who fought against slavery under a demonic England and found their liberty in a new land of freedom belonged to a chosen race. They were "our Israel," who, as Israel of old which was governed directly by God through Moses, knew no "divine right of kings."[24] As in the days of the wilderness fathers, sermons on Old Testament themes predominated, while preachers announced the striking parallel between old and new: "Israel were a free, independent commonwealth, planted by God in Canaan, in much the same manner that he planted us in America."[25] Yet in reality, the colonists were making *two* links as they used the language of "our Israel." They saw themselves in continuity with the first Israel in Canaan, but now they also and more importantly saw themselves in continuity with their fathers. John Winthrop's ringing declaration that "the eies of all people are vppon vs" had worked its way to the core of the collective soul.

"The eyes of the whole world are upon us in these critical times, and, what is yet more, the eyes of Almighty God," preached Phillips Payson in one election sermon.[26] For Mercy Otis Warren, reflecting later on events, America had stood as a "monument of observation, and an asylum of freedom."

The eyes of all Europe were upon her: she was placed in a rank that subjected her to the inspection of mankind abroad, to the jealousy of monarchs, and the envy of nations, all watching for her halting, to avail themselves of her mistakes, and to reap advantages from her difficulties, her embarrassments, her inexperience, or her follies.[27]

In the tradition of its fathers, the favored nation saw with progressive clarity that its exemplary character led to millennial mission. The publication in 1774 of Jonathan Edwards's chiliastic *History of the Work of Redemption* underlined the presence of the past in the revolutionary milieu. Warren seemed to echo the theologian when she wrote as an American patriot:

The western wilds, which for ages have been little known, may arrive to that state of improvement and perfection, beyond which the limits of human genius cannot reach; and this last civilized quarter of the globe may exhibit those striking traits of grandeur and magnificence, which the Divine Oeconomist may have reserved to crown the closing scene, when the angel of his presence will stand upon the sea and upon the earth, lift up his hand to heaven, and swear by Him that liveth for ever and ever, that there shall be time no longer.[28]

Long before the Revolution, a youthful John Adams had had intuitions which were similar. Writing to Nathan Webb, Adams reflected that "soon after the Reformation, a few People came over into this new world for conscience sake. Perhaps this, apparently, trivial incident may transfer the great seat of empire in America. It looks likely to me."[29] It would take the consciousness of the nineteenth century to develop the "secular" version of the doctrine in its fulness, but the seeds were already present as the colonists began to shift the strongest ground of their argument from the rights of British subjects to the rights of humankind. For if the patriots were fighting for the rights which appropriately belonged to all, it was only a short and perhaps implicit deduction that they were fighting *for all*.

The importance of the mythological shift cannot be overestimated. In the switch in language from England to all humanity was buried a transposition which was changing a historical myth into a theological one. When patriots fought British tyrants, they were facing a particular, albeit demonic and corrupt, enemy who was trying to deprive them of particular rights which belonged to Englishmen. When they struggled for human rights in the name of all, their efforts took on a universal and absolute character. Here was an answer to cover every opportunity and an argument to engage each particular. The patriots, as their fathers before them, were building on the strongest and surest foundation. It was true that the language of universal claims had a long history in the patriot past, familiar and comfortable from Puritan pulpits or from mid-eighteenth-century newspapers such as the *Independent Reflector*. But a transformation of symbol occurred in the context of events leading up to the Declaration of Independence. As the natural rights of humankind achieved ascend-

ancy over the particular rights of British subjects, the myth of
Revolution had touched a loadstone of power, and its magnetism
became evident in the growing victory of the patriots over their
unconverted brethren. Curiously, a theological myth of mission
was linked to the philosophy of nature and natural rights. The
amalgamation was only one of the "biformities" which made the
American myth of origins a "two-in-one."[30]

Chosen for an example and imbued with a deep sense of universal mission, Americans, as Israel of old and their fathers before
them, inhabited a promised land. "When we view this country in
its extent and variety," exulted Silas Downer, "we may call it the
promised land, a good land and a large—a land of hills and vallies
[sic], of rivers, brooks, and springs of water—a land of milk and
honey, and wherein we may eat bread to the full."[31] Other patriots agreed. Oratory echoed with the millennial theme in the
land of plenty where, as in Israel's dreams of a future of bliss,
each man would dwell under his own fig tree in the shade of his
vines, while his wife would be a fruitful olive branch surrounded
by her joyful children.

Yet there was a jarring note amid the beauties of Paradise. The
patriots continually announced their fear of the blight which
could hopelessly destroy the new Canaan, for an invasion of sin,
bringing a degeneration and winding down of the world, could
end the millennium. Here was sure evidence that the worldview
of myth was at the core of patriotic awareness, for one recited a
myth in order to bridge the gap between the profane world of
ordinary events and the original world of myth in the strong and
sacred time. The present world had come forth out of the power
of the myth; but in and of itself, the world lacked power and
would speedily return to an inert state. Only contact with living
myth could close the separation, and hence the necessity of drawing strength from remembrance. If one could not be perfect as
the fathers, the solution was to repent and to remember.

It was not surprising that the patriots throughout the Revolution were almost as worried about enslavement through their own

lusts and excesses as they were about enslavement through British tyranny. If there were "deluges of the Old World, drowned in luxury and lewd excess," there could as easily be deluges of the new.[32] John Witherspoon, New Jersey's preacher-delegate to the Congress in 1776, thought nothing "more certain than that a general profligacy and corruption of manners make a people ripe for destruction." A good form of government, he added, might "hold the rotten materials together for some time, but beyond a certain pitch, even the best constitution will be ineffectual, and slavery must ensue."[33] Earlier in 1770, John Adams had seen a parallel between divine government and the human version in which the latter was "more or less perfect, as it approaches nearer or diverges further from an imitation of this perfect plan of divine and moral government." Yet, he warned an invisible audience in the pages of his diary:

In times of simplicity and innocence, ability and integrity will be the principal recommendations to the public service, and the sole title to those honors and emoluments which are in the power of the public to bestow. But when elegance, luxury, and effeminacy begin to be established, these rewards will begin to be distributed to vanity and folly; but when a government becomes totally corrupted, the system of God Almighty in the government of the world, and the rules of all good government upon earth, will be reversed, and virtue, integrity, and ability, will become the objects of the malice, hatred, and revenge of the men in power, and folly, vice, and villany will be cherished and supported.[34]

In this context, George Washington's order to his brigadier-generals in 1777 was representative.

Let vice and immorality of every kind be discouraged as much as possible in your brigade; and, as a chaplain is allowed to each regiment, see that the men regularly attend during worship. Gaming of every kind is expressly forbidden, as being the foundation of evil, and the cause of many a brave and gallant officer's and soldier's ruin.[35]

Writing after the éclat of stirring events, Mercy Warren thought that few would deny that "religion, viewed merely in a political light, is after all the best cement of society, the great barrier of just government, and the only certain restraint of the passions, those dangerous inlets to licentiousness and anarchy."[36] For War- ren and for most of the patriots, luxury and avarice were "totally inconsistent with genuine republicanism." Preachers such as David Tappan regularly inveighed against America's "crimes of the blackest hue" and the "turpitude and guilt of our national provo- cations."[37]

While some, like Nathaniel Whitaker, saw in Toryism a sin against forefathers, contemporaries, and posterity, others, like Samuel Langdon, viewed the cause of the troubles with England as rebellion against God and the loss of a "true spirit of Chris- tianity." "Is it not a fact open to common observation, that pro- faneness, intemperance, unchastity, the love of pleasure, fraud, avarice, and other vices, are increasing among us from year to year? And have not even these young governments been in some measure infected with the corruption of European courts?"[38] Yet, whether sin was a political or a personal reality, it always had a political effect. Citizens must be virtuous because their very com- munal existence as a state could be called into question by their vice. In one instance of a long-standing custom, the Massachusetts Provincial Congress at Watertown legislated against the "unnat- ural War" by condemning "Prophanations" of the Sabbath; thus too the long tradition of congressional proclamations of fasts and thanksgivings which we shall explore in the final chapter.[39]

The most common interpretation of events among the patriots was to see "British oppression" as a visitation for sin, while war defeats required a revival of morality and religion in order to be changed to victory. So, for example, one broadside of 1777 la- mented the "Dreadful Extortion and Other Sins of the Times" (committed against the patriots), offering "a serious EXHORTATION to all to repent and turn from the Evil of their Ways, if they would avert the terrible and heavy JUDGMENTS of the ALMIGHTY that hang over America at this alarming and distressing Day."[40] In another interpretation, the political turmoil acted as a furnace to burn away the dross of sin and purge the new Israel from cor- ruption. Benjamin Rush could write that he hoped the war would "last until it introduces among us the same temperance in pleasure, the same modesty in dress, the same justice in business, and the same veneration for the name of the Deity which distinguished our ancestors."[41]

Whether the actions of England were caused by sin or the cure of it, what emerged was a dualistic view of the world in which the past had been golden and the present stood in peril of decline. The jeremiad, as Perry Miller noted, paid the penny to Jehovah so that Americans could spend the rest of their dollar on their own pursuits.[42] But the jeremiad was also a ritual for mythic remembrance. By clearly experiencing one's sinfulness, one implicitly understood what the opposite condition was about. And so by their lamentation, the patriots underwent a form of *anamnesis*, remembrancing the fathers in such a way that the sons really were present with these ancestors in the golden age of the beginning, *in illo tempore*.

Paradoxically, the jeremiad also looked toward the millennium, for the endtime of peace and plenty was an eschatological transposition of the time of beginning. That is, whether the sacred time of power was seen emerging out of an initial formlessness and chaos, or whether it came as final and perfect form after the world had erupted into the confusion and turmoil of the age before the millennium, it was still the time of the newness when the world experienced the strength of early vigor. In an early nineteenth-century expression, Hesper's words to Columbus in Joel Barlow's *Columbiad* captured the mythic sense.

> Here springs indeed the day, since time began,
> The brightest, broadest, happiest morn of man.
> In these prime settlements thy raptures trace
> The germ, the genius of a sapient race,
> Predestined here to methodize and mold
> New codes of empire to reform the old.
> A work so vast a second world required,
> By oceans bourn'd, from elder states retired;
> Where uncontaminated, unconfined,
> Free contemplation might expand the mind,
> To form, fix, prove the well adjusted plan
> And base and build the commonwealth of man.[43]

As we shall see, the men and women who lived through the Revolution seemed to experience it as that kind of premonitory chaos and anarchy, that dissolution of forms, which would precede the coming of new and perfect form. The jeremiad, the golden age of the fathers, and the future age of the millennium were linked with the strongest of bonds as parallel mythologems of the myth.

But there were further links between their fathers' situation and their own to which the patriots did not allude. It is obvious that the patriots had appropriated the stories of liberty against tyranny and the new Israel in a regenerating wilderness from their understanding of their fathers. At the same time, the men of the Revolution had also received from their ancestors a tradition which had grown more and more comfortable with nature and its laws and increasingly certain that virtuous human activity was the key which would unlock not only the door to salvation but the door to the earthly paradise as well. This tradition is most clearly documented for the Puritan fathers whose past, because it was so well articulated, dominated the revolutionary consciousness, but there are hints that it was more quietly true in the middle and southern colonies. As Richard Merritt has shown, Massachusetts was the earliest articulator of the ideas which culminated in the Revolution, but "the Boston printers by themselves could not produce a symbol revolution."[44] The middle colonies and the southern "nodded their assent" only when, through the processes of inner change, the concerns of the Puritan fathers had been linked to their own understandings and needs.

The records of Puritan experience reveal that the first generation had drawn heart and head together by linking the immediacy of a personal conversion process to reasonable and collective verification in the covenantal community. Yet the much-vaunted "synthesis" seemed to shatter not all at once, with the sudden appearance of revivalism and liberalism as opposing forces, but slowly and gradually. James W. Jones has shown that "throughout the seventeenth century there was an increasing tendency to equate the divine agency with natural causation and human volition. Gradually God's act became simply another name for what, in fact, was happening."[45] Meanwhile, the Great Awakening suggested that perhaps the original Puritan focus on a direct experience of the divine, although it was greatly overshadowed by institutions like the "halfway covenant" and rituals like "owning the covenant," had never really died. Both sides of this Puritan heritage were present in the Revolution, which generated in effect a new and nontraditional religious synthesis, a veritable two-in-one. The lines of the growing crack in the old synthesis had not been so clear as might be supposed. In the mid-eighteenth century, would-be evangelicals could think like liberals when morality and human rights were concerned, and liberals could act as enthusiastically as their Calvinistic brethren.

The religion of nature was already incipiently challenging the ascendancy of the Calvinist God when John Norton began to teach that "God adapts himself to man to the extent of not dealing with man as with a brute creature."[46] It was growing as Giles Firmin began to use human nature as the criterion for deciding what was and what was not correct theology. Ironically, Cotton Mather, that austere preacher of the sovereignty of God, himself helped the humanocentric process along. Mather was a moralist for whom the works of sanctification could be a sign that one was saved, and later Benjamin Franklin would state that Mather's *Essays to do Good* were formative in his (and by implication Poor Richard's) way of living. Moreover, if human nature was raised a notch by Mather's treatment of it, so too was the rest of the natural milieu. Mather indeed was "so enthralled by what he found in nature that he came perilously close to putting nature on a par with Scripture as a source of knowledge about God."[47]

Similarly, Benjamin Colman placed God's sovereignty at the foundation of his theology, yet tied that sovereignty inextricably to God's role as creator of the beauties of the Newtonian cosmos. The God-who-acts was becoming the God whose will was expressed in the laws of nature, since, while humans were as nothing in the sight of God, their reasonable faculties could discover and use the harmonies of the cosmos. For Solomon Stoddard, as the century progressed, God's attractiveness was aesthetic, the effusion of his glory in nature which drew people toward the divine life. Stoddard's grandson, Jonathan Edwards, would himself have a great deal to say about the divine beauty as well as a keen appreciation of the loveliness of natural surroundings.

This sensitivity to the laws of nature as expressed in both human and cosmic form began gradually to take a political shape. With their understanding of themselves as a city on a hill, a theocracy in which God was the true ruler of the political state, the Puritans had always been inclined to treat civic realities as also sacred realities. But the tendency received expression in a manner which would be particularly serviceable for the formation of revolutionary mythology in the writings of John Wise. His *Vindication of the Government of the New England Churches* (1717), written to defend ecclesiastical polity, proved a blueprint for civil democracy and became decidedly influential when it was republished in 1772. Wise had seen himself as opposing Cotton Mather, but when he chose to place his argument from nature before his argument from Scripture in the text of the *Vindication*, he had advanced one side of Mather's thinking toward greater appreciation of the natural world. While it may be an overstatement to say that "some of the most glittering sentences in the immortal Declaration of Independence are almost literal quotations from this essay of John Wise"[48] (since so many were by 1776 speaking in similar vein), the *Vindication* does present an early and emphatic version of the language of reason and nature which became so popular during the Revolution.

Wise, moreover, interwove his use of reason and nature with a mythic view of history. He saw the first three hundred years of the Christian church as an era of near-paradisal perfection, while the next twelve hundred betrayed the "commencement, and Progress of a Direful Apostacy, both as to Worship and Government in the Churches." Yet if the world had wound itself down as it grew further away from the time of origins, it had experienced a mighty regeneration in the Reformation and the New England churches. In language which gloried in the restoration, Wise suggested that "the Churches in New-England; and the Primitive Churches are Eminently parallel in their Government."[49] This perfection for Wise was bound up with early congregational polity which preserved the "Orginal [sic] State and Liberty of Mankind" and was "founded peculiarly in the Light of Nature." The Light of Nature, or alternately, "Light of Reason," was a "Law and Rule of Right" and an "Effect of Christ's goodness, care and creating Power, as well as of Revelation; though Revelation is Natures Law in a fairer and brighter Edition."[50]

The eighteenth century continued to speak in the language of nature and natural religion, as Lemuel Briant asserted human "moral Agency" without trying to relate it to the sovereignty of God and made of Jesus of Nazareth a teacher more than a savior. When, in 1751, Justice Paul Dudley's will set up a fund for the Dudley lectureship on natural and revealed religion, Ebenezer Gay's lecture, "Natural Religion as Distinguished From Revealed," became a milestone for the developing liberal camp. "Revealed Religion is an addition to natural not built upon the Ruins but on the strong and everlasting Foundations of it," Gay had announced.[51] One observer, John Adams, thought that Lemuel Briant and Ebenezer Gay were Unitarians sixty years early.[52]

By the time Jonathan Mayhew and Charles Chauncy were both ministers, New England's preachers had already spent a good part of the century discoursing on such themes as the law of nature and the unalienable rights of human beings, equality, popular sovereignty and the nature of a just constitution, and even life, liberty, and property. Observers of the revolutionary era, many of them unfriendly to the patriots, came to the conclusion that independency in religion and politics went together. Joseph Galloway knew what cognitive consonance was when he wrote:

This kind of popular independence in ecclesiastical, was so nearly allied to that in civil polity, it is scarcely possible to conceive that the human mind could hold the one and reject the other. That kind of reason which led to the one, as strongly inculcated the other; and the principle of either was the principle of both.[53]

If New England sounded the call to which the rest of the colonies responded, the clergy seemed to have the loudest voices. Peter Oliver was contemptuous that the Boston clergy were "esteemed by the others as an Order of Deities." He pointed the finger of accusation especially at Mayhew, Chauncy, and Samuel Cooper, since, he said, they distinguished themselves in encouraging Seditions and Riots, untill [sic] those lesser Offenses were absorbed in Rebellion."[54] One newspaper correspondent identified among the "high sons of liberty" those "ministers of the gospel, who, instead of preaching to their flocks meekness, sobriety, attention to their different employments, and a steady obedience to the laws of Britain, belch from the pulpit liberty, independence, and a steady perseverance in endeavoring to shake off their allegiance to the mother country."[55] "The clergy of New-England," wrote David Ramsay more tamely, "were a numerous, learned and respectable body, who had a great ascendancy over the minds of their hearers. They connected religion and patriotism, and, in their sermons and prayers, represented the cause of America as the cause of Heaven."[56]

While it was true that the preachers tended to be an incendiary lot, it is important to emphasize that part of their rousing argument was couched in the language of natural rights and natural law. Beyond that, their sermons, both liberal and evangelical, suggested strongly that the proper (i.e., natural) behavior of human beings was virtue and the proper arena for the enactment of virtuous pursuits was public. And their message was spreading beyond New England's borders. One example was the sermonizing of the evangelical Samuel Davies, who, as president of the College of New Jersey (Princeton), touched the minds and lives of many of the young men of the Revolution, Benjamin Rush among them. In his *Religion and Public Spirit*, addressed to the graduates of the class of 1760, Davies used the model of King David, a public man whose excellence consisted in "two Things, PUBLICK SPIRIT and

RELIGION.—Publick Spirit, *in serving his Generation*,—and Religion, in doing this *according to the Will of God*." For Davies, a religion without the presence of "public spirit" seemed more a vice than a virtue, for it was "but a sullen, selfish, sour and malignant Humour for Devotion, unworthy that sacred Name." Activity and righteousness, pragmatism and the need to make one's mark were blended in Davies's exhortations.

But if you feel the generous impulses of a publick Spirit, you can never be altogether insignificant, you will never be mere Cyphers in the World, even in the obscurest and most sequestered Vale of Life. Even in the lowest Station, you will be of some Use to Mankind, a sufficient Recompense this for the severe Conflict of sixty or seventy Years.[57]

Generally speaking, despite their Calvinistic doctrines, the Edwardseans who came out of the Great Awakening were preaching the virtuous life which was the external sign of the genuineness of the conversion experience. Revival techniques themselves might be called a step in the direction of "Arminian means," while the Anglicans of the southern colonies seemed already to have been preaching a species of de facto Arminianism for a long time. But it was above all the liberal clergy, now a distinguishable presence, who preached of natural rights and moral duties.

In Boston Jonathan Mayhew was holding forth from the pulpit of the West Church after 1747. As Charles Akers has remarked, "The study of his life makes it easier to understand how a nation of orthodox Christians, led by such near-Deists as Benjamin Franklin, John Adams, and Thomas Jefferson, could undertake a revolution justified by the theory that all men 'are endowed by their Creator with certain unalienable rights.' "[58] If "the liberals transformed the practical nature of Puritan theology into a theological precursor of American pragmatism,"[59] Mayhew's Arminian understanding of the process of salvation as contractual and moralistic was a strong enunciation of the position. Intellectual formulations and theological refinements were distasteful to Mayhew, who saw meaning and value elsewhere, in the life of activity.

"It is infinitely dishonourable to the all good and perfect Governor of the world," he preached, "to imagine that he has suspended the eternal salvation of men upon any niceties of speculation: or that any one who honestly aims at finding the truth, and at doing the will of his maker, shall be finally discarded because he fell into some erroneous opinions."[60] The pastor of the West Church was close here to the religion of righteous deeds on the field of battle and the stage of government, where individuals, as independent entities, gained their places in history.

Moral action, for Mayhew, was grounded not merely in Christian revelation but in the law of nature, a law he considered "obligatory upon all Mankind without exception; because it is promulg'd to all."[61] Mayhew's sermon *Unlimited Submission* (1750) joined the language of natural rights and reason to the motifs of British tyranny and slavery oppressing the true lovers of liberty. This ringing defense of the Puritan and Glorious Revolutions against the canonization of King Charles I, who had died at Puritan hands, became, as time progressed, a defense of the right of revolution per se. Some have seen its language in Thomas Jefferson's Declaration of Independence. It is difficult not to agree when one reads such passages as Mayhew's condemnation of Charles I for excessive and despotic taxation.

He levied many taxes upon the people without consent of parliament; and then imprisoned great numbers of the principal merchants and gentry for not paying them. He erected, or at least revived, several new and arbitrary courts, in which the most unheard-of barbarities were committed with his knowledge and approbation. . . . He sent a large sum of money, which he had raised by his arbitrary taxes, into *Germany*, to raise foreign troops, in order to force more arbitrary taxes upon his subjects.[62]

When the good news reached Boston, in 1766, that the Stamp Act had been repealed, Mayhew's famous sermon, *The Snare Broken*, celebrated the "natural right" that human beings had to their own persons and clearly named the twin sources for the consciousness out of which he spoke.

Having been initiated, in youth, in the doctrines of civil liberty in general, as they were taught by such men as Plato, Demosthenes, Cicero and other renowned persons among the ancients; and such as Sidney and Milton, Locke and Hoadley, among the moderns, I liked them; they seemed rational. Having earlier still learned from the Holy Scriptures that wise, brave and virtuous men were always friends to liberty; that God gave the Israelites a king (or absolute monarch) in his anger, because they had not sense and virtue enough to like a free commonwealth, and to have himself for their king; that the Son of God came down from heaven to make us 'free indeed,' and that where the spirit of the Lord is, there is liberty; this made me conclude that freedom was a great blessing.[63]

Mayhew's geographical and ideological neighbor was Charles Chauncy of the First Church in Boston. God, for Chauncy, gradually reshaped himself in the human image, a transformation which, as we shall see, was being carried out on the plane of activity in the American Revolution, as it more and more conveyed an implicit understanding of a deity found in the midst of human rational energy and control. By denying the imputation of Adam's guilt and the transmission of his sinful nature to others, Chauncy was teaching a kind of truth-in-activity. No human being who came into the world arrived as a "fallen creature who must be reclaimed but rather as a potentiality that must be actualized."[64] The possibility now existed for a morality grounded, not in the traditional tenets of Christian teaching, but transportable to whatever new religious framework might be at hand. Such a framework would be provided in the emerging religion of the American Revolution. Humans for Chauncy controlled their own destinies as *separate* individuals; hence, an atomistic understanding grounded his view of human nature as much as it did the natural rights teaching of the public documents of the Revolution. Although it might be argued that God's benevolence got in the way of human autonomy in his teaching with its emphasis on the salvation of all, Chauncy, despite the theological problem, stood with Mayhew as a prime representative of one source of the moralism of the new religion. Like Mayhew, he had been true to his fathers.

Moralism had been introduced to Boston long before Chauncy was born. No less a Puritan than Cotton Mather made man's duty and moral improvement the focus of his preaching. It was not the invention of the liberals; rather, they were the product of a long line of development in that direction. Chauncy's originality was that he redid all Puritan theology to arrive at a doctrine of man whereby man is able to make himself into whatever he becomes.[65]

At the same time, he was teaching an understanding of faith which also placed it close to the reason of the American Enlightenment. Again, in keeping with the tradition which had developed from the seventeenth-century fathers, Chauncy viewed faith as chiefly an assent of the mind and intellect to certain propositions. As the definition of faith grew more and more external, devotion to duty became a key to the genuineness of each given individual's assent.

By the end of the Revolution, many patriotic laymen could agree with Chauncy. The descendants of the fathers had appropriated and expanded that part of their past which struck the chord most in tune with the "secular" cultural milieu out of which the religion of the Revolution would emerge. The sons of the fathers had more and more seen the mighty acts of God in the unchanging laws of the Newtonian universe; they had seen the reasonableness of the divine plan in nature and the beauty and utility of reason. Above all, it seemed reasonable to these sons of the fathers who became the men of the Revolution to view human life in terms of regular and correct human activity, for the laws of nature could be found in the midst of the human community as well as in the harmony of the universe. Typically in 1768, Silas Downer, the High Son of Liberty, found that the people could not be "governed by laws, in the making of which they had no hand." Their privilege was "*inherent*," not to be "*granted* by any but the Almighty," a "natural right which no creature can *give*, or hath a right to take away."[66] By 1779, Sam-

uel Stillman was only speaking conventionally when he affirmed
the truth of human equality in the law of nature: "The sovereignty resides originally in the people."[67]

While we have been emphasizing understandings of natural
law, reason, and virtue which, part of the inherited Puritan worldview, expressed themselves in the American Revolution, we cannot ignore the "enthusiastic" elements. Alan Heimert's exhaustive
treatment of the relationship between the Great Awakening and
the Revolution is too well known to require more than mention.
And Perry Miller has pointed to the parallels between revivalism
and democracy, both of which require the "man in the bench"
to speak up and act his piece.[68] Still more, the Calvinistic emphasis on the power of God found ready expression during the
era of Revolution in the appeals to Jehovah, God of Battles. At
the same time, contemporaries were linking the new events of the
political sphere to the spirit and language of enthusiasm which
had been used in the great revivals. It was not simply that "enthusiastic" clergy supported the Revolution with their sermons
and their lives, but more that an *enthusiastic spirit*, which was
recognized as such, gripped the populace which perpetrated the
war. We shall discuss this enthusiasm more fully in the next chapter, but it is impossible to omit some reference here. Quite simply,
people knew, and knew that they knew, that political uprisings
were really grand revivals. One hears in their language the echoes
of revivalistic ardor and millennial zeal, for Armageddon was
surely close at hand when divine enthusiasm was unleashed by
righteous patriots against demonic British soldiers.

Therefore, the patriots knit up in their new revolutionary myth
both sides of an older union of head and heart. In a transformation of the old symbolism, they still spoke the language of nature
and moral rectitude at the same time that they experienced the
zeal of revolutionary rage in legions directed by the Lord of
Hosts. The tension between the opposites held the myth together
as a sacred story which shared the archetypal quality of all myth:
the ability to express and sometimes to resolve contradiction.[69]

Structural analysis shows that both sides were present and both sides pulled their weight in the revolutionary story. Historical analysis indicates that the binary opposites which met in the revolutionary motifs were inherited in some measure from the fathers. While it would be emotionally and aesthetically pleasing at this point to launch into a happy-ever-after conclusion about the dualities being resolved into a final unity, the later history of the republic revealed that the myth expressed tension more than resolved it, kept two kinds of concerns in a highly charged balance more than dissolved them into one perfect form. In this respect, the new synthesis was more a statement of the opposites than a resolution of them.

Curiously, the mediating symbol which seemed still to be at hand was the old Puritan covenant, now transmuted into democratic form.[70] Particularly in New England, one notices that when the colonists had dissolved themselves into a state of nature by renouncing their ties with England, they began to constitute themselves anew in covenantal relationships. The Committee of Correspondence at Boston formed a "solemn league and covenant" by which "the subscribers bound themselves in the most solemn manner, and in the presence of God, to suspend all commercial intercourse with Great Britain."[71] Meanwhile, the committee for the town of Plainfield, New Hampshire, formulated a covenant oath which was typical of many in the area. "We the subscribers. . . . Do in the presence of God solemnly and in good faith covenant and engage with each other that from henceforth we will suspend all commercial intercourse with the said Island of Great Britain until the Parliament shall cease to enact laws imposing taxes upon the Colonies without their consent, or until the pretended right of taxing is dropped."[72]

There was an obvious link between the sovereignty of the people and the covenant relationship, a link perhaps most succinctly expressed in the revolutionary era by John Wise's *Vindication*. "The first Humane Subject and Original of Civil Power is the People," Wise had written. "Let us conceive in our Mind a multitude of Men, all Naturally Free & Equal; going about voluntarily, to Erect themselves into a new Common-Wealth." How would they do it? For Wise, the answer was simple and easy: "They must Interchangeably each Man Covenant to joyn in one lasting Society, that they may be capable to concert the measures of their safety, by a Publick Vote."[73] The laws of nature were respected in that humans were treated as the free and equal beings who they were; virtue had been attained because men had *acted* rightly and correctly in covenanting together; passion entered with the sense of need and determination to do something by creating a governmental structure. Finally, for Wise, it was clear that the Lord God must direct the enterprise in order for it to succeed.

Beyond this, the new synthesis was occurring in a form which did not render it easily discernible as religion for the patriots who became a part of it. Previous training had made it clear what religious realities were: they concerned God and his church, sin and grace, death and judgment, heaven and hell. The new revolutionary myth would certainly hold God within its compass—and indeed mold its understanding of him into another two-in-one. The myth would also chart a course of moral action for virtuous citizens. But much of the most colorful language from the traditional religious past was missing, and as the myth developed it became more humanocentric and less concerned with a heavenly realm. Thus, when the Puritan synthesis was partially fused again in the furnace of the Revolution, the amalgamation came in a transformed and "secular" condition as the civil religion of the new United States. The vertical was horizontalized; transcendence was flattened but did not disappear. For now the transcendent object of religion would become more and more America itself. A dynamic thrust had begun: a change which would continue along one gradient—the humanocentric—had been initiated.

Despite the inability of the patriots to recognize their new religion as religion because of the nontraditional language which mediated it, the evolving synthesis did provide a strong vehicle for carrying the values enshrined in the religious mythology of their fathers. The God-who-acted lived on in human beings who continued to imitate his endeavors, exerting themselves strenuously in righteous causes and deeds. Action therefore was, as in the past, a prime bearer of value. More than that, making history and taking one's role upon the public stage extended the life of the city on the hill with its exemplary and missionary import. Moral action was public action, part of the great drama of meaningful and significant events. Finally, right action was action that looked toward the future. Even in the era of the Revolution, the age of progress was at hand, since the patriots who worshiped their fathers seemed as concerned for the future of their sons.

But perhaps the most significant mythologem of the myth which the patriots took from their fathers and transformed unwittingly to their new concerns was the notion of the "fathers" itself. In 1775, Thomas Jefferson had eloquently summarized the myth of the fathers out of which the Revolution began.

Our forefathers, inhabitants of the island of Great Britain, left their native land to seek on these shores a residence for civil and religious freedom at the expense of their blood, to the ruin of their fortunes, with the relinquishment of everything quiet and comfortable in life, they effected settlements in the inhospitable wilds of America.[74]

A decade later, the Reverend Dr. Ladd was delivering an oration before the governor of South Carolina for the Fourth of July. "When we consider this as the natal anniversary of our infant empire," he told the governor and the other members of the audience, "we shall ever be led to call into grateful recollection the fathers of our independence: those to whom (under God) we are indebted for our political existence and salvation."[75] The contrast was telling: within a decade the fathers who trod the wilderness had become the men of the Revolution. These fathers faced the social wilderness of the dissolution of governmental forms in the creation of the new order. Both sets of fathers were patriarchs. But as the civil religion grew with the early nineteenth century and beyond, it was clear that the revolutionary sons had supplanted their ancestral fathers to become the fathers of all America.

A Tree Grows
in Boston

The sons of the fathers became fathers themselves in the course of the Revolution because of a series of events which made them new centers of authority and power. In the midst of their Revolution, the patriots moved from being traditional people to being charismatic people, poised on the edge of equally charismatic events. As traditional people, they had seen themselves as the heirs of a long and indefinite series of heroes and deeds which extended to the first generation of their ancestors in the new world, and beyond them to the conflicts of their fathers in the Puritan Revolution, the struggles of earlier Anglo-Saxons for the rights of Englishmen, and the sufferings of ancient Hebrews in the Exodus which brought them out of slavery and into freedom. Their actions possessed warrant and metaphysical validity because they were patterned on the model which had existed from time immemorial: they in the present were secure because they were repeating an exemplary action from out of the past. Yet while still invoking their fathers, the patriots were finding in their actions a creative power without reference to the models from the past. They began to function as self-constituting and self-commanding figures. Americans and their deeds were standing on their own ground at a new point of mythical beginning. J. G. A. Pocock has put the matter succinctly:

Most societies have their culture-heroes or founding fathers; but to imagine traditions of behaviour originating in specific actions is to imagine actions whose creative power is not explained by any antecedent tradition. Hence the charismatic figure who stands at the mythical beginnings of so many traditions—the gods, heroes, prophets and legislators, who abound in the legends even of highly institutionalised societies and provide the inheritors of tradition with occasion to imagine politics and other activities as consisting of charismatic (which here include rationalist) instead of traditional action, and time as a sequence of such actions instead of as institutional continuity. What stands outside tradition is charismatic; where time itself is envisaged as the continuity of tradition, the charismatic may stand outside time and become the sacred.[1]

Essentially, the movement from tradition to charisma meant passage from old form to new. The ancient forces which had held a world together dissolved. Out of the confusion which resulted, a new order emerged in a mythic process which was analogous to a cosmogony. It was the creation of a world, now not on the physical plane, but in the spiritual realm which Americans inhabited: the social construction of reality *in illo tempore*, a first moment, not outside of history, but in the stream of historical events. The new myth of the Revolution was a work of *bricolage*, a story fashioned out of the bits and pieces of random events which had in common that they had occurred and were malleable enough to be shaped into the structure the patriots were creating even as they honored their fathers.[2]

Collectively experienced and told, the story was also collectively acted out, as a series of rituals grew up to dramatize the inner meaning of outward events, some of the liturgies one-time-only affairs, and some quickly acquiring an annual character. Objects which figured in the sacred theater of public demonstration themselves took on a sacred aura and became symbolic of the developing struggle. Meanwhile, the interrelated structure of event-centered rituals and objects and the collective tale, which made them part of a whole, resembled a grand initiatory schema. The colonies underwent a death to an old order of being, experienced the liminality of existence betwixt and between, and were transfigured in the reality of new birth as a single nation. Dying to the old and on the threshold of the new, the colonists' existential situation was characterized by what Victor Turner has called a state

of *communitas*, an easing of the strict social boundaries which separated person from person and the discovery of a sense of mutual-
ity in the event which made the importance of roles diminish and
the fellowship of the moment grow.[3] The colonists and some who
observed them described this condition as "enthusiasm."

When contemporaries spoke in so many words of the enthusiasm of the Revolution, as we have already noted, they were unconsciously linking the collective changes society was undergoing
to the private and personal initiations of the Great Awakening. It
is worth a glance at the revival experiences to understand more
precisely what the colonists meant. The conversion process which
a person underwent during a revival was a private initiation experience in which the individual died to an old life, encountered
the nebulousness and formlessness of existence in between, and
finally emerged as a person touched by the power of God which
had saved him or her from the results of sin. This work of God
operated not merely in the quiet depths of the soul, but, because
humans were embodied spirits, it could produce physical and
emotional effects. Thus, the death to an old life which the convert experienced might be dramatized in the "falling exercise";
the amorphousness of existence in a marginal and placeless land
of the spirit, convicted of sin and yet not saved by the grace of
God, could occasion the shouts and shrieks which had caused the
liberal clergy to look askance; new birth could generate outbursts
of ecstatic joy or tears and the compulsion to zealous witnessing.
Any or all of these happenings might be described as enthusiasm,
although in practice the term applied more to the second and
third stages of the experience, the states of margin and aggrega-
tion, in which *communitas* seemed indicated.

During the revolutionary era, as event followed event, culmi-
nating in actual hostilities, enthusiasm was paramount. Hermon
Husband's description of a smaller revolution of the period, the
North Carolina Regulator movement, was paradigmatic. Here,
Husband related what happened when an innocent person was
taken into custody as a Regulator and an alarm went forth among

the people. With the exception of the single detail that the men were armed, Husband could have been telling the story of the crowds who went to hear George Whitefield.

This Alarm immediately so engaged almost every Man, Woman and Child, that by Day-Light, next Morning, some Hundreds were assembled near the Town, which Numbers, in an Hour or two, encreased to Odds of seven Hundred armed Men; many of which had traveled forty odd Miles on foot, some bare footed, and some (at least one) had traveled thirty Miles with Shoes slip-shod; but the most part were on Horseback. The whole was actuated by what the World calls the Spirit of Enthusiasm, for I felt it myself as soon as I came into the Company; it catched every Man, good or bad, as Saul was catched among the Prophets.—A man Under the Opperation of this Spirit, I am certain, can do and undergo double what he can at another Time.— It is prodigiously dangerous to raise this Spirit, if it is nothing but Natural, as some imagine; but I believed it was a Work of Providence, and therefore feared no Evil.[4]

Others shared Husband's perceptions and applied them to the larger revolutionary fervor of the colonies. "Perhaps there are no people on earth, in whom a spirit of enthusiastic zeal is so readily enkindled, and burns so remarkably conspicuous, as among the Americans," wrote Mercy Otis Warren as she looked back on revolutionary events. "This characteristic trait may in some measure account for the rapidity with which everything has been brought to maturity there from the first settlement of the colonies."[5] Pondering on the results of the Stamp Act, David Ramsay discussed the effects of the Resolutions of the State of Virginia: "The fire of liberty blazed forth from the press; some well judged publications set the rights of the colonists in a plain, but strong point of view. The tongues and the pens of the well informed citizens laboured in kindling the latent spark of patriotism. The flame spread from breast to breast, till the conflagration become [sic] general."[6]

In Boston, Peter Oliver, the brother of the ill-fated stamp distributor, found that the "*Hydra* was roused" with a "Frenzy of Anarchy" so that "every Man was jealous of his Neighbour, &

such was the political Enthusiasm, that the Minds of the most
pious Men seemed to be wholly absorbed in the Temper of Riot."
When the clergy preached "Manufactures instead of Gospel,"
Oliver sardonically observed that there was abroad a "new Species
of Enthusiasm," which "might be justly termed, the Enthusiasm
of the Spinning Wheel";[7] and after the Boston Massacre had
again electrified public opinion in 1770, the town instructed its
representatives to deport themselves "like the faithful representatives of a freeborn, awakened, and determined people."[8] Warren
told how committees of correspondence began to spring up: the
idea for such committees was "adopted with zeal, and spread with
the rapidity of enthusiasm from town to town, and from province
to province." Writing contemporaneously, John Adams confided
to his diary that the universal cry of the people was "What shall
we do to be saved?"[9]

As Ramsay summarized reaction to the Boston Port Bill, he
wrote of the general state of Americans in all the colonies.

The season of universal distress, exhibited a striking proof, how prac-
ticable it is for mankind to sacrifize [sic] ease, pleasure, and interest,
when the mind is strongly excited by its passion. In the midst of their
sufferings, cheerfulness appeared in the face of all the people. They
counted every thing cheap in comparison with liberty, and readily
gave up whatever tended to endanger it. A noble strain of generosity
and mutual support was generally excited. A great and powerful dif-
fusion of public spirit took place. The animation of the times, raised
the actors in these scene above themselves, and excited them to deeds
of self denial, which the interested prudence of calmer seasons can
scarcely credit.[10]

"There was not a jobber in the street, a peasant in the field, or
a cottager on the rugged mountain's side, whose heart did not
glow with ardent zeal for vigorous or self-denying exertions in
defence of his invaded rights," wrote one correspondent in 1774.[11]
Another assured a British reader that "an enthusiastic love of liberty has pervaded the whole continent of America, which, if
properly directed, would lay the foundation of a great empire."[12]

The enthusiasm which ran through the American populace had its objective correlative in the dissolution of social and governmental forms they were experiencing, a phenomenon which meant that liminality was not simply a state of mind but an external and factual condition. Sometimes the patriots expressed their understanding of what was happening to them by referring to the "state of nature" to which events had caused them to return. There was widespread agreement that a state of nature was a time of social and governmental formlessness, whether that situation was interpreted positively or negatively. For Simeon Howard, who was typical, it was a condition of existence "without any laws or government established . . . by mutual consent" in which everyone had "an equal right to liberty." For Samuel Cooke, who agreed, when a society emerged from a state of nature all were "upon a level" and an individual could "justly challenge a right to make or execute the laws."[13] Charles Woodmason, on the contrary, decried the state of nature among the South Carolinians: "Thro' want of Ministers to marry and thro' the licentiousness of the People, many hundreds live in Concubinage—swopping their Wives as Cattel and living in a State of Nature, more irregularly and unchastely than the Indians."[14]

Even those who saw the state of nature as a moment of wild opportunity sensed that it was fraught with danger. Those who described the colonial state of affairs in these terms communicated the quality of peril it involved. Patrick Henry, debating in the First Continental Congress, announced:

Government is dissolved. Fleets and armies and the present state of things show that government is dissolved. Where are your landmarks, your boundaries of Colonies? We are in a state of nature, sir.

The distinctions between Virginians, Pennsylvanians, New Yorkers, and New Englanders, are no more. I am not a Virginian, but an American.[15]

For Henry, the peril was balanced by the experience of *communitas* in discovering what it meant to be an American. But for Mercy Warren, writing later to describe these same years, the

breakdown of organized forms had assumed more fearful proportions.

While matters hung in this suspense, the people in all the shire towns
collected in prodigious numbers to prevent the sitting of the courts of
common law, forbidding the justices to meet, or the jurors to em-
pannel, and obliging all civil magistrates to bind themselves by oath,
not to conform to the late acts of parliament in any judiciary proceedings; and all military officers were called upon to resign their
commissions. Thus were the bands of society relaxed, law set at
defiance, and government unhinged throughout the province. Perhaps
this may be marked in the annals of time, as one of the most extraordinary eras in the history of man: the exertions of spirit awakened by
the severe hand of power had led to that most alarming experiment
of levelling all ranks, and destroying all subordination.[16]

Warren had put her finger on the insecurity of life in a pre-
existent chaos of the sociopolitical order. Sometimes descriptions
of the dissolution of forms were, however, couched in the language of corruption. It was the British Empire which was undergoing the last throes of disease and death, and heroic colonials
must root and branch for themselves if they wished to enjoy life
and health once again. Richard Bland, in a political tract of 1766,
found that the British Constitution had departed from its "original Purity" and recommended the remedy. "It would be a Work
worthy of the best patriotick Spirits in the Nation to effectuate
an Alteration in this putrid Part of the Constitution; and, by restoring it to its pristine Perfection, prevent any 'Order or Rank
of the Subjects from imposing upon or binding the rest without
their Consent.'" He feared that unfortunately "the Gangrene"
had "taken too deep Hold to be eradicated in these Days of
Venality."[17]

In another tract, Henry Laurens apostrophized: "O America!
how great would be thy happiness and the happiness of that Empire with which thou art so closely united in interest and affection
could a physician be found of sufficient probity and wisdom to
undertake a perfect and radical cure of those disorders under
which thy trade at present languishes!"[18] Preacher Samuel Langdon in 1775 thought that the measures of Parliament might "soon

reduce the body politic to a miserable, dismembered, dying trunk." "We must keep our eyes fixed on the supreme government of the ETERNAL KING," he urged, "suffering the best forms of human government to degenerate and go to ruin by corruption; or restoring the decayed constitutions of kingdoms and states by reviving public virtue and religion, and granting the favorable interpositions of his providence."[19] Earlier, John Adams, writing under the pen name Novanglus, had warned that "the nature of the encroachment upon the American constitution is such, as to grow every day more and more encroaching. Like a cancer, it eats faster and faster every hour."[20]

Elsewhere, Adams had seen the liminal condition of Boston as a kind of death which must precede a new and better form of life. "The town of Boston," he wrote to his wife, Abigail, "for aught I can see, must suffer martyrdom. It must expire. And our principal consolation is, that it dies in a noble cause—the cause of truth, of virtue, of liberty, and of humanity, and that it will probably have a glorious resurrection to greater wealth, splendor, and power, than ever."[21]

Both patriots and Loyalists used natural metaphors to describe what they were perceiving and experiencing; and some of them spoke about its catastrophic quality in terms which suggested the power and terror of events. Jonathan Boucher, a Loyalist, discussed revolution in general in the metaphor of a volcano, whereas Peter Oliver spoke more specifically of Massachusetts Bay, "the *Volcano* from whence issued all the Smoak, Flame & Lava which hath since enveloped the whole British american Continent, for the Length of above 1700 Miles."[22] The letter of one Philadelphia correspondent appeared in a London newspaper warning the British that "we are in danger of being shipwrecked upon your rocks. To avoid these, we are willing to be tossed, without a compass or a guide, for a while upon an ocean of blood."[23]

Those who lived to see the end of the era of Revolution looked back on their past in similar terms. Enos Hitchcock, after the new federal Constitution was officially adopted, mused that "the road to empire has usually been slow and difficult.—As order progres-

sively arose out of Chaos by the forming hand of the great Architect, so must a well-ordered government be collected and formed
from the scattered materials and wild mixture of a chaotic people."[24] And as usual, Mercy Warren spoke from the fund of collective imagery.

It may be observed, that public commotions in human affairs, like the
shocks of nature, convulse the whole system, and level the lofty
mountains, which have arisen for ages above the clouds, beneath the
vallies [sic]; while the hillock, unnoticed before, is raised to a pitch
of elevation, that renders it a landmark for the eye of the weary
seaman to rest upon.[25]

We gain another vehicle of access to the breakdown of form
through Richard Merritt's study of symbols of American community in the colonial newspapers. Merritt's work indicated that
"explicit and royal British symbols all but disappeared from the
language of the colonial press in the decade prior to the outbreak
of the Revolution."[26] But the vacuum in language was quickly
filled. In terms which suggested the human bonding produced in
a liminal situation, American newspapers supplanted their references to British names and places with more and more reminders
of mutual identification. For Merritt, this communal structure of
consciousness preceded the occurrence of major dramatic events
rather than followed them, but such events "most assuredly reinforced the colonists' growing sense of American separatism. It
was this interplay that, more than anything else, led to the Revolution and the formation of the American Union."[27] A growing
sentiment which declared with Patrick Henry, "I am an American," seemed to shape and in turn to be shaped by the events on
which the myth of Revolution began to focus. Already, with the
growing consciousness of being American, a world existed in
which new form had come to be.

But if the patriots sensed their precarious condition, they also
suspected its promise. They reflected their awareness in language
which hinted of the emergence of the new. Three days before his
death in 1766, Jonathan Mayhew wrote a letter to James Otis in

which he suggested what the shape of things to come could be.
"You have heard of the *communion* of *churches*, . . . while I was
thinking of this in my bed, with the dawn of day, the great use
and importance of a *communion* of *colonies*, appeared to me in a
very strong light, which determined me immediately to set down
these hints, in order to transmit them to you."[28] At first in structures such as the committees of correspondence and safety and
later in the continental congresses, the newness was rising. Mercy
Warren marvelled at what had occurred.

It is indeed a singular phenomenon in the story of human conduct,
that when all legal institutions were abolished, and long established
governments at once annihilated in so many distinct states, that the
recommendations of committees and conventions, not enforced by
penal sanctions, should be equally influential and binding with the
severest code of law, backed by royal authority, and strengthened by
the murdering sword of despotism.[29]

New form required re-formers, and John Adams, looking back,
was sure of the religious nature of the American version. James
Otis had been Martin Luther *redivivus*, whom Providence had
raised to "split the knotty lignum vitae block of parliamentary
usurpation over the colonies," just as the first Luther had been a
wedge to split "so hard and knotty a block, as the Papal usurpation upon mankind." Furthermore, "if Otis was Martin Luther,
Samuel Adams was John Calvin. If Luther was rough, hasty, and
loved good cheer, Calvin was cool, abstemious, polished and re-
fined, though more inflexible, uniform and consistent."[30]
    The revivalists of the Great Awakening had seen the converted
soul as a "new creation" and a "new birth" which was "the beginning of all genuine religion and virtue." In like fashion, the
colonists looked on the emerging order as the birth of new form:
it was that toward which their collective initiatory experience was
tending, a new life in sociopolitical flesh and spirit. Adams had
written home to his wife, Abigail, from Philadelphia to tell her
that "great events" were "struggling into birth," and he could not
quit his station.[31] At the end of the war, his friend Benjamin Rush

acknowledged to Granville Sharp that the "language" of American independence "has for many years appeared to me to be the same as that of the heavenly host that announced the birth of the Saviour of mankind. It proclaims 'glory to God in the highest—on earth peace—good will to man.' "[32] With similar sentiments, the "American Whig" in 1768 told the New-York Gazette and Post-Boy that "in proportion to the abatement of national glory in Europe would be the brightness of its resurrection in America."[33]

Fresh and strong from the womb of history, the new order displayed exemplary virtue—at least for some. One popular ballad of the period suggested the remarkable sobriety of American citizens.

> No pleasure-chaises fill the streets,
>   Nor crowd the roads on Sunday,
> So horses ambling thro' the week,
>   Obtain a respite one day.
>
> All gaming, tricking, swearing, lying,
>   Is grown quite out of fashion;
> For modern youth's so self-denying,
>   It flies all lawless passion.[34]

Howard Mumford Jones has pointed to the sense of classical and Roman virtue which prevailed confidently during the years of the war,[35] and even in the postwar era when the jeremiads provided a steady diet of moral woes to be bewailed, the future promised to be an adventure in regeneration. Joel Barlow, if he exceeded others in his bombast, did not exceed them in his assessment. American freedom would recreate the moral frame of the world out of the chaos of spiritual despotism. Here was America's universal vocation:

> Mold a fair model for the realms of earth,
> Call moral nature to a second birth,
> Reach, renovate the world's great social plan
> And here commence the sober sense of man.[36]

The language of the new was also expressed in perceptions of the Revolution as an initiatory passage from childhood to maturity. Barlow was faithful to the revolutionary spirit when he later incorporated this popular conception into his poem. America was the place where Hesper's words to Columbus had been illustrated.

> Man is an infant still; and slow and late
> Must form and fix his adolescent state,
> Mature his manhood and at last behold
> His reason ripen and his force unfold.[37]

Joseph Galloway, although he disagreed, admitted more prosaically in 1780 "the opinion of some men, that Colonies cannot be long kept in subordination to the Parent State. That, like individuals in the different stages of life, they will in their youth be subordinate; but as soon as they are arrived at strength and maturity, they will naturally become discontented, and throw off their connection with their Parent State."[38] One member of the Virginia Convention, earlier in 1776, sharing Galloway's metaphor if not his politics, insisted that "he who would keep a community in a state of infantile dependence, when it became a fit member of the great republic of the world, would be vastly more criminal and infamous than [a private] imaginary family."[39]

The patriots displayed some sort of what can be called a mythic awareness as they participated in the events which were unfolding. Ultimately however, actions, for the patriots, spoke louder than words. Hezekiah Niles remarked in 1822, as he considered the era of Revolution, that "the patriots . . . did not make speeches to be unattended to by their brethren in congress and fill up the columns of newspapers. They only spoke when they had something to say, and preferred *acting* to *talking*."[40] Part of the significant action which prevailed among the patriots was ritual action. Arthur M. Schlesinger, Jr., aptly summarized its importance when he spoke of the planners of popular demonstrations who "by accenting rites rather than rights . . . influenced minds untouched by constitutional and economic issues."[41] It was clear though that the people were not convinced against their will: those who dramatized the myth in collective rituals were touching a sensitive popular nerve, or their presentations would never have produced such impact. The myth, already alive, received an infusion of power by being objectified in ritual action; when internalized again it carried fresh authenticity as the story which was "really real." John Adams noticed the process at a dinner of the Dorchester Sons of Liberty in 1769 when everybody began to sing John Dickinson's "Liberty Song." It was, said Adams, an excellent mode of "cultivating the sensations of freedom."[42]

Indeed, the Sons of Liberty who presided over so many of the early ritual responses to the Stamp Act seemed an advance force of missionaries for the new civil religion. An organization aimed at the working class, the Sons of Liberty possessed no central organization but were effectively knit throughout the colonies by means of a network of committees of correspondence. Elbridge Goss, in his nineteenth-century biography of Paul Revere, hinting strongly at their religious character, explained that the Sons were a secret society with a secret language for recognition. One source told that on public occasions each member wore around his neck a "medal, on one side of which was the figure of a stalwart arm, grasping in its hand a pole surmounted with a Cap of Liberty, and surrounded by the words 'Sons of Liberty.' On the reverse was the emblem of the Liberty Tree."[43]

The medal of the Sons of Liberty, with its symbolic Liberty Tree, was a religious object, for in the early period of the revolutionary era, the custom of using a special tree as the sacramental center for ritual spread throughout the colonies. The Sons of Liberty had been the primary instruments in inaugurating the practice, and when they did so in the Stamp Act crisis, they had unwittingly stumbled upon a religious symbol which would become the focal point for the religion of the American Revolution in its emergent phase. In cultures throughout the world, religious seers and simple people alike had spoken of a Tree which was the axis of the earth, the center of the world that, touching the sky, united the human to the divine realm. Sometimes too they had dramatized their awareness in rituals in which they expressed their affirmations of the life-giving power of the cosmos and their relationship to it. It is to the American version of this tree that we must now turn for a deeper understanding of religious structure in the Revolution. The Liberty Tree became the carrier of the myth of the newness revealed in the unfolding of historical events.

On August 14, 1765, at the height of the protest against the Stamp Act, the formal manifestation of Liberty Tree appeared among Americans. David Ramsay recounted what had happened.

A new mode of displaying resentment against the friends of the stamp act, began in Massachusetts, and was followed by the other colonies. A few gentlemen hung out, early in the morning on the limb of a large tree, towards the entrance of Boston, two effigies, one designed for the stamp master, the other for a jack boot, with a head and horns peeping out at the top. Great numbers both from town and country came to see them. A spirit of enthusiasm was diffused among the spectators. In the evening the whole was cut down, and carried in procession by the populace, shouting "liberty and property forever, no stamps."[44]

So began a pattern which would repeat itself often in the months and years that followed, as each new occasion or crisis brought the crowds together for meetings, protests, and processions at "Liberty Hall," under the great elm tree at Washington and Essex Streets in Boston, or its counterparts in towns and villages throughout the colonies. Andrew Oliver and Lord Bute were replaced on other occasions by other effigies, but the pattern remained constant.

The colonial appropriation of the cosmic tree in the Liberty Tree expressed and reinforced the direction that the national myth was taking. This tree was a self-conscious, historicized symbol, and the nature of the ritual activities around it suggested the humanocentric quality of the American myth even as it was unfolding. While other cultures had oriented themselves toward a tree with roots in the sky and branches touching the earth as in the Upanishads, or like Yggdrasil of Northern Europe with roots which pierced the bowels of the earth, the patriots understood their Tree in terms of themselves and their collective deeds in the public arena in which they made history.[45] Even the wood of the Christian cross, which was a distinctly historicized valorization of a sacred tree, appeared remote and abstract by comparison.

Yet the self-consciousness of the American variant did not obliterate its universalist and cosmological implications. For the Tree was still a sacred space which functioned at the center of a world, albeit a historicized and humanocentric one. Just as the May poles of English life and seventeenth-century Merry Mount in Massachusetts Bay, the Liberty Tree possessed a kind of sexual significance as a source of fertility and renewal of life: it symbolically stated that these were to be found only in the region of Liberty, and without Liberty there was death. Far from being simply an expression of vindictiveness, the effigy figures which everywhere dangled from the Liberty Tree proved that, as with the Cross of Jesus, fertilization required blood, and the forces of life, now identified with Liberty, would prevail over death itself. Combining the sacred trees in the garden of Eden of old, this tree of life was also a tree of good and evil. If it separated American life from British "death," it also separated New World innocence and virtue from Old World corruption and vice.

The forces of life and spirit had been challenged by tyranny and death, but at each new manifestation of Liberty Tree, the good prevailed. When the Stamp Act took effect on November 1, appropriate ceremonies were held at the Tree,

the people of the town assembling under the tree, and passing to and from it until evening, when the images [John Huske and George Grenville] were cut down, and carried in a cart, thousands following them, to the town house, where the assembly was sitting, and from thence to the gallows, where, after hanging some time, they were cut down, torn in pieces, and flung into the air; all to shew the detestation, which the people had, of the men whom the images were intended to represent.

About a month later, Andrew Oliver was required to appear in person at noon "under liberty tree; to make a publick resignation" which would be pleasing to the "true-born sons of liberty."[46]

In 1766, when the Stamp Act was repealed, there was jubilant celebration around Liberty Tree with cannon announcing the glad event. A formal liturgy planned the use of an obelisk constructed of oil paper by Paul Revere. The design of the obelisk was instructive: One side contained some verse to the Goddess of Liberty, including the cry, "GODDESS! we cannot part, thou must not fly;/Be SLAVES! we dare to Scorn it—dare to die." Beneath was a sketch of America as an Indian chief lying under a pine tree while the angel of Liberty hovered above. At the same time, the prime minister, Lord Bute, a bishop, and others stood menacingly by, as overhead the devil flew with the Stamp Act in his claw. Another side bore the sketch of Liberty Tree with an eagle feeding its young in the top branches while an angel advanced carrying an aegis. The brief title told that "She endures the Conflict, for a short Season."[47]

Some of the responses to historical events which involved Liberty Tree, as some of the other ritual demonstrations of the era, were spontaneous and unrepeated. Yet others, such as the anniversary of the Fourteenth of August, when the stamp distributors had resigned, became annual events. Here, the high theater of a single demonstration gained in solemnity by its repetitive character. Thomas Hutchinson described such an anniversary in 1768.

The anniversary of the 14th of August, the day on which the distributor of stamps had been compelled to resign, was celebrated this year with great parade. A vast concourse of people assembled at Liberty Tree, and, after rejoicing there, a procession of two or three chariots, and fifty or sixty chaises, went from thence to Roxbury, to an entertainment provided for them.[48]

When the violent death of Christopher Snyder occurred in 1770 in the tense atmosphere which preceded the Boston Massacre, the coffin of the boy was taken to Liberty Tree where a large crowd formed a procession to accompany the body. Four or five hundred schoolboys led the march as city and church bells tolled, and an inscription on the coffin protested that "innocence itself is not safe." John Adams recollected the incident in his diary and confessed, "My eyes never beheld such a funeral; the procession extended further than can well be imagined."[49] Again in 1773, the trading consignees in the famous tea controversy were called to appear at the Tree and resign their offices at the spot.

The British responded to the meaning of Liberty Tree by indicating that they understood it. When they gained control of Boston, the *Essex Gazette* reported what happened.

They made a furious attack upon it. After a long spell of laughing and grinning, sweating, swearing, and foaming with malice diabolical, they cut down the tree because it bore the name of liberty. A soldier was killed by falling from one of its branches during the operation.[50]

The British could not, however, erase the memory of the place. As late as the mid-nineteenth century, when David Sears erected a row of buildings on the site of the old elm grove where Liberty Tree had stood, he paid homage to the place with a niche and sculpture of the tree.

The story was much the same in other towns throughout the colonies, as the custom quickly spread of finding a center for orientation at Liberty Tree. Norwich, Connecticut, for example, had its Tree which was brought from the forest and set in the open plain. The stamp distributor for Connecticut was burned in effigy on a high hill overlooking it, but when the Stamp Act was repealed, the Tree was decorated lavishly and "crowned with a Phrygian cap. A tent, or booth, was erected beneath it, called a pavilion. Here, almost daily, people assembled to hear news and encourage each other to resist every kind of oppression."[51] In Charleston, South Carolina, there was a "wide-spreading live oak" near the home of Christopher Gadsden which assumed the function of Liberty Tree. Some years later, the Declaration of Inde-

pendence was read to the people under its branches, and it continued as the sign of liberty until 1780 when Sir Henry Clinton
ordered that it be cut down and burned. The British were out-
done, however, for after the war pieces of the stump became
relics as they were carved into cane heads. One of them even
found its way into the possession of Thomas Jefferson. Boards cut
from the stump were also used to build a ballot box.

Where Liberty Trees were unavailable or destroyed, they were
supplanted by Liberty Poles. The historian William Gordon recounted how "the *May poles* in different parts of the continent
had changed their names, or given place to *liberty poles*, after the
exhibition upon the liberty trees at Boston during the stamp-
act."[52] A Liberty Pole stood at Concord, where one Englishman
reported that the royal army had fired at the colonials and "pursued them with charged bayonets till we entered the town of
Concord, where we cut down what they call their Liberty
Pole."[53] Another Loyalist source spoke of a riot in Elizabethtown,
New Jersey, in which the people had "fixed up a liberty pole in
the middle of the town." When authority intervened, "their deity,
the liberty pole, was struck by an order from the committee."[54]
Meanwhile, in Poughkeepsie, New York, "a few friends of liberty . . . erected a pole . . . with a flag on it, bearing on one side,
THE KING, and on the other, THE CONGRESS AND LIBERTY," but
this one too was cut down "as a public nuisance."[55] The Liberty
Pole in New York City had figured prominently in commemorations of such events as the Boston Massacre and had already progressed through its fifth version by 1776, as one by one, previous
poles were destroyed in encounters with British soldiers. The destruction in 1770 of one of these poles, which had been reinforced
with iron hoops, probably provoked the most intense excitement,
when British soldiers piled the sawed-up wood in front of the
meeting-place of the Sons of Liberty in New York. It was said
that three thousand people afterward encircled the stump and
went through a series of declarations of their rights and their intentions to maintain them.[56]

There was a structural continuity from Liberty Tree to Liberty Pole to Liberty Monument. Thus Dedham, Massachusetts, decided to erect a Pillar of Liberty at the repeal of the Stamp Act. The four-foot granite cube was dedicated to the memory of William Pitt of England for his activities against the act, and it was surmounted by an eight-foot painted wooden column with a bust of Pitt on the top. Part of the inscription, which had been composed by Nathaniel Ames, read: "To the honor of Willm Pitt, esq., & other patriots who saved America from impending slavery."[57]

Both the patriots and their opponents recognized the religious character of the Liberty Tree or Pole and responded with either reverence or sacrilege according to their commitments. We have already discussed the activities of British soldiers in terms which suggested as much, and Peter Oliver named what the soldiers had enacted. This Liberty Tree, he said, was "consecrated as an Idol for the Mob to worship; it was properly the *Tree ordeal*, where those, whom the Rioters pitched upon as State delinquents, were carried to for Trial, or brought to as the Test of political Orthodoxy. It flourished until the British Troops possessed *Boston*, when it was desecrated by being cut down & carried to the Fire ordeal to warm the natural Body."[58] In similar vein, a letter from South Carolina to a British correspondent derided "our American creed, which every saint at Boston rehearsed at that Indian shrine of freedom, the Tree of Liberty, with more enthusiastic frenzy than what is expressed by the frantic infidel at the tomb of Mecca, or the bigotted pilgrim at the chapel of Loretto."[59]

At Providence, in 1768, Silas Downer delivered an oration for the dedication of a Liberty Tree. After his discourse, there was a ceremony, "conducted with great order and quiet," in which the people laid their hands upon the tree and Downer pronounced on their behalf.

We do, in the name and behalf of the true sons of Liberty, in America, Great Britain, Ireland, Corsica, or wherever they may be dispersed throughout the world, dedicate and solemnize thereto, this tree, to be a Tree of Liberty. May all our councils and deliberations under its venerable branches, be guided by wisdom, and directed for the support and maintenance of that liberty which our renowned Forefathers sought out, and found under trees, and in the wilderness. May it long flourish, and may the sons of Liberty often repair hither, to confirm and strengthen each other. When they look towards their sacred Elm, may they be penetrated with a sense of their duty to themselves and their posterity; and may they, like the House of David, grow stronger and stronger, while their enemies, like the House of Saul, shall grow weaker and weaker. Amen.[60]

In Philadelphia, Francis Hopkinson's *Prophecy*, written as part of the controversy which Thomas Paine's *Common Sense* had generated, portrayed an ancient seer who, out of the past, predicted the future of the American continent:

And in process of time, the people shall root up the rotten tree [British growth], and in its place they shall plant a young and vigorous tree, and shall effectually defend it from the winds of the North by an high wall. And they shall dress it, and prune it, and cultivate it to their own liking. And the young tree shall grow and flourish and spread its branches far abroad; and the people shall dwell under the shadow of its branches, and shall become an exceeding great, and powerful, and happy nation."[61]

Familiar with the Bible, the men of the Revolution participated in the general ethos of their time with its interest in the mystical and millennial numerology of the Book of Revelation. Although they did not engage in numerical interpretation of events, they often attached significant numbers from their immediate history to Liberty Tree. When the Massachusetts Assembly, by a margin of 92–17 voted not to rescind their circular letter sent to the other colonies for support and unification, Hutchinson noted that "the number 92 was auspicious, and 17 of ill omen, for many months after, not only in Massachusetts Bay, but in most of the colonies on the continent."[62] This provoked a spate of prunings of Liberty Trees which thereafter bore precisely ninety-two branches with seventeen stubs. Similarly, when issue no. 45 of John Wilkes's magazine in England was suppressed and this friend of American liberty was having difficulty remaining in the British

House of Commons, forty-five lanterns appeared on Liberty Tree in Boston while in various places it became customary for ninety-two Sons of Liberty to raise a forty-five-foot Liberty Pole.

In the events which followed the formation of a national government, Liberty Poles were co-opted by the Antifederalists in the context of protest against the Alien and Sedition Acts. The religious meaning of the symbol was perhaps obscured, but it did not end. As late as the age of Andrew Jackson, Michel de Chevalier, who had seen democratic festivals and processions as religious celebrations of a piece with Methodist camp meetings, described the hickory poles of the Jacksonians:

I stopped involuntarily at the sight of the gigantic hickory poles which made their solemn entry on eight wheels for the purpose of being planted by the democracy on the eve of the election. I remember one of these poles, its top still crowned with green foliage, which came on to the sound of fifes and drums and was preceded by ranks of Democrats, bearing no other badge than a twig of the sacred tree in their hats. It was drawn by eight horses, decorated with ribands and mottoes. Astride the tree itself were a dozen Jackson men of the first water, waving flags with an air of anticipated triumph and shouting, *Hurrah for Jackson!*[63]

The impact which Liberty Tree made on contemporaries may be judged by the frequency of allusions to it in the popular literature of the period as well as the fondness of the patriots for the symbolic language of the Tree in their discussions of liberty. Thomas Paine's poem "Liberty Tree" appeared in the *Pennsylvania Magazine* in 1775, while he was a contributing editor, and with studied classicism told of the Goddess of Liberty who with "ten thousand celestials" conducted to America:

> A fair budding branch from the gardens above,
>   Where millions with millions agree,
> She brought in her hand as a pledge of her love,
>   And the plant she named Liberty Tree.[64]

Other ballads, such as "A Voyage to Boston," were narratives of events, telling how "The Tory Williams and the Butcher Gage/

Rush'd to the tree, a nameless number near," where they "Each, axe in hand, attack'd the honor'd tree,/Swearing eternal war with Liberty."[65] Parodies by both patriots and Loyalists mentioned Liberty Tree, liberty songs celebrated it, and broadsides represented it.[66] Hutchinson included an account in his history of how "the spirit of liberty spread where it was not intended." Undergraduates at Harvard had become past masters of the art of avoiding "prayers and college exercises" until the tutors decided on the initiation of a new and less flexible regime. "This gave such offence, that the scholars met in a body, under, and about a great tree, to which they gave the name of the tree of liberty! There, they came into several resolves in favour of liberty; one of them, that the rule or order of the tutors was *unconstitutional*."[67]

Like the sacrament that it was, Liberty Tree was the reality which oriented the patriots, and yet it pointed beyond itself to another source of power. The Tree that had grown in many a town commons throughout the colonies was also spreading its branches in patriotic heads and hearts. As early as 1766, Jonathan Mayhew had preached in the revolutionary context that "the stately oaks of the forest take the deeper root, extend their arms the farther, and exalt their venerable heads the higher, for being agitated by storms and tempests."[68] John Dickinson, issuing a warning with a millennial ring in his *Letters from a Farmer* of 1768, prophesied that "the axe is laid to the root of the tree; and the whole body must infallibly perish, if we remain idle spectators of the work."[69] Later, with growing urgency, Boston sent a letter of correspondence to other towns, exhorting them not to "set supinely indifferent on the brink of destruction, while the Iron hand of oppression is dayly tearing the choicest Fruit from the fair Tree of Liberty, planted by our worthy Predecessors, at the expense of their treasure, & abundantly water'd with their blood."[70]

Even Daniel Leonard, a Tory, ruminated on the "small seed of sedition" which had become "a great tree; the vilest reptiles that crawl upon the earth, are at the root; the foulest birds of the air rest upon its branches."[71] But when in 1775, the British did succeed in destroying Boston's Liberty Tree, the *Constitutional Gazette* declared emphatically that the reality of Liberty Tree was more than physical.

Be it known to this infamous band of traitors, that the GRAND AMERICAN TREE OF LIBERTY, planted in the centre of the united colonies of North America, now flourishes with unrivalled, increasing beauty; and bids fair in a short time to afford under its wide-spreading branches a safe and happy retreat for all the sons of liberty, however numerous and dispersed.[72]

Thomas Jefferson's declaration on *Taking Up Arms* for the Continental Congress expressed concern for "the tender plant of liberty which we have brought over, & with so much affection fostered on these our own shores."[73] At the beginning of the federal era, a dozen years afterward, Jefferson wrote to friends, confiding to them that "the tree of liberty must be refreshed from time to time with the blood of patriots and tyrants. It is it's natural manure."[74] Enos Hitchcock, celebrating the ratification of the new federal Constitution, echoed Jefferson's sentiments, though less approvingly. It was a "dishonour to human nature that wherever liberty has been planted and flourished, it has commonly required the blood of her sons to water and enrich the soil."[75] Indeed, one wonders if the Liberty Tree did not form the unconscious symbolic backdrop for the message in a reader of 1796: the future of America would be "as the towering cedar upon the trees of the wood, or the sun in the presence of the stars."[76] Certainly, Daniel Webster had heard of Liberty Tree in 1826 when he eulogized the auspicious deaths of both Adams and Jefferson on the Fourth of July of that year.

The tree which they assisted to plant will flourish, although they water it and protect it no longer; for it has struck its roots deep, it has sent them to the very centre; no storm, not of force to burst the orb, can overturn it; its branches spread wide; they stretch their protecting arms broader and broader, and its top is destined to reach the heavens.[77]

While Liberty Tree functioned as the sacramental center for ritual demonstrations in the colonies, the patriots expressed their dramatic and liturgical response to events in a variety of ways. The rituals of the Revolution were instructive, for they supported, buttressed, and often disclosed hidden nuances of the evolving myth. More than that, as we have already maintained, they shaped and directed the myth so that out of collective action emerged new or stronger collective realities. At least from the time of the Stamp Act, contemporaries recognized the significance of the kind of community demonstration that the rituals involved. Thus, David Ramsay observed that the collective remonstrances against the Stamp Act were organized by "leading men of character and influence" who well knew that "the bulk of mankind are more led by their senses, than by their reason."[78] And John Adams reported in his diary how universal the witness seemed: "Our presses have groaned, our pulpits have thundered, our legislatures have resolved, our towns have voted; the crown officers have everywhere trembled, and all their little tools and creatures been afraid to speak and ashamed to be seen."[79] The liturgical quality of the scenario, as leaders and followers acted it out, was everywhere apparent.

Gordon, Ramsay, and Warren, recording many of the details, waxed eloquent on the dramatic response of Philadelphia to the arrival of the stamps in 1765. As William Gordon had it, "Upon the appearance of the ships having on board the stamps, all the vessels in the harbour hoisted their colours half staff high; the bells were muffled and continued to toll till evening; and every countenance added to the marks of sincere mourning."[80] In Charleston, South Carolina, ritual action included the tolling of muffled church bells, the ceremonial burning of nineteen effigies, and a funeral procession for Liberty which ended solemnly at the burial ground, where at the eleventh hour Liberty revived. The interment of Liberty became a common ceremony throughout the colonies, with towns such as Portsmouth, (New Hampshire), Newport (Rhode Island), Baltimore, and Wilmington (North

Carolina) all burying an effigy of American Liberty. The ceremonial at Portsmouth seemed particularly striking, and David
Ramsay recounted it with attention.

At Portsmouth, in New-Hampshire, the morning was ushered in, with
tolling all the bells in town. In the course of the day, notice was given
to the friends of liberty, to attend her funeral. A coffin, neatly ornamented inscribed with the word *Liberty* in large letters, was carried
to the grave. The funeral procession began from the state-house, attended with two unbraced drums. While the inhabitants who followed
the coffin were in motion, minute guns were fired, and continued till
the corpse arrived at the place of interment. Then an oration in favour
of the deceased was pronounced. It was scarcely ended before the
corpse was taken up, it having been perceived that some remains of
life were left, at which the inscription was immediately altered to
'Liberty revived.' The bells immediately exchanged their melancholy,
for a more joyful sound, and satisfaction appeared in every countenance.[81]

By November 1, Boston itself was only a typical colonial town in
its liturgy of protest: muffled bells tolled, vessels in port showed
their flags at half mast, and Liberty Tree dangled its two effigy
figures, the "spirit" bodies of George Grenville and John Huske.

When news reached the colonies that the Stamp Act had been
repealed, ritual outbursts proceeded apace. The elements seemed
common to all as church bells were rung, ship colors raised, cannons fired, toasts drunk by ebullient Sons of Liberty, bonfires and
illuminations produced, ceremonial dinners eaten with speeches
usual and sometimes parades. In Boston, as Loyalist an individual
as Governor Francis Bernard proclaimed a Day of Thanksgiving,
while John Adams dutifully told his diary that the Sons of Liberty had initiated preparations far beyond the usual for rejoicing,
"such illuminations, bonfires, pyramids, obelisks, such grand exhibitions and such fireworks as were never before seen in America."[82] Preaching with fervor that the snare had indeed been
broken, Jonathan Mayhew estimated that there had never before
been "so great external demonstrations of joy among the people
of America; not even when all Canada was reduced."[83] With ob-

vious relish, nearly a century later, Benson Lossing dwelt on the lavishness of the spectacle: "The dawn, bright and rosy, was ushered in by salvos of cannon, ringing of bells, and martial music. Through the liberality of some citizens, every debtor in the jail was ransomed and set at liberty, to unite in the general joy." John Hancock held a huge celebration and "treated the populace to a pipe of Madeira wine, erected at the front of his house, which was magnificently illuminated, a stage for the exhibition of his fire-works." James Otis and others held open house, while a horizontal fire-wheel, atop the Sons of Liberty pyramid, began to revolve until it discharged "sixteen dozen serpents in the air, which concluded the show."[84]

In Philadelphia, similar jubilation prevailed. The captain who brought the news of repeal drank punch at the coffeehouse "where a gold-laced hat was given him and presents were distributed among his crew." The punch became a community gesture, and "first men played hob-and-nob over their glasses with sailors and common people." Illuminations and bonfires appeared; "many barrels of beer were distributed among the populace; and the next day the governor and mayoralty gave a feast to three hundred persons at the State House gallery."[85]

Governor Bernard's departure occasioned another ceremonial display in Boston in 1769, with bells rung, cannon fired, Liberty Tree adorned with flags, and a bonfire on Fort Hill. Spontaneity itself had by this time assumed a structure. When the Boston Massacre in 1770 produced a new event around which ritual activity could center, the result became an anniversary liturgy, formal and expressive, which remained a primary event until 1784 and continued even afterward. Years later, John Adams pondered its significance in a letter to Jedidiah Morse, telling him that "how slightly soever historians may have passed over this event, the blood of the martyrs, right or wrong, proved to be the seeds of the congregation." Even though Adams had defended the British captain and soldiers who were involved in the incident, he thought with mythic sympathy that there was "no reason why the town should not call the action of that night a massacre."[86] Before the trials, Peter Oliver remembered more bitterly, "the Pulpits rung their Chimes upon blood Guiltiness, in Order to incite the People, some of whom were to be Jurors, to Revenge, in cleansing the Land of the Blood which had been Shed."[87] Earlier, at the funeral of the victims, a solemn drama had unfolded, while the shops in Boston closed and the bells were tolled there and in neighboring towns. The bodies of two of the slain were carried in procession from Faneuil Hall until they joined with the hearses of the remaining victims on King Street near the site of the massacre. Then the whole entourage processed through the main street to the place of burial in a common vault.

In 1771, the first annual solemnity was observed. Hutchinson, though an unsympathetic witness, related what happened:

Upon the anniversary of the 5th of March, the bells in the town of Boston were tolled from twelve to one o'clock at noon, and from nine to ten in the evening, and, during the last, figures to represent the murder of the inhabitants were exhibited from a window in a square at the north part of town. In a town meeting, the usher of one of the publick grammar schools [James Lovell] was appointed to deliver an oration at Faneuil Hall, to commemorate the 'barbarous murder' of their fellow citizens, and to impress upon the minds of the people the necessity of 'such noble exertions' in all future times, as the inhabitants of the town then made.[88]

Salem too remembered with "religious solemnity" and "prayer and sermon" before a "crowded assembly by one of the ministers" [Nathaniel Whitaker].[89] Sources agreed that the orators who annually graced these spectacles were chosen for their oral virtuosity and the crowds who listened were stirred to higher and higher pitches of intensity. Adams, who heard John Hancock's oration in 1774, recollected the "vast crowd" with "rainy eyes." "The composition, the pronunciation, the action, all exceeded the expectations of everybody. They exceeded even mine, which were very considerable."[90] Held in the evening so that the darkness heightened the religious awe of the spectators, the orations would be preceded by dramatic tableaux of the "murderers" and the "martyred." For those who did not or could not attend, there were graphic broadsides to help the processes of remembering. With borders of engraved black coffins, and emotion-laden prose or poetry to accompany the printed orations, they sang their paeans to the slaughter of the innocents and urged the patriots to action on their behalf.[91]

Structurally and thematically, the Boston Massacre orations were a glorious recital of the myth of Revolution. Often they would begin with a lofty declamation on the ideals of government with frequent citation of Greek and Roman models. "Our fathers" haunted the presentations as living spectres out of the past, and their memory corroborated the oppressiveness of the British taxation the colonists were experiencing. Ultimately, the orations aimed at the renewal of mythic innocence, ever under the threat of "corruption," through action in the public cause. As the years passed, the emphasis of the call to action fell more and more on human effort, sometimes with the apology "under God," but usually with appeals to the Goddess of Liberty far more frequent than invocations to the Judaeo-Christian God. Yet the central mythologem of this rendering of the myth came out of the Christian past and was shaped by the patriots to their present needs. For in the slaughtered and martyred innocents whose blood had been spilt by "British butchers," the patriots had a powerful symbol around which to orient themselves. The *Boston Gazette* captured some of the vigor of that mythic center in the intensity of its beginning in 1770.

A mercenary, licentious rabble of banditti are encouraged to riot uncontrol'd, and tear the bowels and vitals of their brave but peaceable fellow subjects, and *to wash the ground with a profusion of innocent blood* . . . which like the blood of Abel and Zechariah, *still* cries ALOUD for *pointed* vengeance to blast the ORIGINAL PROCURERS as well as the *execrable instruments* of that horrid massacre.[92]

Two years later, Joseph Warren delivered the charge with what must have been a ringing display of oratory.

THE FATAL FIFTH OF MARCH, 1770, CAN NEVER BE FORGOTTEN—The horrors of THAT DREADFUL NIGHT are but too deeply impressed on our hearts—Language is too feeble to paint the emotion of our souls, when our streets were stained with the BLOOD OF OUR BRETHREN,—when our ears were wounded by the groans of the *dying*, and our eyes were tormented with the sight of the mangled bodies of the *dead*.[93]

By 1775, his mythic recital was even more dramatic:

The baleful images of terror croud around me—and discontented ghosts, with hollow groans, appear to solemnize the anniversary of the FIFTH OF MARCH.

Approach we then the melancholy walk of death . . . hither let me lead the tender mother to weep over her beloved son—come widowed mourner, here satiate thy grief; behold thy murdered husband gasping on the ground, and to complete the pompous show of wretchedness, bring in each hand thy infant children to bewail their father's fate— take heed, ye orphan babes, lest, whilst your streaming eyes are fixed upon the ghastly corpse, *your feet slide on the stones bespattered with your father's brains*. Enough! this tragedy need not be heightened by an infant weltering in the blood of him that gave it birth.[94]

Benjamin Church had been equally fascinated by the necessity of gazing on the "mangled corpses of our *brethren* and grinning *furies*, glotting o'er their carnage." Likewise, John Hancock had harangued: "Ye dark designing knaves, ye murderers, parricides! how dare you tread upon the earth, which has drank in the blood of slaughtered innocents, shed by your wicked hands?"[95] If the rhetoric seemed gruesome and sensational, it was in keeping with the hyperbolic and melodramatic quality of the rest of the patriotic myth. To see at all, the patriots seemed to require as vivid and dramatic telling of the story as could be contrived. They were a history-making people. As with those who would follow them, sensation had become their way of establishing a truth: the biggest splash was the sign of the most authentic tale and the means by which one kept the "real" world in view.

The tea controversy of 1773 stirred up new displays of patriotic fervor and a new occasion for ritual. Protest rose throughout the colonies but came to its most celebrated liturgical culmination in the Boston Tea Party, a rite created and perpetrated in the context of one event, but powerful in its mythic impact nonetheless. Ringing bells tolled the story of protest, patriots assembled at Faneuil Hall, and then in the words of Mercy Warren:

There appeared a great number of persons, clad like the aborigines of the wilderness, with tomahawks in their hands, and clubs on their shoulders, who without the least molestation marched through the streets with silent solemnity, and amidst innumerable spectators, proceeded to the wharves, boarded the ships, demanded the keys, and with much deliberation knocked open the chests, and emptied several thousand weight of the finest teas into the ocean. No opposition was made, though surrounded by the king's ships; all was silence and dismay.

This done, the procession returned through the town in the same order and solemnity as observed in the outset of their attempt. No other disorder took place, and it was observed, the stillest night ensued that Boston had enjoyed for many months.[96]

John Adams sensed profound implications in the event and shared enthusiastic observations with his diary of "a dignity, a majesty, a sublimity, in this last effort of the patriots." Adams knew what it was to be a history-maker, and he thought that "the people should never rise without doing something to be remembered, something notable and striking." The destruction of the tea had qualified, "so bold, so daring, so firm, intrepid and inflexible." It would surely have "so important consequences, and so lasting, that I cannot but consider it as an epocha in history."[97] Others celebrated the ritual of the tea in their own style, as broadsides memorialized the "Tea, Destroyed by Indians" and "Ye Glorious Sons of Freedom," and the *Pennsylvania Packet* published yet another "New Song" heralding the "Sons of freedom" over whose heads "Three bright angel forms were seen."[98] One enterprising author composed a scriptural parody which began: "And behold! when the tidings came to the great city that is afar oft, the city that is in the land of Britain, how the men of Boston, even the Bostonites, had arose, a great multitude, and destroyed the Tea."[99]

A year later came the British response to the Tea Party, as the Boston Port Bill closed the port of Boston to further trade. News of the act was greeted throughout the colonies with ritual lamentation. William Gordon noted how swiftly the message spread. In some places, copies of the act "were printed upon mourning paper with a black border, and cried upon the streets under the title of *a barbarous, cruel, bloody and inhuman murder*." Elsewhere, people were gathered and the "obnoxious law burned with great solemnity."[100] This "uncommon solemnity" was particularly noteworthy, according to Mercy Warren, on June 1, the day when the bill went into effect and a day of fasting and prayer throughout the colonies.[101] The fast was "devoutly kept at Williamsburgh"; in Philadelphia, "it was solemnized with every manifestation of public calamity and grief," as "the inhabitants shut up their houses" and "after divine service a stillness reigned over the city, which exhibited an appearance of the deepest distress."[102] Thomas Jefferson gave testimony to the self-consciousness and pragmatism of the Virginia effort by recollecting that the House of Burgesses was "under the conviction of the necessity of arousing our people from the lethargy into which they had fallen as to passing events." Since the last fast day had occurred during the French and Indian War and "a new generation had grown up," Jefferson and his friends "rummaged over . . . the revolutionary precedents and forms of the Puritans" and "made up a resolution, somewhat modernizing their phrases."[103] Later in the year, the Provincial Congress of Massachusetts, with perhaps a similar self-consciousness, ordered a day of thanksgiving, "from a consideration of the union which so remarkably prevails, not only in this province, but throughout the continent, at this alarming crisis."[104]

When finally the first shots of war echoed at Lexington and Concord, convincing John Adams and many of his compatriots that "the die was cast, the Rubicon passed," the same need to memorialize and ritualize engulfed Americans. "The Americans who fell," observed David Ramsay, "were revered by their countrymen, as martyrs who had died in the cause of liberty." "Combinations were formed and associations subscribed, binding the inhabitants to each other by the sacred ties of honour, religion, and love of country, to do whatever their public bodies directed for the preservation of their liberties."[105] The anniversary of Lexington and Concord provided, especially in New England, still another occasion for ritual remembrance, and ministers lamented from their pulpits the shedding of innocent blood. As in the previous year, Massachusetts stubbornly proclaimed a public thanksgiving in the fall of 1775, despite British arms, droughts, and a "wasting sickness." The significance of the document could not be lost on those who read it or heard it read, for it ended with "God save the People" instead of "God save the King."[106]

We have already paid a good deal of attention to the mythology which undergirded the various ritual responses to events. Much of it was cast in the language of liberty which would triumph over slavery and of slain innocents who were pitted against demonic tyrants. Yet a new mythologem had become more and more prominent, as the patriots began to discover in acting out their liturgies that they were their own men as well as sons of the fathers. With a generalized classical and pagan inspiration to guide them, they stretched their consciousness beyond their Judaeo-Christian past to encompass the Goddess of Liberty and the twin altars of freedom and patriotism. Already, in 1752 and 1753, the *Independent Reflector* had extended its Presbyterian heritage to include a personified Liberty which, it had found, "imparts a Relish to the most indifferent Pleasure, and renders the highest Gratification the more consummately delightful." It was in fact the "GENIUS OF LIBERTY dispensing unnumber'd Blessings" and the "SPIRIT OF PATRIOTISM ever watchful for the public Good!"[107] From the first, the Boston Massacre orations were particularly assiduous in bringing the Goddess to the fore. Thus, James Lovell in 1771 instructed his fellow-Bostonians in the dimensions of the new religion:

Watchful, hawk-eyed jealousy, ever guards the portal of the temple of the GODDESS LIBERTY. This is known to those who frequent her altars. Our whole conduct therefore, I am sure, will meet with the utmost candor of her VOTARIES: but I am wishing we may be able to convert even her basest APOSTATES.[108]

Songs began to appear which celebrated the Goddess, while Bickerstaff's Boston Almanack for the year 1770 boasted a title page with an engraved portrait of James Otis, centered between Liberty and Hercules or Perseverance.[109] Ramsay reported that after the Boston Port Bill, "a sense of common danger, extinguished selfish passions," and "local attachments and partialities, were sacrificed on the altar of patriotism."[110] Preachers took up the cause of the Goddess in their turn. Jacob Duché shared with his congregation in 1775 his considered opinion that "liberty, traced to her true source, is of heavenly extraction, that divine virtue is her illustrious parent, that from eternity to eternity they have been and must be inseparable companions, and that the hearts of all intelligent beings are the living temples in which they ought to be jointly worshipped."[111] Later, in 1777, John Hurt would extol Liberty before the North Carolina troops and lament that in former ages Britain had been the place where "the heavenly goddess seemed to have fixed her temple." There her "sacred fires" had been kept alive, and there she had had "her saints and her confessors, and a whole army of martyrs." "But alas!" Hurt mourned, "how are the mighty fallen! The gates of hell have prevailed against her."[112] By 1780, Simeon Howard was warning that if the enemies of America should prevail, then Liberty,

the heaven-born virgin, seeing her votaries slain, her altars overthrown, and her temples demolished, and finding no safe habitation on earth, would be obliged, like the great patron of liberty the First-born of God, to ascend to her God and our God, her Father and our Father, from whom she was sent to bless mankind, leaving an ungrateful world, after she had, like him, been 'rejected and despised of men,' in slavery and misery, till with him she shall again descend to reign and triumph on earth.[113]

Some years earlier, the Anglican Loyalist Jonathan Boucher had bid farewell to his flock to sail for England, admitting the while that he had sinned: in the days of the Stamp Act, he said, "I too bowed at the altar of Liberty; and sacrificed to this idol of our groves, *upon the high mountains, and upon the hills, and under every green tree.*" Providence had intervened, however, and he had been converted "with sincerity in my heart, and my Bible in my hand."[114] Indeed, well into the nineteenth century, the personified Liberty wove her charms to entice patriotic hearts and could even on occasion merge her identity with that of Liberty Tree. Writing of the life of Liberty's eldest son, George Washington, James K. Paulding took time to remember her.

The first years of the new-born child of liberty were those of danger and suffering. Her cradle was assailed by the serpent, but she proved the sister of Hercules, and slew him at last. She was nurtured in bloody strife and cruel vicissitudes, but she grew only the wiser and stronger for the buffeting of the waves and violence of the storm. Like the oak in the whirlwind, she became only the more deeply rooted in the soil of freedom from the energy with which she withstood its lashings.[115]

While it would be tempting to dismiss such flourishes as "just oratory" or "just metaphor," it follows logically that references to Providence, the Lord of Hosts, the Governor of the Universe, and other intangible realities ought then to be relegated to the poetic attic in similar fashion. It is hard to find some criterion to distinguish between these references, since the patriots seemed held as securely captive by the power of Liberty as their fathers had been by the sovereignty of God. "Free" patriots were literally unfree as they walked in the service of the Goddess, yet enslavement to her virtues, which living out of her mythic center involved, created for them another form of freedom or at least the illusion of it. Furthermore, the fleeting glimpse which the patriots caught from time to time of the illusory quality of their invocations to Liberty—glimpses which constituted the self-consciousness and pragmatism of their most basic appeals—seemed shared in their references to either an orthodox or deistic God. They were facing the problem that had faced every high culture since the Fall: nature had drawn away from culture, and the growing chasm between them could less and less be healed by the myth which partook of the contrivance and artifice which unfailingly attended human cultural forms. Quite simply, the patriots could not go home again to Paradise.

When coupled with pleas for the help of a more traditional deity, whether biblical or deistic, the apostrophes to the Goddess Liberty formed for the patriots a second two-in-one. If, in their own way, they had forged a synthesis of head and heart in the shadow of the old Puritan covenant, they were also celebrating a marriage between the Goddess and their God. There would be no need in America to ponder the question of the union of religion and nation under the collective symbols of church and state because when Liberty celebrated her *hieros gamos* with Providence, the reality toward which these symbols pointed had already been made present. The sacred marriage meant that the Absolute was moving from the fathers and the fathers' God into a world in which human values were more and more becoming the transcendent and the absolute. While it might be argued historically, sociologically, and even psychologically, that the prominence of the Goddess in the American consciousness arose from the need to supplant the British model with another equally commanding, a figure who evoked the classical prowess of Greece and Rome, such an argument does not alter the religious meaning and significance which infused the event. The patriots were subtly transferring their awareness to new forms of mythic consciousness which would affect the later history and lifestyle of the republic more deeply than they knew. Still, the facts were curious indeed. As Americans continued invoking the Goddess of Liberty at the altars of freedom and patriotism, the war became a reality. And it was clear that the Lord God of Hosts had armed himself for battle and was fighting on the patriotic side.

Chapter 3

Jehovah, God
of Battles

Ever since America first entered the consciousness of its European settlers, it had been the place and the occasion for the exploration of ambiguity and tension. Throughout their history, Americans seemed drawn by opposites which they found impossible to reconcile. Torn between wild places and cities, innocence and experience, spontaneity and control, reason and passion, tradition and newness, Americans ran toward both poles of each opposition at once, and Michael Kammen has not been the first to suggest the fascination with contradictory extremes which this people of paradox displayed. The American Revolution was a case par excellence: "during the passion of revolutionary fervor, Utopia itself appeared as a biformity, the 'Christian Sparta' of Sam Adams's dreams: vigorous and tender, primitive and sophisticated, Christian and pagan, free yet bound to a moral mission."[1]

The "biformity" in Utopia was, however, far from static. As Americans moved between Christian and "natural" religious forms in their New World paradise, a subtle change in their awareness was occurring. The transformation was expressed and channelled in their encounters with the old Calvinist God. As God of Battles, he had girded on his armor to join patriots fighting in righteous combat the veritable war of the world. Yet somehow, Jehovah, God of Battles, got lost in the fray. The patriots emerged after the dust of war had cleared, without chagrin at the fact—and instead with a keener sense of the reality of one another. Still, the disappearance of Jehovah was no clear-cut event.

When the Revolution was over, as an old soldier, he had not died but was simply fading away from the action. Meanwhile, his colleague, the Great Governor who was Nature's God, had continued after a fashion to preside.

At the beginning, though, Jehovah's outlines were clear. The patriots traced his action in their world through the "remarkable providences" with which he had visited them as he had of old visited their fathers. Jonathan Mayhew's liberalism did not deter him from celebrating the repeal of the Stamp Act as the heir of the seventeenth century Puritan tradition that he saw himself. He reminded his congregation that, if God numbered the very hairs of their heads, "how much more then, is his providence to be acknowledged in the rise, in the preservation, in the great events, the revolutions, or the fall of mighty states and kingdoms?"[2] Later, as event followed event in the Revolutionary War skirmishes, the patriots were quick to interpret their outcome as the mark of a God who was acting in history to supply their wants and needs. At Charleston Neck, South Carolina, in 1775, the *Constitutional Gazette* was certain it had caught God in the act when American sailors who needed a particular kind of lantern, unavailable in America, captured a cruiser. A correspondent described the uncanny coincidence when "in her there is found, not only the kind of lanthorns which we so much wanted, but the exact number we wanted, and not one more or less. Surely we may, without being charged with superstition, be permitted to say, 'The Lord hath done this, and it is marvellous in our eyes.'"[3]

After the Battle of the Great Bridge near Norfolk (1775), the *Pennsylvania Evening Post* reported the British body count (thirty-one killed and wounded) and, like many another newspaper, editorialized on its meaning.

What is not to be paralleled in history, and will scarcely appear credible, except to such as acknowledge a Providence over human affairs, this victory was gained at the expense of no more than a slight wound in a soldier's hand; and one circumstance which renders it still more amazing is, that the field-pieces raked the whole length of the street, and absolutely threw double-headed shot as far as the church; and afterwards, as our troops approached, cannonaded them heavily with grape-shot.[4]

After the Nantasket expedition, the *Pennsylvania Journal* told its readers that "the enemy were compelled once more to make a disgraceful precipitate flight; and we have it now in our power to congratulate our friends on our being in full possession of the lowest harbor of Boston." "Through Divine Providence," the newspaper continued, "not one of our men were hurt."[5]

Politicians and preachers agreed that God was acting for them, although the clergy, it was true, mitigated their confidence with appeals for repentance. Early in the war Elbridge Gerry wrote to Samuel Adams, acknowledging that history could "hardly produce such a series of events as has taken place in favor of American opposition. The hand of Heaven seems to have directed every occurrence."[6] His colleague thought the same. Speaking from the steps of the statehouse at Philadelphia, Adams told a crowd in 1776 that "the hand of Heaven appears to have led us on to be, perhaps, humble instruments and means in the great providential dispensation which is completing."[7] Meanwhile, John Witherspoon thought it would be "a criminal inattention not to observe the singular interposition of Providence hitherto, in behalf of the American colonies," while Samuel West could not "but take notice how wonderfully Providence has smiled upon us by causing the several colonies to unite so firmly together against the tyranny of Great Britain."[8] Congress itself, in a circular letter to Americans in 1779 found that England had behaved in ways which were tantamount to "courting the vengeance of heaven and revolting from the protection of Providence," under which, it was assumed, Americans were dwelling.[9]

Indeed, after the great victory at Yorktown, George Washington ordered that "divine service shall be performed to-morrow in the different brigades and divisions. The commander in chief recommends, that all the troops that are not upon duty, do assist at it with a serious deportment, and that sensibility of heart, which the recollection of the surprizing and particular interposition of Providence in our favour claims."[10] Songs celebrated praise to the Lord, for the snare was broken and the patriots were escaped.[11] Looking back at the victory from the vantage of the nineteenth century, Mercy Warren had to "pause a moment, to reflect on the vicissitudes of human life, the accidents of war, or rather the designations of Providence, that one day lift to the pinnacle of human triumph, and another, smite the laurel from the brow of the conqueror, and humble the proud victor at the feet of his former prisoner."[12]

At the close of hostilities, Ezra Stiles found that there would not be enough time to "recount the wonder-working providence of God in the events of this war" and hoped for a "tranquil period for the unmolested accomplishment of the *Magnalia Dei*—the great events in God's moral government designed from eternal ages to be displayed in these ends of the earth."[13] For David Tappan, even "the poor Indian savages" recognized that "the Lord hath done great things for America," while later in her history, Warren assessed that America's soldiers and statesmen "seemed to have been remarkably directed by the finger of Divine Providence, and led on from step to step beyond their own expectations, to exhibit to the view of distant nations, millions freed from the bondage of a foreign yoke."[14] Nineteenth-century school texts took up the cry by claiming that Britain's failure in the war with its greater resources implied "that it had neither courage nor a just cause protected by God."[15] No one, it seemed, quarrelled with the manifest truth that

the seeds of separation were sewn, and the *ball* of empire rolled westward with such astonishing rapidity, that the pious mind is naturally excited to acknowledge a superintending Providence, that led to the period of independence, even before America was conscious of her maturity.[16]

Still more, the Providence which aided Americans was no abstract being which directed destiny from metaphysical distances. Rather, it was the stern God of Battles who as a warlord intervened on behalf of the patriots. Bearing the thunderbolts from his tribal past, more recently energized in his Calvinistic ascendancy, this rain-and-storm god left the aloofness of the skies and, like the elements, sped to earth. Because he had come from out of the skies which stretched through interminable space, he could see the complete shape of things, knowing the whole and knowing the particular, scrutinizing each individual heart. He was a true *deus pluviosus*, and his cloudbursts were action on behalf of the Americans who were a particular people and dear to his jealous heart. Already during the French and Indian War, Samuel Davies had recognized his lineaments and had urged the continental troops onward, praying, "May the Lord of hosts, the God of the armies of Israel, go forth along with you! May he teach your hands to war, and gird you with strength in battle.!"[17] Especially in the years when the clouds of war were gathering and the early years after they had broken, the colonists made it clear that they recognized his face not merely in the clouds but on the earth alongside themselves. Sometimes he stayed their arms, as in the tense moment in 1773 when Benjamin Church heard him after the Boston Massacre: "But hark! the guardian God of New England issues his awful mandate, 'PEACE, BE STILL:' hush'd was the bursting war, the louring tempest frowned its rage away."[18]

But overwhelmingly, God urged them on to battle, as Jacob Duché assumed a year later when he prayed in the Continental Congress: "Plead my cause, O Lord, with them that strive with me; fight against them that fight against me; take hold of shield and buckler, and stand up for my help; draw out also the spear, and stop the way against them." The Anglican Collect of the day was fortuitous, and after he had read it, Duché began to pray extemporaneously and "filled every bosom present." "It seemed as if Heaven had ordained that Psalm to be read on that morning," John Adams, who had been present, wrote to his wife.[19]

Benjamin Rush agreed and wrote to his friend Granville Sharp across the ocean that "the God of armies cannot be an indifferent spectator of these things. Victory must at last declare herself in favor of justice. Our cause is a righteous one. It is the cause of Heaven."[20] Preachers throughout the colonies took up the theme vigorously. The sermons of the period indicated that, providing Americans were properly faithful, the Lord God of Hosts was fighting on their side. William Gordon pleaded with his flock for repentance so that they might "hope He will be on our side: and, *if the Lord is for us, what can men do unto us?* Have we the God of hosts for our ally, we might bid adieu to fear, tho' the world was united against us!"[21] Gordon later found that American repentance had been sufficient, for at Long Island, to aid the patriot's retreat, the Lord of Hosts interposed "by sending a thick fog about two o'clock in the morning which hung over Long-Island, while on New-York side it was clear."

Had it not been for the providential shifting of the wind, not more than half the army could possibly have crossed, and the remainder, with a number of general officers, and all the heavy ordnance at least, must inevitably have fallen into the enemy's hand. Had it not been also for that heavenly messenger, the fog, to cover the first desertion of the lines, and the several proceedings of the Americans after day-break, they must have sustained considerable losses. The fog resembled a thick small mist, so that you could see but a little way before you. It was very unusual also to have a fog at that time of the year. My informer, a citizen of New-York, could not recollect his having known any at that season, within the space of twenty or thirty years.[22]

Not to cooperate with such a war god by beating ploughshares into swords and pruning-hooks into spears would expose the patriots "to the displeasure of God Almighty."[23] "Remember, soldiers," Joab Trout had exhorted on the eve of Brandywine, "that God is with you! The eternal God fights for you! He rides on the battle-cloud; he sweeps onward with the march, or the hurricane charge! God, the awful and the infinite, fights for you, and will triumph!"[24]

The popular voice echoed an answer which was corroboration. The American soldier had his own hymn which assured him that God girded each one's armor on and taught him the art of wielding "manly weapons" and other lessons of war.[25] The Battle of

Hog Island, in which estimates suggested that one hundred to three hundred Britons had been killed or wounded, while only three Americans were hurt, inspired the *Virginia Gazette* and the *Pennsylvania Journal* to print the same editorial comment: "Heaven apparently, and most evidently, fights for us, covers our heads in the day of battle, and shields our people from the assaults of our common enemies." Not two months later, the *Gazette* reported a skirmish at Gloucester in which it was equally evident that "the Almighty was on our side. Not a ball struck or wounded an individual person, although they went through our houses in almost every direction when filled with women and children."[26]

One British newspaper published a letter from a Philadelphia correspondent of 1775 who declared that "in the hour of danger, the Lord took us under his protection, and our delivery was miraculous. The gray-headed Putnam was our guardian-angel, and his revelation proved our salvation."[27] Where the British were at issue, the *Freeman's Journal* could not contain itself and harangued its overseas cousins: "Why do YE suffer YOUR Fleets and Armies again to be sent against America? Are YE not yet convinced that the GREAT JEHOVAH is on her Side? and that God helping her the Gates of Hell shall never prevail against her."[28] And when the unhappy British abandoned Elizabethtown, New Jersey, in 1777 the *Journal* printed a letter which proved that its warnings had not been mistaken: "The enemy appear to be panic-struck in the extreme. God prospers our arms in an extraordinary manner."[29] Similarly, at the Battle of Bennington which produced an American victory, the *Pennsylvania Evening Post* included an account by "a gentleman who was present in the action." "This action," he wrote, "which redounds so much to the glory of the Great Lord of the heavens, and God of armies, affords the Americans a lasting monument of the Divine power and goodness, and a most powerful argument of love to and trust in God."[30]

Congress was inclined to share the sentiment and, addressing United States citizens in 1778, assured them that "at length that

God of battles, in whom was our trust, hath conducted us thro' the paths of danger and distress to the thresholds of security." A year later, Congress again reminded them how "America, without arms, ammunition, discipline, revenue, government or ally, with a 'staff and a sling' only, dared, 'in the name of the Lord of Hosts,' to engage a gigantic adversary, prepared at all points, boasting of his strength, and of whom even mighty warriors 'were greatly afraid.' "[31]

Jehovah, God of Battles, fought on the American side because America was "our Israel," as we have already noted and as the sermons of the period especially made clear. One particular event in the long history of Israel, which they saw themselves repeating, fascinated the Americans. They turned to the Exodus to understand the course of their affairs. The symbolism of the Exodus had been part of the heritage from their fathers, who had escaped from the fleshpots of England to the milk and honey of the American Canaan. Now the patriots shaped the past anew to their present concerns. As early as the time of the Stamp Act, one pamphlet had employed the motif of Exodus, portraying William Pitt as Moses and Lord Bute as Aaron in the context of a temptation to sacrifice to false gods.[32] Charles Chauncy in 1766 had likened the colonists' plight to the children of Israel in Egypt: " 'We are denied straw, and yet the full tale of bricks is required of us!' Or, as it was otherwise uttered, We must soon be obliged 'to borrow money for the king's tribute, and that upon our lands.' "[33] When the British evacuated Boston early in 1776, the sermon preached at Cambridge in the presence of George Washington interpreted the scripture: "And took off their chariot which, that they drove them heavily; so that the Egyptians said, Let us flee from the face of Israel, for the Lord fighteth for them against the Egyptians."[34]

David Ramsay, as historian of the Revolution, solemnly uncovered the face of events at Trenton.

The more effectually to disguise the departure of the Americans from Trenton, fires were lighted up in front of their camp. These not only gave an appearance of going to rest, but as flame cannot be seen through, concealed from the British, what was transacting behind them. In this relative position they were a pillar of fire to the one army, and a pillar of cloud to the other. Providence favoured this movement of the Americans. The weather had been for some time so warm and moist, that the ground was soft and the roads so deep as to be scarcely passable: but the wind suddenly changed to the north-west, and the ground in a short time was frozen so hard, that when the Americans took up their line of march, they were no more re-tarded, than if they had been upon a solid pavement.[35]

If the patriots were Israelites embroiled in a grand Exodus-event, the British easily qualified as Egyptians. "Surely the people at large of Great Britain, are involved in worse than Egyptian darkness, while their rulers are madly rushing, like Pharaoh and his host, through a sea of blood, on their utter destruction," wrote one Philadelphia correspondent after Lexington and Concord had mobilized popular response throughout the colonies.[36] Patrick Henry had "no doubt that that God who, in former ages, had hardened Pharaoh's heart, that he might show his power and glory in the redemption of his chosen people," for similar pur-poses had acted in the present.[37] When General William Howe and the British failed to take Philadelphia, Mercy Warren mused that no one could tell "why he stopped short on the borders of the river, as if afraid the waters of the Deleware [sic], like an-other Red Sea, would overwhelm the pursuers of the injured Americans, who had in many instances as manifestly experienced the protecting hand of Providence, as the favored Israelites."[38] One broadside on the evacuation of Boston found that "notwith-standing the finger of God,/ . . . Howe, Pharoah like, did harden his heart,/ Being thirsty for victory to maintain his part."[39] On Long Island in 1776, Lydia Post quietly celebrated the return of domestic tranquillity in her diary, absorbing even the Hessians into the myth. "The neighborhood has been more quiet for a week past, and the Hessians have really left, bag and baggage, for which Heaven be praised! They are like the locusts of Egypt, desolating the land, and eating up every green thing."[40]

As the Israelites who had been tested in the Exodus and their subsequent desert existence, the Americans were enduring a time of trial which pointed to their special place in the divine dispensation. And as they contemplated their collective destiny as Israel chosen of God, the patriots were accepting a cosmological schema which was figurative. Occurrences in the present conformed to an antitype from the past so that later time fulfilled the earlier moment and the early moment contained in itself the mystery of a later age. Thinking in figures gave to tradition an added twist, for instead of repeating what had been done from time immemorial, types and antitypes dwelt in the immediacy of a divine present. Americans might have ceased thinking figuratively by beginning to think historically in terms of causal connections between events which followed each other serially, or even in terms of the haphazard progression of one thing after another. But they did not. As "our Israel" they had skipped over centuries, which they had found unconnected with their condition, to live in the power of the mythical moment of Exodus. When they began to move out of Israel, the patriots did so only relatively, and they did so by moving to a new form of mythic thinking in which they themselves became *the* center of mankind on their own recognizance and their action, a foundational event.

This centrality of their independent existence and action became clear to the patriots gradually and indirectly in both a negative and a positive manner. Couched negatively, the patriots' discovery of themselves came as they extended the figurative "Egyptian" condemnation of the enemy to an absolute and categorical demonization of the British and their supporters. If British supporters were personified Evil eager to enslave them, Americans—in a dualistic schema—had to be at the very least angelic, godly, and even gods. And British partisans were demonic in patriot consciousness as early as the time of the Stamp Act confrontation.

The *Boston Gazette*, from the first, minced no words about those who attempted to enforce the Act.

Let therefore all those apostate sons of venality, those wretched hire-lings, and execrable parricides, those first-born sons of Hell, who for a little filthy lucre, have thus as far as they were able, betray'd and murder'd their country, with the vile slander of their contagious breath and dire hissing of their forked tongues, conscious of their base perfidious lies, blush and be confounded at the light of the sun, and tremble at the countenance of the sons of honour and vertue.[41]

Peter Oliver who complained that "the common People had had that [Stamp] Act, & all the Acts of Parliament since, dressed up by their seditious Leaders, either with raw Head & bloody Bones, or with Horns, Tails & cloven Feet, which were sufficient to affright their weak Followers," did not seem to be exaggerating.[42] One address to the Sons of Liberty at Liberty Tree cheerfully compared Lord Bute to the seven-headed monster of the Book of Revelation and George Grenville to the second monster, men-tioned later in the book.

In an engraving in 1768, Paul Revere caricatured the infamous seventeen rescinders of the Massachusetts Circular Letter. He had sketched huge jaws opening to swallow up the rescinders while flames belched forth and overhead the devil with his pitchfork forced them forward.[43] Governor Bernard was castigated, though unnamed, in a letter to the *Boston Gazette*, including the dog-gerel: "If such Men are by God appointed,/ The Devil may be the Lord's annointed."[44] The while, broadsides and songs reit-erated the theme. "American Taxation" was a good example, as Satan, "arch traitor" and ruler of the "burning lake," journeyed across the "Britannic ocean" to North America.[45]

Community leaders both led and followed the collective intui-tion. Samuel West inveighed against the "horrible wild beast" of Revelation 13, "having seven heads and ten horns, and upon his heads the names of blasphemy." The monster had been consti-tuted by the devil to be his vicegerent on earth, an event which meant for West and his hearers that "tyrants are the ministers of Satan, ordained by him for the destruction of mankind." The daily peril became worshiping the dragon (Satan) through the tyrant.[46] "Projected in the blackest principles of the human mind," declared Benjamin Hichborn in 1777 at a Boston Massacre oration, "and supported by ambition and a lust of unbounded sway, this *armed monster* both spread havoc and misery throughout the world."[47] The poet Philip Freneau imagined a soliloquy by King George III:

> Curs'd be the day when first I saw the sun,
> Curs'd be the hour when I this war begun;
> The fiends of darkness then inspir'd my mind,
> And powers unfriendly to the human kind;
> My future years I consecrate to woe,
> For this great loss my soul in tears shall flow.[48]

Just as the acts of God had made their mark on human history, the cruelties of Britons and their partisans were public facts accomplished in the arena of time and history. Their demonic nature was particularly evident in British attacks on churches. The *Pennsylvania Journal* reported that the British in Boston, "by order of their general, Howe, have taken down the pulpit, and all the pews in the Old South meeting-house, and are using it for a riding school. . . . Thus we see the house once set apart for true worship and service of God, turned into a den for thieves!"[49] When later the British began to burn churches, the *New Hampshire Gazette* commented that "they manifest peculiar malice against the Presbyterian churches, having, during this month, burnt three in New York State, and two in Connecticut."[50]

Writing to his wife, Abigail, in the spring of 1777, John Adams pondered the matter of British atrocity with some depth. It was "full of important lessons," and "if the facts only were known, in the utmost simplicity of narration, they would strike every pious and humane bosom in Great Britain with horror." Adams went on to suggest that "not only history should perform her office, but painting, sculpture, statuary, and poetry ought to assist, in publishing to the world and perpetuating to posterity the horrid deeds of our enemies."[51] Another letter writer of the period spoke accusingly to his correspondent overseas: "You rob us of our birth-rights, you destroy our charters, you burn our towns and villages, you murder our wives and children, you block up our trade, and you plunder us of our property, and for remonstrating against such cruelty, we are deemed Rebels."[52]

Nowhere did the horrors of British treatment appear more manifest than in the campaign in New Jersey. Mercy Warren echoed the collective sentiment when she wrote in her history:

The footsteps of the British army in their route through the Jersies, were every where marked with the most wanton instances of rapine and bloodshed: even the sacred repositories of the dead were not unmolested by the sacrilegious hands of the soldiery; while the licentiousness of their officers spread rape, misery, and despair, indiscriminately through every village.[53]

William Gordon agreed in his own history and spared no words, decrying the "licentious ravages of the soldiery, both British and foreigners [Hessians], who were shamefully permitted, with unrelenting hand, to pillage friend and foe in the Jerseys." Gordon could be more explicit, and he detailed for his readers the case of the sixteen young women who fled to the woods but were seized there and carried off. "One man had the cruel mortification to have his wife and only daughter (a child of ten years) ravished. Another girl of thirteen was taken from her father's house, carried to a barn about a mile off, there dishonored, and afterward abused by five others."[54] For Ramsay, likewise, soldiers and especially Hessians "gave full scope to the selfish and ferocious passions of human nature. . . . Infants, children, old men and women were stripped of their blankets and clothing. Furniture was burnt or otherwise destroyed. Domestic animals were carried off, and the people robbed of their necessary household provisions."[55]

British treatment of American prisoners of war also received the hue and cry and was denounced in the press, in the pulpit, and in the Congress. John Witherspoon, as he looked back on the war years, condemned "the inhumane treatment of the American prisoners by the British," which, he said, "was not more remarkable than their insolence and rapacity towards the people of the country wherever their power extended."[56] In 1777, the congressional "Committee to enquire into the conduct of the enemy" filed a report which it had divided into four parts: "First, The wanton and oppressive devastation of the country, and destruction of property: Second, the inhuman treatment of those who were so unhappy as to become prisoners: Third, The savage butchery of many who had submitted or were incapable of resistance: Fourth, The lust and brutality of the soldiers in the abusing of women."[57]

The lowest places in hell, however, seemed reserved for those Americans who turned their back on the patriot cause, and betrayed their fellow-countrymen to the enemy. The *cas célèbre* was Benedict Arnold. David Ramsay's assessment was mild when he concluded that it was "to the honour of human nature, that a great revolution and an eight years war produced but one."[58] Other writers of the Revolution seldom mentioned the name of Arnold without, as Moses Coit Tyler described it, "its being coupled with that of Satan, between whom and the traitor the intercourse was assumed to be both familiar and without intermission."[59] Even more striking were the ritual demonstrations which appeared to rise spontaneously, expressing, and themselves creating, a popular mythology of the traitor who incarnated the inversion of the myth of Revolution.

In Philadelphia, an effigy of Arnold was carted through the streets, dressed in regimentals, two-faced, with a mask in his left hand and a letter to Beelzebub in his right. Behind him stood the black-robed Devil with pitchfork in hand, shaking a purse of money at the ill-fated general. Before the cart, a large lantern formed a transparency which depicted scenes in the story of Arnold's treachery. The *Pennsylvania Packet* reported that "the procession was attended with a numerous concourse of people, who after expressing their abhorrence of the treason and the traitor, committed him to the flames, and left both the effigy and the original to sink into ashes and oblivion."[60]

The story was the same elsewhere, as Arnold was hung in effigy and consigned to the fire at Boston, Providence, and other places throughout New England. In Providence, the Liberty Tree was the site of his execution. In New Milford, Connecticut, Arnold appeared "sitting on his coffin, in a horse-cart, hung round with several pair of splendid lanterns," while behind him the Devil looked "ashamed of so unprofitable a servant." The people, who were not excluded from the liturgy, expressed "their universal contempt of the traitor, by the hissing explosion of a multitude of squibs and crackers," while "thirteen volleys were fired by the guards, and three cheers given by the people in testimony of their joy that the States were rid of the traitor." The *Pennsylvania Packet* hoped "the ever memorable 25th of September (the day when the blackest of crimes was unfolded) will be observed yearly throughout the United States of America, and handed down to the latest posterity, to the eternal disgrace of the traitor."[61]

But the patriots became their own center through affirmation as well as negation. Couched positively, the patriots' discovery of themselves came, first, through their involvement in the attainment or the continuance of their liberty against the backdrop of British attempts to enslave them. It came, second, in the urgency of their calls for the virtues—powers—which were the condition of their freedom. The American cult of liberty took some curious turns as it shifted in articulation from liberty versus slavery, with the God of Battles as liberator, to liberty *and* property, with Americans themselves as acquisitors. Sometimes, indeed, one wondered whether liberty were not simply a Sunday dress for property.

Moral denunciation at the materialism of the patriots does not succeed in illuminating the concern which animated them and which was, in its own way, a religious one. The Calvinist heritage of some Americans had taught them that wealth, although it could lead to corruption, was the blessing of Jehovah on virtue. Property, in the colonial consciousness, was also a general concern which had been heightened by the ethos of natural rights. Thus, possession and ownership had assumed transcendent meaning.

Both symbolized and presented to the patriots that sense of themselves as centers of self-actualizing power in which they delighted.
If liberty was the Sunday dress for property, the reason was that
property was the everyday form of liberty, and liberty, the state
of existence of strong and confident men and women.

It was apparent that property came to be equated with life
itself. One need only cite the venerable custom of debtors' prison,
where even so eminent a patriot as Robert Morris spent some
time, or the later penal codes which Americans adopted instead.
One's life was not too high a price to exact for the violation of
property rights of another, since property, as transcendent, became more valuable than life. Religiously, the transcendence of
property meant that natural and man-made entities had been elevated to a plane previously inhabited by gods and divine beings;
that pedestrian, everydayish things and productions eked out by
the sweat of the brow occupied a place which other cultures had
reserved for inspired creations in art, music, and poetry. Beyond
that, it hinted at part of the inner dynamic in the problematic
ambivalence of Americans toward their black slaves, the enduring
signs of contradiction in the patriotic vision.

The hidden transcendent, property, crept out regularly during
the era of Revolution. When the dramatic wails of outraged liberty rose the loudest, property usually lurked in the wings, a
situation true in the crises produced by the Stamp Act, by the
Townshend Acts, by the Tea Act, by the Boston Port Bill. One
broadside on "Tea destroyed by Indians" urged:

> Bostonian's SONS *keep up your Courage good,*
> *Or Dye, like Martyrs, in fair Free-born Blood.*
>
> Our LIBERTY, and LIFE is now invaded,
> And FREEDOM's brightest Charms are darkly shaded!
> But, we will STAND—and think it noble mirth,
> To DART the man that dare oppress the Earth.[62]

Ramsay recorded that in 1774 "every news paper teemed with
dissertations in favour of liberty," while in the *London Chronicle*

a letter from an overseas correspondent announced that Americans were "prepared to die freemen, rather than live what they call slaves."[63]

On other occasions, the transcendence of property was not so hidden. John Dickinson's "Liberty Song," which was universally popular, spoke to the profit motive of Americans.

> In freedom we're born, and in freedom we'll live;
> Our purses are ready,—
> Steady, friends, steady,—
> Not as slaves, but as freemen, our money we'll give!
>
> How sweet are the labors that freemen endure,
> That they shall enjoy all the profit secure;
> No more such sweet labors Americans know,
> If Britons shall reap what Americans sow.[64]

At the dedication of the Liberty Tree in Providence, Silas Downer complained that "the *common people* of *Great Britain* very liberally give and grant away the property of the *Americans* without their consent, which if yielded to by us must fix us in the lowest bottom of slavery." "If they have such power over our properties," he inveighed, "they must have a proportionable power over our persons; and from hence it will follow, that they can demand and take away our lives, whensoever it shall be agreeable to their sovereign wills and pleasure."[65] Gad Hitchcock's election sermon of 1775 closed with the solemn judgment: "Our danger is not visionary but real; our contention is not about trifles, but about liberty and property, and not ours only, but those of posterity to the latest generation."[66] One need only remember the cries of the Boston mob, which rallied around invocations of "liberty and property" as they displayed their unhappiness with Lieutenant-Governor Hutchinson, the stamp distributors, and the Stamp Act, to appreciate how deeply ingrained in the collective consciousness was the union of liberty and property.

As Americans began to understand that the liberty they sought must extend itself ultimately throughout the world, the transcendence of property could only gain thereby. Liberty as Goddess meant property as God. It was no accident that, as America grew more prosperous in the nineteenth century than even the millennialists of the Revolution had dreamed, the paeans to universal liberty rose louder and longer than they had in the turmoil of events. It was not a colonial newspaper or a contemporary history, but the nineteenth-century Democrat George Bancroft, who wrote of Lexington: "Alarm guns were fired, and the drums beat, not a call to village husbandmen only, but the reveille to humanity. . . . These are the village heroes, who were more than of noble blood, proving by their spirit that they were of a race divine. They gave their lives in testimony to the rights of mankind. . . . their action was the slowly ripened fruit of Providence and of time.'[67]

The patriots' discovery of themselves, which came in their pleas for virtue, was really the discovery, despite their jeremiads, of their own righteousness. By the era of Revolution, it seemed as if every formative element in American consciousness had shaped virtue into a central concern. Liberal Christianity had tilted its weight toward Arminianism with its emphasis on the good which humans could accomplish. Evangelicals had already begun to take a keen interest in the lives of their converts whose behavior would provide a telling indication of the reality of the experience of awakening. Even Freemasonry, which had become a force among the leaders of the Revolution, set its sights on the perfect ashlar which a human being might become. "Favor'd by Heaven," ran one song of 1775, "the virtuous few,/Tyrannish legions shall subdue." William Gordon reminded the patriots that "the obligations this people are under to holiness, are special, from the many appearances of God in their favour, and his having so multiplied and exalted them."[68]

By the end of the Revolution, Ezra Stiles and his fellow-countrymen knew that "the history of the Hebrew theocracy shows that the secular welfare of God's ancient people depended upon their virtue, their religion, their observance of that holy covenant

which Israel entered into with God on the plains at the foot of
Nebo, on the other side Jordan."[69] It followed that the welfare of
the Americans depended upon *themselves*. Put another way, the
patriots *controlled* Jehovah, for their virtuous action was the lever
which pushed his outstretched arm. As time went on, they would
find less and less need to bother Jehovah at all, since their virtue
led them to a sense of their own power.

One gains some sense of the subtle transition in an article in the
New York Journal for 1779. In conventional terms, the writer
affirmed how "strangely blind and inattentive" an observer would
be who did not "discern . . . the overruling hand of Divine Providence" in events. Then he went on to indicate why, with such
powerful aid, the war had not already been won: "the general
prevalence of wickedness among us renders us unfit for the blessings of peace, lengthens out the calumnities of war upon us, and
prevents the success of our arms."[70] In order to succeed, the patriots had merely to straighten up and fly soberly. Then Jehovah
would be compelled to intervene on their behalf. The cynical
Peter Oliver understood what was happening when he castigated
the clergy:

Those pious Men were as saucy to the supreme Being, in their publick
Prayers, that a Bystander would imagine that he was only their Ex-
ecutioner. . . . They arrogated to themselves the Power of the Keys,
& could let in & shut out whom they pleased: but they were more
fond of the Key of the bottomless Pit, & dealt their Curses pretty
illiberally; for one of that sacred Order used this Expression in his
publick Prayers, vizt. "O Lord! Bind up all the Tories on this and
the other Side of the Water, into one Bundle, & cast them into the
bottomless Pit, & let the Smoke of their Torrent ascend forever &
ever."[71]

Similarly, the *Freeman's Journal* was sure that Providence had
"retaliated" when British vessels were banned from an American
port in 1776. William Gordon, a year later, affirmed that the
"God of nature" had "declared again and again his disapproba-
tion" of the British by "scattering their fleets, staying their voy-

ages, disconcerting their plans, delivering many of their stores into our hands, and plunging them continually into greater difficulties."[72] "The American republicans," grumbled an unfriendly source of the same period, "like the rebels of all ages, from their *justice, peace-loving, and mercy*, pretend to have the especial favors of God, and none of the devil's, on their side, and for this reason we rarely see a proclamation from the rebel camp, without a pious sentence bringing up the rear."[73]

When, at Ticonderoga in 1775, Ethan Allen demanded the surrender of the fort "in the name of the great Jehovah, and of the continental congress," he—or David Ramsay who reported his words—was unconsciously pointing toward the vector along which British devils, liberty, property, and virtue were enticing the patriots to run.[74] Jehovah had found his peer in colonial authority. As the war progressed, fewer came the assertions that God was on the American side, and the war seemed increasingly to be a *human* event wrought by human means. John Witherspoon, who recognized the process as early as 1776, warned that it had given him "great uneasiness to read some ostentatious, vaunting expressions in our newspapers" though he was relieved to find them "much restrained of late."[75]

But on July 4, 1776, anthropocentrism already in large measure characterized American civil religion as Hezekiah Hayden, a private in the army which lay camped in New York, wrote home:

Let us therefore rely upon the goodness of our cause, and the aid of the Supreme Being, in whose hand the decree is to animate and encourage us to great and noble actions. The eyes of all our countrymen are upon us, and we shall have their blessings and praises, if happily we are the means of saving them. Let us therefore animate and encourage each other,—and shew the whole world, that freemen contending for liberty on their own ground are superiour to any slavish mercenary on earth.[76]

John Winthrop and his associates among the Puritan fathers might have been faintly bemused at this latter-day version of "A Modell of Christian Charity." The sons, however, had begun to authorize themselves. The Almighty, while echoing divine decrees from an inscrutable Calvinistic sovereignty, had benevolently facilitated the human exploits of Americans. At the same time, the "Supreme Being" who, already by title more distant than the God of the past, would animate and encourage the patriots was fading from view. The patriots would "animate and encourage each other." Instead of the eyes of all the world, there were the eyes of countrymen whose political salvation depended on military action. No longer should Americans show the world the greatness of their God, but rather "that freemen contending for liberty" would not be made slaves.

In this context, the military "enthusiasm," a more specific version of the general patriotic enthusiasm we have already discussed, became indicative of self-authorization. If, as Perry Miller has suggested, the Puritans had transformed their role in the "errand into the wilderness" from "errand boy" to "doer of errands," the patriots were effecting a similar transposition. Still hailing Jehovah, God of Battles, their vision moved to the exuberant spectacle of impending war. Already in 1775, the *rage militaire* had "taken possession of the whole Continent," according to one correspondent. "The City of Philadelphia has turned out 4000 men, 300 of whom are Quakers. Every County in our Province is awakened, and several thousand Riflemen on our Frontiers are in readiness to march down to our assistance at a moment's warning, if necessary."[77] John Adams was ready to estimate that Philadelphia turned out "two thousand every day," and meanwhile he told Abigail, "Oh that I were a soldier! I will be. I am reading military books. Everybody must, and will, and shall be a soldier." Abigail was not indifferent to the martial fever and wrote eagerly in 1776 to say that she had been sitting on Penn's hill "to hear the amazing roar of cannon, and from whence I could see every shell which was thrown. The sound, I think, is one of the grandest in nature, and is of the true species of the sublime.[78] Another correspondent from Philadelphia agreed that everyone was learning the "military exercise" and owned that he himself took "great pleasure" in learning. The exercise was performed every day, he added, "upon a fine common near the city, with an almost enchanting wood at the back of us, where we regale ourselves after we are done."[79]

One sign of the times was the number of servants of Jehovah who had recruited soldiers or marched from the pulpit into the battlefield to become servants of battle instead. When a military officer begged Samuel Eaton of Harpswell, Maine, for help in the recruitment of troops, Eaton called his people back to the church green on a Sunday evening and thundered scripturally, "Cursed be he that keepeth back his sword from blood."[80] Peter Muhlenburg of Woodstock, Virginia, dramatically left his congregation at the head of a Virginia regiment after news of the Battle of Bunker Hill reached him. Joel Headley told the tale with relish.

> Closing the services he stepped into the vestry-room, and laying aside his gown, put on his colonel's uniform, and stood before his astonished congregation in full regimentals. This sudden apparition of a Virginia colonel, in full uniform, walking down the broad aisle, in the place of their pastor, took every one by surprise. Turning neither to the right hand nor to the left, he strode sternly on to the door, and ordered the drum to beat for recruits.
> The silence that had reigned, while this extraordinary scene was passing, was suddenly broken by the loud and rapid roll of the drum. The congregation rose simultaneously to their feet, and the men gathered in a mass around their former pastor—scarcely one capable of bearing arms remaining behind.[81]

John Gano, a Baptist chaplain with the army, got caught in the midst of a fierce skirmish and confessed: "My station in time of action *I knew to be among the surgeons, but in this battle I somehow got in front of the regiment, yet I durst not quit my place for fear of dampening the spirits of the soldiers,* or of bringing on me an imputation of cowardice."[82] In Gaysboro, Vermont, the news of the battle at Lexington compelled a preacher, David Avery, to join the army, taking twenty parishioners with him. In Danvers, "the deacon of the parish was elected captain of the minute-men, and the minister his lieutenant."[83]

Militarism became the center of a new conversion experience. It was altogether fitting that Samuel Spring should preach over the grave of George Whitefield before the American expedition which attempted the conquest of Quebec. After the service, he reported what happened.

Some one requested a visit to Whitfield's tomb. The sexton was hunted up, the key procured, and we descended to his coffin. It had lain in the tomb six years, but was in good preservation. The officers induced the sexton to take off the lid of the coffin. The body had nearly all returned to dust. Some portions of his grave-clothes remained. His collar and wristbands, in the best preservation were taken and carefully cut in little pieces, and divided among them.[84]

The relics of the enthusiast had gone to bless a new enthusiasm, and after the victory of Yorktown sealed the success of the patriot cause, the intensity of the American response prompted David Ramsay's later description.

The reduction of such an army occasioned unusual transports of joy, in the breasts of the whole body of the people. Well authenticated testimony asserts, that the nerves of some were so agitated, as to produce convulsions, and that at least one man expired under the tide of pleasure which flowed in upon him, when informed of his lordship's surrender.[85]

When the transports had calmed and the enthusiasm quieted, as inevitably it must, the patriots had entered a religious universe which centered on American society. The ministers in their military zeal had been representative of their compatriots, and with other Americans they continued to turn distinctly toward the human. George Duffield was not unusual in preaching the necessity of "a diligent attention to the use of means."[86] In the meantime, Abner Benedict became an inventor for submarine warfare and "made various experiments in the manufacture of saltpetre from materials never before used." The chaplain for Durkee's Regiment, the Reverend Mr. Boardman, kept a diary which was totally "secular" in its account of events.[87] And when the Connecticut Valley lay under the threat of General John Burgoyne

in 1777, President Eleazar Wheelock of Dartmouth sent to the
Committees of Safety in convention to exhort the "appointment
of a day of prayer, the repression of vice and profaneness, a revival of Christian spirit among the churches, and a concert of
prayer, besides a *practical exertion in every rational mode of self-
protection.*"[88]

Clearly, the patriotic discovery of self was the discovery of a
common identity in action. Although the American myth involved the discovery of manyness, as we shall see the natural
rights philosophy hinted, still it told of the origins of *one* people.
For David Ramsay, the Americans had known "but little of one
another, previous to the revolution." But:

A continental army, and congress, composed of men from all the
states, by freely mixing together, were assimilated into one mass. Individuals of both, mingling with the citizens, disseminated principles
of union among them. Local prejudices abated. By frequent collision
asperities were worn off, and a foundation was laid for the establishment of a nation, out of discordant materials.[89]

Repeatedly, exuberant witnesses testified that the nation was in
the process of becoming, was indeed at hand. "Persevere, YE
GUARDIANS OF LIBERTY!" one "Freeman" urged the army camps.
"May success be your constant attendant, until the enemies of
freedom are no more, and all future generations, as they successively tread the stage of time, and taste the JOYS OF LIBERTY, will
rise up and call YOU blessed.[90] John Adams marked the second
anniversary of Lexington by writing to Abigail that "after all our
difficulties and misfortunes, [we] are much abler to cope with
them now than we were at the beginning." Abigail answered in
kind: "We are no wise dispirited here. We possess a spirit that
will not be conquered. If our men are all drawn off and we should
be attacked, you would find a race of Amazons in America."[91] A
broadside in 1778 printed the congressional message urging the
citizens to "exert the means of defence which God and Nature
have given you." A year later, it was clear to the *New Hampshire*

Gazette that they had done so: "Nothing can exceed the spirit and intrepidity of our countrymen in storming and capturing the British fortress at Stony Point. It demonstrates that the Americans have soldiers equal to any in the world; and that they can attack and vanquish the British in their strongest works."[92]

Likewise, in the *Virginia Gazette* of 1780, Timothy Standfast found "a dignity in the soul of man, which, when interwoven with the interest of his country, makes him act as if he was immortal; every power of his mind seems heightened to a peculiar greatness, and all his actions blaze with the refulgency of magnanimity and patriotism."[93] It seemed certain that Jehovah had at least removed himself to the sidelines when, after the Battle of the Cowpens in 1781, the *New Jersey Gazette* reported the body count: big losses on the British side and "but ten killed and fifty-three wounded of the Americans." What did it mean? The *Gazette* answered sensibly enough: "This is but a prelude to the era of 1781, the close of which, we hope, will prove memorable in the annals of history, as the happy period of peace, liberty, and independence to America.[94]

Jehovah had stopped making history, while the nation of patriots was obligingly making it for him. The new nationals did so with dramatic flair, as contemporaries regularly observed. Simeon Baldwin in 1781 looked back on the era of Revolution and thought it would be "impossible to do justice to the merits of those patriots who performed conspicuous parts on the theatre of those actions we . . . commemorate."[95] Mercy Warren thought that James Otis, her brother, was "justly deemed the first martyr to American freedom"; his name would be enrolled "among the most distinguished patriots who have expired on the 'bloodstained theatre of human action.' "[96] Significantly, as General Washington issued his orders to the army at the close of the war, he told its members: "Nothing now remains but for the actors of this mighty scene to preserve a perfect unvarying consistency of character through the very last act, to close the drama with applause; and to retire from the military theatre with the same approbation of angels and men which have crowned all their former actions."[97]

Not only did the patriots make history with all the accoutrements of high drama, but they were aware that they did so. This awareness of making history seemed to revolve chiefly around military ventures. Military enthusiasm had been an ephemeral manifestation, but beneath it lay an enduring American structure of consciousness. The historians of the Revolution, who provided a window into the public concern, overwhelmingly centered their accounts on the details of battles, the celebrations of military encounters, the deeds of warriors and heroes. This was true for David Ramsay and William Gordon; for John Marshall, whose five volumes were intended to be a life of George Washington; for Mercy Warren, who tempered the narration of the annals of war with frequent Puritan sermonizing. Jedidiah Morse continued the tradition as the nineteenth century progressed. More recently, Ruth Miller Elson's study of schoolbooks of that era has established that the American Revolution, and particularly its military exploits, occupied more space in the texts than any other single event.[98] Already in 1772, at a Boston Massacre oration, Joseph Warren was pondering what it meant to "turn over the historic page, and trace the rise and fall of states and empires, [in which] the mighty revolutions which have so often varied the face of the world strike our minds with solemn surprise."[99] Another Bostonian wrote an enthusiastic letter abroad to England: "I would only ask if in all your reading of history, you have found an instance of irregular troops, hurried together at a moment's warning, with half the number at first, attacking and driving veterans, pick'd men, 17 miles, and continually firing the whole way, and not losing one third the number they killed?"[100] John Adams in 1777 sent along a piece of fatherly advice to the youthful John Quincy: "If it should be the design of Providence that you should live to grow up, you will naturally feel a curiosity to learn the history of the causes which have produced the late Revolution of our Government. No study in which you can engage will be more worthy of you."[101] "What are the most esteemed paintings?" queried the text of a reader in 1806. "Those representing historical events," came the ready answer of its author.[102] The Revolution was the "event next in importance to the birth of Christ," and it stood above all other wars of the same genre because "it had its origin, neither in ambition nor avarice, nor envy, nor in any gross passion; but in the nature and relation of things and in the thence resulting necessity of separation from the parent state."[103]

When Daniel Webster eulogized the Revolution in 1825 at the laying of the cornerstone of the Bunker Hill Monument, he spoke out of a myth which had pushed patriotic history-makers to stage center and left Jehovah hovering behind the scenes. The action of Americans in the Revolution had taught "how admirably the character of our people was calculated for setting the great example of popular government." It urged Webster and the others to extend their ideas "over the whole of the vast field in which we are called to act." Their object should be "OUR COUNTRY, OUR WHOLE COUNTRY, AND NOTHING BUT OUR COUNTRY." When the monument was at last completed in 1843 and Webster spoke again, his enthusiasm suggested the direction which militant patriotism had taken. "Even if civilization should be subverted, and the truths of the Christian religion obscured by a new deluge of barbarism," thundered Webster, "the memory of Bunker Hill and the American Revolution will still be elements and parts of the knowledge which shall be possessed by the last man to whom the light of civilization and Christianity shall be extended." "Woe betide the man who brings to this day's worship feeling less than wholly American!" he warned.

We know, that if we cause this structure to ascend, not only till it reached the skies, but till it pierced them, its broad surfaces could still contain but part of that which, in an age of knowledge, hath already been spread over the earth, and which history charges itself with making known to all future times. We know that no inscription on entablatures less broad than the earth itself can carry information of the events we commemorate where it has not already gone; and that no structure which shall not outlive the direction of letters and knowledge among men, can prolong the memorial.[104]

War had become the center of a ritual cult in which the original patriots and their descendants realized who they were and what their existence meant. Just as in the Old Testament—which the patriots had seen as a figure of their own condition—war assumed crucial importance. Necessary in ancient times for the creation and maintenance of the city-state with its sacred king, war in America created a nation-state with the military hero of the Revolution, as we shall see, the high priest of an American presidency. More than that, as the expression of human transcendence, the war cult demanded ultimate sacrifices: death was not too large a price to pay for identification as a patriot. Herbert Richardson was correct in his critique of the relationship between war and civil religion, in 1974, when he suggested that Americans no longer sacrificed their children to nature, but fed them instead to the state.[105]

In the actual experience of the Revolution, the ultimacy and transcendence which the patriots found in war provoked a double consciousness among them. We have already pointed to a connection between the woes of the jeremiad and the joys of the millennium, but here it is important to notice the tension generated by the relationship. On the one hand, as each day delivered the patriots further from the time of the Revolution, they experienced the perennial plight of mythic conceptualization: the world was traveling downhill as it grew away from the sacred event. On the other hand, the product of their righteous endeavor announced that a natural millennium was at hand and that the moment which had split time in two could be extended in secular time. The myth had in fact bred a discord in American consciousness which would grow larger through the years. Americans would strain to remember their originating event in an enduring and virtuous paradise and at the same time keep discover-

ing that some serious elements had been disturbed and the world
was in decline.

Mercy Warren was a good example of the predicament. Caught
between her glorification of the people in republicanism and her
equal sense of their weakness and ability to be seduced, between
her understanding of the grand destiny of America and the reality
of human sin, she conceived a nation *simul justus et peccator*.

[America] . . . has been conducted through a revolution that will be
ever memorable, both for its origin, its success, and the new prospects
it has opened both at home and abroad. The consequences of this
revolution have not been confined to one quarter of the globe, but the
dissemination of more liberal principles in government, and more honorable opinions of the rights of man, and the melioration of his condition, have been spread over a considerable part of the earth.

At the same time, Warren continually feared the "unpleasing part
of history, when 'corruption begins to prevail, when degeneracy
marks the manners of the people, and weakens the sinews of state.' "

If this should ever become the deplorable situation of the United
States, let some unborn historian, in a far distant day, detail the lapse,
and hold up the contrast between a simple, virtuous, and free people,
and a degenerate, servile race of beings, corrupted by wealth, effemi-
nated by luxury, impoverished by licentiousness, and become the *au-
tomatons* of intoxicated ambition.[106]

At the beginning, though, when the patriots were in the midst
of the time of Revolution, the consciousness of their presence in a
millennial dream which had taken flesh prevailed. Different from
the inherited millennium of the fathers, this new millennium was
manifestly political and national. Warren herself recalled that in
1774, "there were some who viewed the step of their summoning
a general congress, under exciting circumstances of peculiar em-
barrassment, as a *prelude* to a *revolution* which appeared pregnant
with events, that might affect not only the political systems, but
the character and manners of a considerable part of the habitable
globe."[107] The *New Jersey Gazette* in 1779 was already agreeing

with its correspondent that America had "now become an open asylum to all that are oppressed by the old corrupt governments in Europe," and Hector St. John Crèvecoeur, although he ultimately left it, exuberantly declared America "as the asylum of freedom; as the cradle of future nations, and the refuge of distressed Europeans."[108] After the war, Elias Boudinot remembered, perhaps with a certain wry humor, that he had "read an excellent treatise, said to have been written by Lord Kaim, which in a very extraordinary manner foretold the certainity of American Independence, in some future day, and that founded on a train of solid reasoning, but we talked of it and treated it as the generality of People now do the accounts they read of the Millinium."[109]

When peace came in 1783, the preachers articulated in the language of Christian orthodoxy the common sentiment which spread through the fledgling United States. "Our late convulsion," announced David Tappan, "with its present happy termination, tends to wake up and encourage the dormant flame of liberty in all quarters of the earth—to rouse up an oppressed, enslaved world from that stupor which has so long benumbed it." There was, he said, a "grand chain of Providence—in which the American revolution is a principal link—a chain which is gradually drawing after it the most glorious consequences to mankind, which is hastening on the accomplishment of the Scripture prophecies relative to the millennial state, the golden age of the church and the world in the latter days."[110] Ezra Stiles found that already the "new constellation of the United States" was beginning to realize its glory.

It has already risen to an acknowledged sovereignty among the republics and kingdoms of the world. And we have reason to hope, and, I believe, to expect, that God has still greater blessings in store for this vine which his own right hand hath planted, to make us high among the nations in praise, and in name, and in honor.[111]

The United States, George Duffield proclaimed, was a nation "born at once," and when the "American Zion began to travail, . . . without experiencing the pangs and pains which apprehensive fear expected, she brought forth her children, more numerous

than the tribes of Jacob, to possess the land from the north to the
south, and from the east to the yet unexplored, far distant
west."[112] In South Carolina, two years later, the Reverend Dr.
Ladd prophesied that "succeeding ages shall turn the historic page,
and catch inspiration from the era of 1776; they shall bow to the
rising glory of America; and Rome, once mistress of the world,
shall face on their remembrance."[113]

The new birth of the millennium was the completion of the
rite of passage which the Revolution had been. The sons had begun their struggle relying on their forefathers and their forefathers' God, but as their war grew in size and stature so did their
unconscious estimate of themselves. Although they were not
ready to disown Jehovah at the end of their encounter, and although they no doubt listened approvingly to preachers who
bound the natural millennium to the Christian version which
revelation had endorsed, effectually many of the patriots had begun to run their own lives. By 1825, Hesper's words to Columbus,
in Barlow's *Columbiad*, were signs of the times which the Revolution had brought about.

> There lies the path thy future sons shall trace,
> Plant here their arts and rear their vigorous race:
> A race predestined, in these choice abodes,
> To teach mankind to tame their fluvial floods,
> Retain from ocean, as their work requires,
> These great auxiliars, raised by solar fires,
> Force them to form ten thousand roads, and girth
> With liquid belts each verdant mound of earth,
> To aid the colon's as the carrier's toil,
> To drive the coulter and to fat the soil,
> Learn all mechanic arts and oft regain
> Their native hills in vapor and in rain.[114]

War and empire, making history and dramatic action, pragmatism
and an incarnational understanding which found the sacred in the
midst of things, all were of a piece. The God of the fathers, the
deus pluviosus, who rained and stormed and searched the hearts
of men, had become another face for the retiring God of Nature.

Chapter 4

The Greatest Governor
Governs Least

On September 8, 1774, the Continental Congress was debating the American controversy with Great Britain. John Adams, a delegate, had preserved notes of the occasion. Richard Henry Lee of Virginia was arguing that he could not see "why we should not lay our rights upon the broadest bottom, the ground of nature. Our ancestors found here no government." Edward Rutledge of South Carolina disagreed and said that American claims were founded on the British constitution and not on the law of nature. The contrary opinions were tossed back and forth by the delegates for some time, until it became clear that they were struggling to ascertain which line of reasoning would present the best legal case. For New York's James Duane, the law of nature would "be a feeble support."[1] In an unguarded moment, the patriots had revealed themselves: they knew intuitively what they wanted to do and why, but a "decent respect for the opinions of mankind" required them to turn their intuitions into rational justifications.

More than that, a "decent respect" for their own mental world and the experiences out of which it had arisen required rational justifications. The patriots had begun by appealing to the king against Parliament, a procedure in which there was a certain comfort. The waning of the Middle Ages and the rise of modernity had occurred in a world in which new nation-states were ruled by kings who held power by divine right and thus supplied an absolute to replace the diminishing imperium of the medieval church and papacy. Although English Whig political theory had

112

already significantly undercut the divine right of the king, the patriots still dwelt in a climate which demanded an unqualified foundation for authority and action. Accustomed to orient themselves in terms of an absolute, they needed a new one to replace the British sovereign.

It was here that the prior sovereignty which belonged to the people in conformity with the law of nature under God became immensely important. Far from being the "feeble support" which James Duane labeled it, the law of nature and the God who bequeathed it provided just that logical and psychological ground which the patriots' condition demanded. For this necessary divinity and his law would guarantee the stability of the human foundation while furthering the maximization of value placed on the human. In short, this God would provide merely by existing and would act by remaining inactive. He would be a *deus otiosus*, and it was this "lazy creator" who was the God of deism as well as so many of the public documents of the American Revolution.

As early as 1750, Jonathan Mayhew gave voice to what would become the rationale of the future, that the divine right of kings and nonresistance to royal authority were notions "fetched neither from divine revelation nor human reason" *because* the authority of God was absolute.[2] Mayhew's friend, James Otis, was representative over a decade later, when he saw that "the power of GOD Almighty is the power that can properly and strictly be called supreme and absolute." Besides linking him to his fathers, the realization led Otis to a subsequent one that "in the order of nature immediately under him [God] comes the power of a simple *democracy* or the power of the whole over the whole."[3] From here it was a small step to begin to regard the people as primary, while God was more and more relegated to the conventionalities, a kind of cosmic backdrop which did not interfere in the everyday conduct of human affairs. A broadside which printed the letter of a town meeting in 1774 was typical: "To you Gentlemen, our brethren and dear companions in the Cause of God *and our Country*, we apply; . . . To you, therefore, we look for that *Wis-*

dom, Advice and *Example,* which, giving strength to our understanding, and vigor to our actions, shall, with the blessing of God,
save us from destruction."[4] The letter was in fact a prayer, and
it was addressed, "under God," to the almighty people.

But the links to the world of the fathers were not so perfunc-
tory for all. As the language of Nature and Nature's God became
the possession of everybody's people, it was clear that the mental
world of the patriots required a double-facing divinity. Both
Christian pietists and Christian rationalists wanted a God who
acted in history even as he supported it. A curious situation developed: while Jehovah God of Battles, got lost in the war, Nature's God apparently found his armor lying there, put it on, and
began to direct events. The language of the God of Nature became inseparable for some from the *actions* of a God of History.
The anomaly of Nature's God directing the course of battle was
an incongruity which did not seem to disturb the patriots. And
when the God of Nature went out of style in the nineteenth
century as the evangelical impulse swept America, the new patriots had no difficulty in identifying with the God of the Revolution. For, to a significant extent, he had acted as they expected
a God of History to act, and his eighteenth-century name had not
been a disclaimer.

Less radical than clothing the God of Nature in the garments
of battle was the patriots' tendency to compromise by seeing him
as the Great Governor or Grand Architect of the universe. With
all of the colonies under either royal or proprietary governors
and many of the colonists chafing under their authority, it seemed
a reasonable conclusion that the greatest governor would be one
who governed least, by leaving Americans to shape their own
lives and fortunes in the context of liberty.[5] Thus, there was an
otiose content in descriptions of the Great Governor which approached the understanding of the God of Nature, while the
political epithet tied this God to history. Similarly, a Grand Architect achieved importance through his product, a free-standing
and enduring structure. Yet he had acted in a manner which was

more than natural and had entailed a direct intervention. Again, he was at once otiose—"alive" in his construction—and historical, the maker of a definite configuration of material and energies best understood in terms of human artifice. Freemasonry, as it waxed in importance among the patriots, would assert its identity in its proclamations of the Architect.

The God of Nature had come to America with the Enlightenment which, as in England and in France, had been grounded on Newtonian cosmic philosophy and the religious system of deism. Neither anticlerical nor antiecclesiastical, the deism which permeated the religious structure of the Revolution was one with which a broad spectrum of Americans could be at home. For it posited simply a general and benevolent Providence, an afterlife of reward and punishment, and the necessity of a life of virtue in the present. Herbert Morais has documented the widespread presence of rationalistic works in libraries and schools throughout the colonies as well as the publication of deistic tracts and periodicals during the period.[6] Harvard seemed particularly susceptible, and already in the early eighteenth century, its latitudinarian tendencies provided one of the strongest arguments for the foundation of Yale. By mid-century, deism was more than an undefined rumble at Cambridge, since the God of Nature had made an official appearance with the establishment in 1755 of the Dudleian lectureship in Natural Religion. Significantly, in 1775 King's College, New York, was imitating the gesture as the Regius Professorship of Divinity was inaugurated "in defense of the Christian, and on the principles of natural religion."[7]

Contact between American militiamen and British soldiers in the French and Indian War brought skepticism within the reach of ordinary folk. Later, according to New England accounts of the period, French officers and soldiers were responsible for spreading deism during the Revolution.[8] At the same time, the gradual evolution of Unitarianism in New England was transforming Arminian activism more and more in the direction of the deists, while the pragmatic necessity of uniting the colonies inclined the men who led the Revolution to regard deism benignly. It provided a core or skeleton of religious belief which was, as Sidney Mead has described it, the "relevant religion" of the churches,[9] a hidden bond which undergirded the peculiarities of sects and denominations. In the realization that there was such an underlying agreement and the need to valorize it for immediate and practical purposes, the patriots implicitly blessed the intellectual windfall from the European Enlightenment.

Natural religion grew in popularity with the Revolution and, as we shall see, found an *institutional* vehicle in the Freemasonry of the leaders. By the end of the war, some could deplore, as did Ezra Stiles, the presence of "declension" with a pervading "deism and skeptical indifferentism in religion," or with David Ramsay lament that the institutions of religion had been "deranged, the public worship of the deity suspended, and a great number of the inhabitants deprived of the ordinary means of obtaining that religious knowledge, which tames the fierceness and softens the rudeness of human passions and manners."[10] When in 1784 Ethan Allen published his *Reason the Only Oracle of Man*, Timothy Dwight accusingly called it "the first formal publication in the United States, openly directed against the Christian religion."[11] Yet the irreligion which some of the patriots decried among their fellow-countrymen was in reality another form of religion, not Christian as Timothy Dwight had recognized, but nevertheless a structure of religious order which only appeared to be disorder because a number of Americans had identified religion exclusively with Judaeo-Christian symbols. The God who got lost in the sky to let humans run the world had much in common with Jehovah, but he had some differences too. It was these that the patriots who were offended by outright deism had noticed.

During the era of Revolution, however, Nature's God had gained a public following. *Deus otiosus* that he was, he was recognized everywhere as creator. Unlike the rain-and-storm God who interfered with the state of the earth, this God had fashioned the world but then remained aloof. His power was so overwhelming that if he should reenter the natural domain that he once had set in motion, he would—like the bull in the proverbial china shop—upset the delicate balance.

In popular usage, frequent and continued testimonies to the Creator God enunciated the understanding of the deity that accompanied one side of the myth of the Revolution. Indeed, the patriots perceived their God far more as Creator than Redeemer. A rigorous Baptist such as Isaac Backus could find with ease that the "real cause of all the *disorders* in the world" came from "*hearkening* to a creature instead of the Creator" and "*worshipping* and *serving* the *creature* more than the *Creator*, who is over-all, God blessed forever."[12] At the other end of the spectrum, George Washington was fond of referring to God in public speeches and private letters by a number of deistic terms, among them "Author" and "Divine Disposer." Daniel Boorstin has pointed out that there was "wide disagreement among the Jeffersonians . . . as to the possibility and extent of revelation; but all appear to have believed that the creation itself was the primary source of knowledge of God."[13] A judicious "Patriot's Prayer," appended to an edition of Thomas Paine's *Common Sense*, was addressed for the edification of Americans to the "Parent of all, omnipotent," whose "streams of goodness" flowed "through all creation's bounds." The suppliant begged his Creator to teach him to heed his country's voice which was "nature's call" and God's as well.[14]

It was the Continental Congress, above all, which esteemed the Creator in its official proclamations. As we have noted, the Creator found such a ready congregation among the patriots precisely because he could give to government a solid foundation. Thus Congress announced to the colonies initially that "in every case of opposition by a people to their rulers, or of one state to another, duty to Almighty God, the creator of all, requires that a true and impartial judgment be formed of the measures leading to such opposition." Again, the "Declaration on the Reasons for Taking Up Arms" declared in favor of the "divine Author of our existence," "our beneficent Creator," and a "reverence for our great Creator."[15] Over a decade earlier, in 1764, James Otis had adumbrated the stance of the Congress clearly, if floridly.

I think it [government] has an everlasting foundation in the *unchangeable will* of GOD, the author of nature, whose laws never vary. The same omniscient, omnipotent, infinitely good and gracious Creator of the universe who has been pleased to make it necessary that what we call matter should *gravitate* for the celestial bodies to roll round their axes, dance their orbits, and perform their various revolutions in that beautiful order and concert which we all admire has made it *equally necessary* that from *Adam* and *Eve* to these degenerate days the different sexes should sweetly *attract* each other, form societies of *single* families, of which *larger* bodies and communities are as naturally, mechanically, and necessarily combined as the dew of heaven and the soft distilling rain is collected by the all enlivening heat of the sun.[16]

The Creator God had wound the springs of a great natural machine which worked according to prescribed and predictable laws. Once the process had been initiated, it was self-regulating. Interference by either God or demon was unnecessary, for this God was Nature's God and the Law of Nature which ruled over all. In such a system, there was no place for a particular revelation to a special people, since general providence meant *universal* law. The regular motion of heaven and earth in accordance with the law paradoxically guaranteed nonmotion: the God of Nature would not interrupt his law to enter the human arena and act in the public lives of human beings. Instead, Nature conformed in its objective dimensions to the general outline of the human mind which could discern the character of divinity by tracing its imprint on the harmonious rhythms of the cosmos. There was, as Carl Becker observed, a new absolute, Nature, and reason became the human oracle for distinguishing between "nature drunk" and "nature sober."[17]

God, Nature, Nature's God, and the Law of Nature were interchangeable terms in the evolving American structure of consciousness. George Washington was being true to the patriot tradition when in 1788 he told Sir Edward Newenham that if Americans used "these blessings which God and Nature seemed to have intended us," they would see "scenes of National happiness, which have not heretofore been offered for the fruition of the most favoured Nations."[18] Earlier, Ethan Allen had pondered the meaning of the God of Nature and had also come to the conclusion that he could be identified with the Law of Nature. Allen's *Reason the Only Oracle* (1784) had been brewing for many years, and its publication at the end of the war was a clear and fitting summary of the religious consciousness which seemed more or less prevalent among the patriot leaders.[19] Even though most of them, if they had known Allen's book at all, would not have endorsed his extreme statements of their own half-hidden opinions, his work is illuminating as an articulation of the logical structure of the patriots' views.

Allen understood that the God of Nature stood in opposition to Jehovah, who, Allen hinted, was really an idol, a being who had "no existence but in the mere imagination of the human mind." "An idea of a jealous God," he said directly, was "of this sort," for jealousy was "the offspring of finite minds proceeding from the want of knowledge, which in dubious matters makes us suspicious and distrustful." Nor was there "any propriety in ascribing the passion of anger or wrath to God," since "any being, who is capable of the passion of anger or wrath, must be admitted to be mutable, which is incompatible with the divine perfection." In this context, Allen attacked the biblical understanding of predestination, of Jehovah's displeasure toward Pharoah, of his choice of Jacob over Esau. Instead, it was the purposive order of nature which disclosed the meaning of God. If Allen's contemporaries would but imagine "a compendious idea of the harmony of the universe," it would be "the same as calling God by the name of harmony, for there would be no harmony without regulation, and no regulation without a regulator, which is expressive of the idea of God." The creation of God could not be "confined or limited to the order of time, or successively connected with its fleeting moments like ours." Such a system would subject God to "a capacity or condition, which is manifestly finite," and "infinitude" could not be "compounded of parts, or measured by time, nor repleted by anything which pertains to, or operates by succession."

This meant in effect that God could not *act*, for to act *in time* would be a limiting condition. Nature, by contrast, was the true revelation of God:

The whole, which we denominate by the term *nature*, which is the same as creation perfectly regulated, was eternally connected together by the creator to answer the same all glorious purpose, *to wit*; the display of the divine nature, the consequences of which are existence and happiness to being in general, so that creation with all its productions, operates according to the laws of nature, and is sustained by the self-existent cause in perfect order and decorum, agreeable to the eternal wisdom, unalterable rectitude, impartial justice and immense goodness of the divine nature, which is a summary of God's providence. It is from the established ordinances of nature that summer and winter, rainy and fair seasons, monsoons, refreshing breezes, seed time and harvest, day and night interchangeably succeed each other, and diffuse their extensive blessings to man.

Providence was simply the way the world turned; it was ludicrous to think of it taking sides in tribal confrontations. Answering prayers was impossible for Providence because it would imply some change in the eternal wisdom. "Our great proficients in prayer must need think themselves to be of great importance on the scale of being, otherwise they would not indulge themselves in the notion, that the God of nature would subvert his laws, or bend his providence in conformity to their prayers."[20] And yet, implicit in Allen's scheme, was a way in which God could be on the side of the Americans, for if their claims and desires were one with the natural order of things, as Allen and the other patriots claimed that they were, Providence *of necessity* would operate in their favor. Right would make might, and it is in this sense that the deists of the Revolution felt perfectly comfortable with the language of divine Providence. There was an ambiguity about the expression which made it possible for the patriots to affirm an interposition which was purely natural, or specific and historical, as they chose. Sometimes, it seemed, the same patriots were affirming both kinds of Providence at once.

We have seen that throughout the eighteenth century, Americans had felt no conflict in identifying God with the Law of Nature. John Wise had announced in his *Vindication of the Government of the New England Churches* that he intended to go about "plainly discovering the Law of Nature." Now, in the time of Revolution, Wise and the heritage he represented took on new and pointed meaning in the context of the growing struggle with England. "God has Established the Law of Nature, as the General Rule of Government," Wise told his readers, and man was born with "an Original Liberty Instampt upon his Rational Nature."[21] Sir Edward Coke, whose commentary on Littleton's *Tenures* was the "universal lawbook of students" in the revolutionary period, had from the legal point of view corroborated Wise's argument, for Coke taught the doctrine of a fundamental law which bound king and Parliament alike.[22] In 1761, the Law of Nature supplied the backdrop for James Otis's famous argument in the Writs of Assistance Case, in which he enunciated the notion of judicial review that became fundamental in the American system of government. Three years later in his *Rights of the British Colonies*, Otis continued his probing of the nature of government with the grand tool of the natural law. His friend Samuel Adams shared the mode of discourse and pointed to the Law of Nature, the rights which stemmed from it, and the "institutes of the great Lawgiver and head of the Christian Church."[23]

Nor were the preachers of the period, as they aided the politicians, indifferent to the beauties of the natural law. When Charles Chauncy delivered his thanksgiving sermon on the repeal of the Stamp Act, he began by discoursing on how humans had been "formed by the God of nature," a situation which had decisive implications for the piece of history he was that day considering.[24] Later in 1770, Samuel Cooke, in attempting to establish criteria for rulers, found that the "solemn charge given to rulers" was not "an arbitrary injunction imposed by God, but . . . founded in the most obvious laws of nature and reason." Seen in this light, the faithful ruler must hold fast to the truth that he ruled over men who were "of the same species with himself, and by nature equal."[25] By 1776, Samuel West quoted John Locke to the effect that men were naturally in a "state of perfect freedom" if "within the bounds of the law of nature," and followed with observations on what the natural law included and what the state of nature involved.[26] Phillips Payson preached during the war that "Nature has given us the claim, and the God of nature appears to be helping us to assert and maintain it."[27]

The Continental Congress had of course taken a leadership role in the trend by establishing its case on the "broad bottom" of natural law. In its Declaration and Resolves of October 14, 1774, Congress asserted that "the inhabitants of the English Colonies in North America, by the immutable laws of nature, the principles of the English Constitution, and the several charters or compacts, have . . . rights."[28] Moreover, the language of political and ecclesiastical leaders had slipped easily into the consciousness of all. The popularity of the message was clear from a ballad of 1776.

> Great nature's law inspires,
> All free-born souls unite,
> While common interest fires
> Us to defend our rights.[29]

One wonders if the mystical relationship which Americans perceived between their land and their liberty did not have something to do with the God who lived in the Law of Nature. The covenant with nature which Thomas Jefferson affirmed throughout his writings seemed to be the other side of his reflections on natural law, for Jefferson was one of a multitude who were united in the consciousness that "the *principle* of free government adheres to the American soil. It is bedded in it: immovable as its mountains."[30] Because the land and the human beings who lived on it were both part of inscrutable nature, the land was a kind of guarantor for natural law as it applied to the human condition: it literally grounded the equality which was the natural state of men, the reason which was natural law expressed in intelligence, and the unalienable rights which were laws that primed men for action. With its power of agriculture to nourish human life, the land was a sacred place outside of historical time and its changes; and it gave its produce in recurring cycles like the rhythm of the planetary spheres. The newness of living in a first time seemed to possess its spatial equivalent in the newness of a first place, the America which was both wilderness and garden. The nineteenth century would make much of these growing perceptions.

During the era of Revolution, however, Nature's God appeared in historicized form as the Great Governor of the world. American identification with the land did not prevent an enthusiastic espousal of the Governor's cause, a cause which in fact had been nascent even before the revolutionary period.[31] In 1766, Jonathan Mayhew's exuberance over the repeal of the Stamp Act provided a model of the way in which patriots acknowledged the Governor. "Blessed revolution! glorious change!" he had exclaimed. "How great are our obligations for it to the supreme Governor of the world?"[32] Here Mayhew had unconsciously discovered the key to the Governor's utility: one did not know if the change which the Governor had induced had come from the nature of things (governing least) or through direct interference in the course of events, since, for those who desired, the Great Governor could obligingly wear the trappings of Jehovah. Mayhew's compatriot, Charles Chauncy, had come to a similar intuition. Again the Governor was sufficiently ambiguous in his providential activity to please patriots of several leanings: "Though our civil joy has been expressed in a decent, orderly way, it would be a poor, pitiful thing should we rest here, and not make our religious, grateful acknowledgements to the Supreme Ruler of the world, to whose superintending providence it is principally to be ascribed that we have had 'given us so great deliverance.' "[33]

Later, others followed suit. The Continental Congress ordained a fast day in 1775 by calling paradoxically for prayer to a Great Governor who had manifested himself very much as a *deus otiosus.*

As the great Governor of the world, by his supreme and universal providence, not only conducts the course of nature with unerring wisdom and rectitude, but frequently influences the minds of men to serve the wise and gracious purposes of his providential government; and it being, at all times, our indispensable duty devoutly to acknowledge his superintending providence, especially in times of impending danger and public calamity, to reverence and adore his immutable justice, as well as to implore his merciful interposition for our deliverance . . .[34]

By contrast, the Pennsylvania Constitution of 1776 seemed to link the Governor more clearly with Jehovah when it required of members of the House of Representatives the affirmation: "I do believe in one God, the Creator and Governour of the universe, the rewarder of the good and the punisher of the wicked, and I do acknowledge the Scriptures of the Old and New Testament to be given by Divine Inspiration."[35] It was significant for the deistic progress of the Governor that religious tests for office were eliminated quickly in Pennsylvania and most other early state constitutions.

The Governor continued to wear his coat of many colors throughout the revolutionary era. No one appeared to be upset by the lack of definition in his scheme. Thus, John Adams could write to Abigail in 1776 that "the arbiter of events, the sovereign of the world, only knows which way the torrent will be turned," while, at the conclusion of the French alliance in 1778, George Washington issued general orders for a day of prayer, "It having pleased the Almighty ruler of the Universe propitiously to defend the Cause of the United American-States and finally by raising us up a powerful Friend among the Princes of the Earth to establish our liberty and Independence."[36] One newspaper correspondent during the war exhorted his fellow-countrymen to free the slaves since they would "one day give an account to the Supreme Governor of the world." Earlier in 1775, another looked up "to the Supreme Disposer of all human events for his timely interposition."[37] Congress itself ratified the Articles of Confederation after a formal acknowledgment to the Great Governor of the world, while the historian William Gordon found that "the Governor of the Universe" had so "ordered events that peace is at length fully restored."[38] Meanwhile, Ethan Allen saw clearly in his own mind that "the governor of the universe . . . rules not by our proscriptions but by eternal and infinite reason. To pray to God, or to make supplication to him, requesting certain favors for ourselves, or for any, or all of the species, is inconsistent with the relation which subsists between God and man."[39] George Bancroft had indeed read the patriots closely when he concluded in the mid-nineteenth century: "Believing in the justice of 'the Great Governor of the world,' and conscious of their own honest zeal in the cause of freedom and mankind, they looked with astonishment at their present success and at the future with unclouded hope."[40]

In this context, the Grand Architect seemed a friendly variation on the Governor or perhaps the Governor himself appearing in yet another garb. The Architect was a Creator God who had been historicized. Daniel Boorstin understood him well as he wrote of the Jeffersonians:

Throughout Jeffersonian thought recurs this vision of God as the Supreme Maker. He was a Being of boundless energy and ingenuity who in six days had transformed the universal wilderness into an orderly, replete and self-governing cosmos. The Jeffersonian God was not the Omnipotent Sovereign of the Puritans nor the Omnipresent Essence of the Transcendentalists, but was essentially Architect and Builder.[41]

God had been cast in the Jeffersonians' own image, and the Masonic brotherhood, which many of Thomas Jefferson's friends shared, no doubt formed a background for their collective understanding. Ethan Allen, who also counted himself a member of the Masonic order, found a ready place for the Grand Architect in *Reason the Only Oracle*.

God, the great architect of nature, has so constructed its machinery, that it never needs to be altered or rectified. . . . The machine of the universe admits of no rectification, but continues its never ceasing operations, under the unerring guidance of the providence of God. Human architects make and unmake things. . . . But that mind, which is infinitely perfect, gains nothing by experience, but surveys the immense universality of things, with all their possible relations, fitnesses and unfitnesses, of both a natural or moral kind, with one comprehensive view.[42]

Whether in natural or historicized form, as Creator or Architect, Nature's God and Law, or Governor, the God of the Revolution was above all concerned with human rights and values. As the ground of being and activity, he encouraged others to imitate his productivity and providence in the work of self-creation. The collective identity of the Christian community was dissolving in a new atomism of nature which the canopy of united nationhood would not obliterate. Each individual understood that he was alone in the crowd of patriots as, in the condition of equality, he used natural reason and unalienable rights in pursuit of those goals which could be summarized as the good life: life itself and liberty, property and happiness. Even so thoroughly Christian a believer as Isaac Backus discovered in his quest for Baptist religious freedom that the virtues of right and reason were manifold: "All men are born equally free and independent, and have certain natural, inherent and unalienable rights, among which are the enjoying and defending life and liberty, acquiring, possessing, and protecting property, and pursuing and obtaining happiness and safety."[43]

Both Christian rationalists and Christian pietists, in fact, could agree. The New England language of natural law, to which we have already pointed, had taught as much, but so had the sectarian concern for the salvation of the individual. As Sidney Mead has shown, both "fostered the idea of individual human autonomy" since "all the lines of thinking of the eighteenth century converged on the idea of free, uncoerced, individual consent as the

only proper basis for all man's organizations, civil and ecclesiastical."[44]

Yet the anomaly of latter-day Calvinists and other sober Christians running to embrace the divinity of right and reason was not
lost on some of the colonists. Six years before the Declaration of
Independence, John Trumbull was satirizing the evidence of
"self-evidence" in the "New System of Logic." The scheme, he
caustically remarked, was erected on two grand principles: "First,
That the common sense and reason of mankind is so weak and
fallacious a guide, that its dictates ought never to be regarded;
Secondly, That nevertheless nothing is so great that it can surpass,
or so perplexing that it can entangle, the understanding of a true
metaphysician." He added that he took these points to "be so
nearly self-evident, that although I can say very little in proof of
them, the reader ought for this very reason the more firmly to
believe them."[45] The language of right and reason was enticing
the patriots to the affirmation of a new two-in-one, for it was
suggesting to sinners that their persons contained a divinity which
corresponded to the divinity in the nature of things. Why should
Jehovah need to intervene with a particular revelation when the
patriots did not need special information or gifts to observe what
was plainly visible in their heads and all around them? How could
patriots who had the power to see and to do for every eventuality,
because of the vigor of the natural creation which they embodied,
be considered in any sense alienated from their God?

Different from either rationalist or pietist Christianity, the new
religion of the Revolution was espousing natural rights and liberties on its own humanocentric terms. God, the source of nature,
did not interfere during the unravelling of the plan, since it contained in its beginnings the power and secret of its destiny. Jonathan Mayhew spoke prophetically in 1750 when he preached in
another context: "For a nation thus abused to arise unanimously
and to resist their prince, even to the dethroning him, is not criminal, but a reasonable way of vindicating their liberties and just

rights; *it is making use of the means, and the only means, which God has put into their power* for mutual and self-defense."[46] More than that, the self-creation which was mediated by natural rights and indwelling reason fostered the mythic consciousness of the patriots. In their allegiance to the "rights of man" instead of the "rights of Englishmen," Americans had pronounced themselves in alienation from the organic past, a veritable "rebuke to time." Fred Somkin has observed that "the notion of unprecedentedness, of utterly new beginnings, remained for a long time a primitive assumption of the American mind."[47] The presumption of newness, which constituted the innocence of Americans, constituted also the core of their myth.

By the 1760s, proclaiming the good news of natural rights had become the province of a new class of preachers. The politicians were zealous in their task, their words suggesting that at some level they knew their work was religious. Thus, James Otis numbered among the natural rights of patriots the proviso that *"the supreme and subordinate powers of legislation should be free and sacred in the hands where the community have once rightfully placed them."*[48] The Circular Letter of the Province of Massachusetts solemnly asserted that it was "an essential, unalterable right in nature, engrafted into the British constitution as a fundamental law, and ever held sacred and irrevocable by the subjects within the realm, that what a man hath honestly acquired, is absolutely his own, which he may freely give, but cannot be taken from him without his consent."[49] By 1775, Alexander Hamilton was writing with upper-case emphasis that "THE SACRED RIGHTS OF MANKIND ARE NOT TO BE RUMMAGED FOR AMONG OLD PARCHMENTS OR MUSTY RECORDS. THEY ARE WRITTEN, AS WITH A SUNBEAM, IN THE WHOLE VOLUME OF HUMAN NATURE, BY THE HAND OF DIVINITY ITSELF, AND CAN NEVER BE ERASED OR OBSCURED BY MORTAL POWER."[50] At the end of the war, the center of space and time lay in America, as Congress triumphantly announced to the states the universal and transcendent implications of American action: "Let it be remembered finally, that it has ever been the pride and boast of America, that the rights for which she contended, were the rights of human nature. . . . No instance has heretofore occurred, nor can any instance be expected hereafter to occur, in which the unadulterated forms of republican government can pretend to so fair an opportunity of justifying themselves by their fruits."[51]

Throughout the revolutionary era, the God of Revelation had had an institutional home in the Christian church, from which he operated in a general way on the popular perceptions of society. Similarly, the God who grounded natural rights and governed through natural law found institutional affiliation in Freemasonry, but in his case he directly affected the operations of the few who were patriot leaders. Yet it is important to trace the interactions of these Americans with the Grand Architect and with one another in the Masonic lodges since, in the circularity of mythic construction, the leaders not only articulated the concerns of the masses but shaped and informed them as well. A digression in favor of Freemasonry will lead us to a fuller comprehension of the popular civil religion if we pursue the inner as well as the outer history of the brotherhood, paying close attention to the religious structures of consciousness which it embodied and their complementary role in relation to the general myth of civil religion.

The outer history of the brotherhood formally began in the colonies in 1731 when St. John's Lodge in Philadelphia was recognized by the Grand Lodge in London. In the years which ensued, lodges appeared in Massachusetts, Georgia, New Hampshire, New York, Virginia, Rhode Island, Maryland, Connecticut, and North Carolina so that, as one student of the phenomenon has maintained, by 1760 "there was no town, big or small, where Masonry had not spun its web."[52] There were in fact over forty lodges before 1776. From the beginning, the Masons spread from place to place a spirit and an organization which could work for unity. Daniel Coxe, first Grand Master for the Central Colonies, had also been the first public personage to advise that the colonies form a federation, while it was Brother Benjamin Franklin who in

1754 drafted the Albany Plan of Union. As Masonic brothers traveled throughout the colonies, it was customary for them to visit the lodge in each area, so that a kind of aristocracy of community leadership developed. Thus, for example, when George Washington traveled from Virginia to Boston, he visited lodges in Philadelphia, New York, and Boston as well as the other places where he stopped. Bernard Faÿ has gone so far as to suggest that Masonry laid a foundation for national unity in America,

because, through the very nature of its organization, it could spread throughout all the colonies and work steadily and silently. It created in a limited but very prominent class of people a feeling of American unity without which the American liberty could not have developed—without which there would have been no United States.[53]

The Sons of Liberty and the committees of correspondence, Faÿ believed, were "puppet" societies for Freemasonry. Indeed, the majority of the Continental Congress and fifty-two of the fifty-six signers of the Declaration of Independence were Masonic.[54] Benjamin Franklin acted as an intermediary between the Grand Lodge of Pennsylvania and the American Philosophical Society which, although not officially Masonic, became a kind of extension society for the brotherhood. Meanwhile, Franklin, by owning and directing a series of newspapers and lending money to fellow Masons to start papers in Charleston and New York, spread Masonic understandings through the press.

While politics was kept as much as possible out of the meetings of the Ancient Lodges, it flourished in the ubiquitous ceremonial toasts which accompanied the informal social gatherings brothers attended. A lodge met most commonly in the backroom of a tavern, where it was an easy transition to the mood of conviviality and shared perceptions which the public room of the tavern invited. Here, Masons mingled with working folk, and in port cities, with sailors, so that a free exchange of opinion could flow. Since each tavern kept at hand current newspapers and almanacs, the exchange could include printed sources. Newspapers, taverns, and lodges in fact formed a tinder blend which worked in unison as the revolutionary movement in America began. One needed only to add preachers and merchants for the mixture to catch fire.

Although a few lodges did remain Loyalist in the Revolution and others kept to neutrality, the overwhelming majority sided with the patriot cause. Even in New York, the stronghold of loyalism, all of the lodges except one stood with the Congress in the struggle, but in revolutionary Boston, the Grand Lodge of St. Andrew of the Scottish rite seemed, in the early years of friction with Britain, to be a miniature Congress. Headed by Joseph Warren, prominent Boston surgeon and patriot, the Lodge met at the Green Dragon, a local tavern where the North End Caucus, the radical political club of the area, also held official meetings. Warren obligingly officiated in this organization as well. The Indians of the Boston Tea Party, it was said, had exited from the Green Dragon and reentered it later during the memorable evening of their liturgy.

> Then rally boys and hasten on
> To meet our chiefs at the Green Dragon
> Our Warrior's there and bold Revere
> With hands to do and words to cheer
> For Liberty and Laws.[55]

In the American army, Masonic lodges counted about fifteen thousand men as members, and the American Union Lodge No. One became the prestigious center of the brotherhood. When on the Feast of John the Evangelist in 1778, a Masonic procession solemnized the retaking of Philadelphia by the patriots, George Washington marched in full Masonic dress, sword at his side, with three hundred others to Christ Church. Here they celebrated Divine Service according to the rite of the order. The event was hailed as the "greatest Masonic parade that has ever been seen in the New World," as the *Pennsylvania Packet* provided editorial coverage with relish, detailing the order of the procession in seventeen separate categories.[56]

It was only with the nineteenth century and its evangelical backlash that Freemasonry became less respectable and less popular, but in the context of the Revolution it functioned smoothly alongside of traditional Christianity. The brotherhood officially neither endorsed nor condemned the religious structure of Christianity but at the same time subtly operated as a vehicle for the promulgation of a new religious structure, the religion of the Revolution. On the conceptual plane, Masonry accepted Christianity as a historical fact although it did not deem it "divine revelation." But it also saw the "decay" of Christianity as another important fact. In its universalist ethic of tolerance toward all, Freemasonry was suggesting that Christianity was acceptable as part of a larger whole and that the whole was the Masonic brotherhood.

One gets an inkling of the delicate balance the Masons had encouraged between religious forces in its two annual sacred celebrations on June 24 and December 27. From the Christian context, these recalled the great medieval festivals of the Johns—John the Baptist, who had been the last prophet of Judaism, and John the Evangelist, the beloved disciple of Jesus and the new dispensation. From the point of view of the God of Nature, on the other hand, they were the sacred times of summer and winter solstice, when the sun had climbed to its zenith and descended to its nadir. They represented the great annual cycle of nature as well as the individual cycle of a human lifetime.

On this level of myth and ritual, although it had been historicized to include a Christian interpretation, the edifice of Masonry had been erected predominately on a natural and anthropocentric foundation. It was true that the myth of the order dwelt on its links with the building of the Temple of Solomon in ancient Israel as well as the medieval guild system in which practical masons were considered the predecessors of the speculative Masons of the eighteenth century. It was also true that the Bible, along with the Square and Compass, was honored after 1760 in England as a Great Light of the Lodge and that a number of the ritual motifs were susceptible to a Judaeo-Christian interpretation. Yet the great symbolic themes of the Ancient Craft were elements of natural religion. In his quest for light and labor in the building of character, the Masonic initiate enacted his own spiritual pilgrimage in terms which did not require the Christian revelation to support them. Masonry seemed in fact to be a species of sun religion, and Thomas Paine at least was clear in his understanding of its origins:

To come then at once to the point, *Masonry* . . . is derived and is the remains of the religion of the ancient Druids; who, like the magi of Persia and the priests of Heliopolis in Egypt, were priests of the sun. They paid worship to this great luminary, as the great visible agent of a great invisible first cause, whom they styled "Time without limits."

Paine noted for his readers that the sun was "the great emblematical ornament of Masonic lodges and Masonic dresses," "the central figure in their aprons," and the "pendant on their breasts in their lodges and in their processions."[57] The ritual dramatization of this impulse came in the festivals of summer and winter solstice and in the orientation of Masonic initiates toward the east as the sacred and preferred direction in the conferring of the degrees of the order. Conveniently, the east was the direction of the Holy Land, but most prominently in Masonic ritual it was the place of the rising sun.

With the Square and Compass, the pragmatic and anthropocentric concern of Masonry came into its own. Each Mason engaged in the task of utilizing the working tools of the speculative science to complete the Perfect Ashlar, the true square stone which represented the work of self-creation. Just as the atomism of the natural rights doctrine had put the premium on individual existence, just as Arminianism and the new life of the sectarian convert had in their own way achieved the same end, the Square and Compass directed the Masonic initiate in his personal quest for a new form of perfection. The Square as symbol of earth needed to be used in tandem with the Compass which represented the arc or circle of the sky. Together the two suggested the duality of human nature, body and spirit at once, achieving spiritual goals with physical means. As the practical mason whose square measured a stone in order to fit it into the structure of a building, the Masonic brother was to use the Square in the achievement of morality and virtue. He must live "on the Square" and "be square" in his dealings with his fellows. But it required the circle of divine life to support the Square. Here the Compass entered its own since it was within its arc that the Square was drawn. Moreover, because it drew the boundaries with its sweeping lines, the Compass enabled the Masonic initiate to set limits for his own life, to know what he could and could not undertake and achieve, and to learn the precision task of self-mastery. The brother placed the point of the Compass at the center of himself and began to draw concentric circles, enlarging the bounds as he succeeded in each facet of the work of building the spiritual edifice.

There were lesser lights and lesser working tools which commanded respect among the brothers, the Level and the Plumb-line among them. The Level measured equality, symbolizing the fellowship of the lodge where all economic and social distinctions disappeared in the *communitas* of initiation. The Plumb-line suggested at once precision and judgment. Level and Plumb-line together told the initiate whether or not he had created a Square, for this would be true if the Level were straight and the Plumb-line hanging evenly. Meanwhile, the Common Gavel, symbolic of a hammer or ax, was used by each brother to refine the imperfections of the Rough Ashlar of his own character as he worked toward the goal of becoming a Perfect Ashlar.[58] Mysticism and practicality thus mingled freely in Masonic myth and ritual: the work which the Masons were undertaking was not unlike the "work" of the medieval alchemists in seeking the true gold of the spirit, the Philosopher's Stone, which as both Mircea Eliade and Carl Jung have pointed out, was the Self of self.[59] Yet, different from the alchemy of the spirit, the Masonry of self-creation was understood in the moralistic terms which befitted a nation with a strong Protestant and Calvinist heritage. The practical commands of ethical endeavor seemed to put the mystical life at the disposal of every patriot in the street. Beyond that, reason blended with the pursuit of virtue, for Masonry was an exact science as well as an art. One realized reason in action, it was true, but the practicality of reason did not destroy its precision as the great measuring device by which the cosmos and individual human life were judged. Bernard Fay remarked aptly:

The Catholic Church worshiped openly a mysterious God. Free-masonry honored mysteriously a logical principle. The Great Architect was simply an idea, a tool of the human mind which needed it for its scientific work and for social peace. The Masonic god had no mystery, while the Masonic society was all a mystery.[60]

Reason *was* the Grand Architect, and the Almighty operated through his works so that it was in the adventure of perfecting his own Self that each Mason met God. But unlike the mystical tradition which had developed in Christianity, the Mason did not "let go" to allow God to work in him. His was a far more active effort which might be described as a "will power" variety of endeavor. Now consciousness and moral determination effected what mystical prayer and self-effacing penance had only prepared the way for in the monastic life. In short, the myth and ritual of Freemasonry had turned mysticism inside out so that it became the "work" not of other worldly contemplatives but the task of Americans who were, already in the eighteenth century, offering a square deal to the world.

Beyond this, the religious structure of Masonry complemented the God of Revolution because it fostered the values of maleness and patriarchy which were preeminently those of the Governor and Architect. Each Masonic lodge was in the ritual sense a men's club, in some respects not unlike the men's clubs of primitive societies. The same secrecy prevailed and heightened the bond of brotherhood which the initiation ceremony formed. The initiation itself, divided into its three degrees, in symbolic form presented terrors or obstacles which the initiate had to face, dramatic events which "made a man" of him. Even the morality of being "on the square" was, culturally speaking, appropriate to males more than females. Thus Freemasonry provided a support and buttress for the sons of the fathers as they encountered the obstacles which the field of battle and the stage of politics presented for them to surmount. The patriots were living out their hero myth in the initiatory experience of the Revolution. Those sons who also counted themselves Freemasons were pursuing harmonious projects in the lodge and in the world.

"Virtue and vice are the only things in this world, which, with our souls, are capable of surviving death," Ethan Allen had observed. His brother Mason, George Washington, had asked rhetorically in his Farewell Address, "Can it be, that Providence has not coñected the permanent felicity of a Nation with its virtue?"[61] The perceptions of the brothers flowed into the general cultural stream which carried the religion of the Revolution and became indistinguishable from the perceptions of other patriots. The lovers of liberty had all celebrated their awareness and oriented themselves in their world through ritual action. They had all freely blended morality with pragmatism and seen value more than truth or beauty as their absolute. An American structure of consciousness had emerged in which, with Claude Lévi-Strauss, what was "good to think" was preeminently good for exchange.[62] Useful goods and services were items which, on the material level, facilitated the process of exchange in society and were therefore valuable. Useful goods and services on a more intangible level were those moral qualities and activities which smoothed the gears of the machinery of society and oiled the rough edges of individual existence. Morality thus was also valuable. Americans unconsciously made the connection in terms of value so that a kind of trinity developed in which moralism, pragmatism, and the economy of exchange were three aspects of an absolute which Americans discovered, not in metaphysical speculation, but in the midst of their everyday encounters in the world.

Significantly, the full title of that "Masonic extension," the American Philosophical Society, included the qualifying phrase "for Promoting Useful Knowledge." The first volume of its *Transactions* clarified any confusion as to what useful knowledge might consist in. The *Transactions* were, in the words of Daniel Boorstin,

laden with articles on how to preserve wine, cure figs and distil persimmons; suggestions on the culture of the silkworm and the uses of sunflower seed; prescriptions against the fly weevil that destroyed wheat and the worm that attacked the pea; hints on curing sore throat; instructions on shipping seeds; and plans for a horizontal windmill. Except for those on astronomical subjects, virtually all the Society's papers were justified by a practical utility—and even astronomy was only an apparent exception, for it was studied mainly for its relevance to climate and navigation.[63]

The Reason of Nature's God, the Architect and Governor, had revealed that its true nature was practical. Useful knowledge meant "natural facts," and for Jeffersonian philosophers and other Americans, these facts were normative as well as descriptive. The "is" of affairs became a kind of "ought" with moral commands implicit in material states and events.

What finally characterized their thought was less its specific theological or metaphysical doctrines than its attitude toward all theology and metaphysics. Philosophy was to be a by-product of right and fruitful activity: the fulfillment of man was not in theoretical formulation nor in abstract comprehension of the universe, but in the life he led and the society he built. The genius of Jeffersonian philosophy was intuitive and practical; reflection, speculation and contemplation were given second place.[64]

It was as if American philosophers had taken from the maternal bosom of the earth its inclination to continual productivity and its prerational mode of awareness and linked these to the meanings and values which were protected by a paternal sky: they kept the universalism of the sky, which became in the political sphere, imperialism; they cherished the military might and public activity which were the means to empire; they continued to foster the making of history in the clear light of the sun which created the contrasts of brightness and shadow enabling the patriots to separate good from evil.

For everybody's people, the pursuit of agriculture, which was the focus for the central exchange of the economy, led in similar directions. Farming, the universal occupation of humankind in its long history, became particularized in America in a context in which it complemented a number of the meanings and values the Revolution focused. Perhaps the experience of land without limit and vast open spaces heightened the mystique of agrarian life in the New World. Here the land possessed a givenness which, as for the philosophers, compelled as well as asked. Indeed, it was not surprising that a "philosopher" like Thomas Jefferson was also a gentleman farmer. Agriculture oriented a man to the practical side of life, and, as Arthur Schlesinger has observed:

The farmer's pressing concern with the practical and utilitarian made him indifferent if not hostile to the life of the mind. Intellectual activity for its own sake, though allowable perhaps for idle townfolk, had no place in his scheme of things. The doer, not the thinker, achieved results in the world as he knew it; anything else was a form of malingering.[65]

The ritual exchange of ploughshares for swords, over which the patriots often lingered affectionately in the language of their myth, suggested the strength of the bond between the pragmatism of the farmer and the militarism of the soldier. Both lived in a world in which action was equated with value, and value was the description of ultimacy. Both were joined in their practicality by the politician who, with his fellows, controlled the public destiny of the new nation. Thomas Jefferson was only being a typical American when he ended a letter, which had been a long statement of his religious beliefs, with a thisworldly wish for an afterlife for John Adams and himself: "May we meet there again, in Congress, with our antient Colleagues, and receive with them the seal of approbation 'Well done, good and faithful servants.' "[66]

If value more than truth or beauty was the absolute, Americans would understand education—to initiate succeeding generations of new Americans into the religion of the Revolution—as education to utility. Already, in 1789, Benjamin Rush had written to John Adams to ask with dudgeon: "Who are guilty of the greatest absurdity—the Chinese who press the feet into deformity by small shoes, or the Europeans and Americans who press the brain into obliquity by Greek and Latin?"[67] Useful citizens obviously did not need dead languages. Rush's thinking was representative of the spirit in which Benjamin Franklin founded the University of Pennsylvania, and Thomas Jefferson the University of Virginia. Later throughout the nineteenth century, useful knowledge would continue to function as the highest good in the public school system. Ruth Miller Elson's study of nineteenth-century schoolbooks has indicated just how thoroughly the notion was inculcated for the benefit of America's youth.[68]

By the era of Revolution, the God of Nature had left the public arena free for the activity of a myriad Americans who were enjoying the delights of immersion in the business of war and government. Both leaders and followers acknowledged the God of Nature, while many of the leaders and most of the followers cheerfully venerated Jehovah as well. Without recourse to the convenient ambiguity of the Great Governor, which we have already noticed, a good number of the patriots not only moved comfortably between the God of Nature and Jehovah but sometimes conflated the two in a manner which suggested that they did not perceive a difference. The makers of a new tradition had done their work well: Nature's God, the natural rights he guaranteed, the Law of Nature, and even the Grand Architect had become familiar mythologems in the world of everyday. Logical consistency proved a poor second to the power of words. In their myth, as they recited it, the patriots had created again a ritual exchange, this time in the two-in-one of language. One Boston correspondent, writing abroad to England, explained that Americans claimed their rights "not only under a charter from a temporary king, but from one under the broad seal of heaven—from the king of kings, and Lord of all the earth. They say these rights

were created in them by the decree of providence; that they were
born with them—exist with them—are founded upon the immutable and eternal maxims of right, reason, and the never failing
principles of strict justice." He hastened to add that they would,
if they must, "take the sword, and appeal to the God of battles—
the great general of the universe."[69] Joseph Barrell, a prominent
merchant, wrote to a friend in 1775 and told him emphatically
that the Yankees would "prove that they have a true sense of that
freedom wch the God of nature gave & by whose Assistance they
will Defend it."[70] About a year later in Charleston, Judge William
Henry Drayton delivered a charge to his court which seemed a
masterpiece of mythic combination.

The fortitude with which America has endured these civil and military outrages; the union of her people, as astonishing as unprecedented,
when we consider their various manners and religious tenets; their
distance from each other; their various and clashing local interests,
their self denial; and their *miraculous* success in the prosecution of
war: I say, these things demonstrate that the Lord of Hosts is on our
side! So it is apparent, that the Almighty Constructor of the universe,
having formed this continent of materials to compose a state preemi-
nent in the world, is now making use of the tyranny of the British
rulers, as an instrument to fashion and arrange those materials for the
end for which, in his wisdom he had formed them. . . . In short I
think it my duty to declare in the awful seat of justice and before
Almighty God, that in my opinion, the Americans can have no safety
but by the Divine favor, their own virtue, and their being so prudent
as NOT TO LEAVE IT IN THE POWER OF THE BRITISH RULERS TO INJURE
THEM.[71]

Official documents shared the ambivalence, as a double consciousness about God pervaded them. The Declaration of Independence, as an example, proclaimed in 1776 the necessity for
Americans "to assume among the powers of earth, the separate
and equal station to which the Laws of Nature and of Nature's
God entitle them," and underlined as a "self-evident truth" that
all were "endowed by their Creator with certain unalienable
Rights." At the same time, the signers of the document appealed

to "the Supreme Judge of the World" to uphold the rightness of their intentions and found support in a "firm reliance on the protection of divine Providence."[72] The following year it was evident that the Congress still believed that God helped those who helped themselves. A draft of a circular letter to accompany the Articles of Confederation read:

It [the Articles of Confederation] seems essential to our very existence as a free people, and without it we may soon be constrained to bid adieu to independence, to liberty and safety; blessings which, from the justice of our cause and the favour of our Almighty Creator visibly manifested in our protection, we have reason to expect, if in an humble dependence on his divine providence we strenuously exert the means which are placed in our power.[73]

As we have seen, the mingling perceptions of God as an actor in human history and God as the inactive ground of being were not surprising in the context of the heritage of the patriots. The jealous and interfering Jehovah, however, had always presented the possibility of being understood differently. Not only had he been a rain-and-thunder God who drove his forces to the earth and there, with the knowledge he had obtained in the sky, meddled in the affairs of humans, but he had also been an omnipotent creator. His power had formed earth and sky in six days out of nothingness. For this reason, as for any other Creator God, his power could be viewed as too awesome for active intervention in the world process. Like a mighty overseer who had originally created with some overplus of cosmic energy, Jehovah could retire from business in the world and studiously avoid any motion other than the regular cycles of nature. In other words, while he had been traditionally perceived as an all-knowing *deus pluviosus*, the possibility had existed because of Jehovah's role as creator to understand him as *deus otiosus*. No one could condemn a "lazy Creator" when his lack of involvement provided just the foundation which the republic needed. Now to meet their urgent needs the patriots had discovered that Jehovah had two faces or, if you will, that he mediated a two-sided religious structure.[74]

From his own orbit, the God of Nature had also shown that he could acquire some of the characteristics of a history-making God, for he had flourished under acknowledgments as Governor and Architect. The religion of the Revolution had become a huge generator for symbolic transformation: Jehovah, God of Battles, had come to express the reality of human activity, while the God of Nature, who rarely governed, had learned how to defend the rights of Americans. Jehovah and the God of Nature both kept their names. Yet, unobtrusively and unconsciously, both began to display a substantive content which suggested that they had interfused their identity. They had in fact become such soulmates that their two-in-oneness was hopelessly crossed and crisscrossed in a manner which suggested the extent of the ambiguity Americans experienced. Christian rationalists and Christian pietists had seen their active God grow less and less involved as human reason and the human experience of enthusiasm combined to produce a new humanocentrism. Deists, meanwhile, had seen their otiose creator blend with the Christian trappings of their culture so that, like a magnet attracting metal, he began to absorb more and more activity. His reasonableness was united with patriotic enthusiasm to become a providence which did care and concern itself in the world. Yet over all, the inactivity of God became more striking as the Revolution progressed. The nation-state had become a hierophany and George Washington, founder and father, its clearest Sign. Both Jehovah and the Governor had learned that the greatest and wisest government was achieved, as we shall see, by letting George do it.

Chapter 5

Our Father,
Our Washington

As the call to arms sounded, many sons of many fathers had come together, pledging "their lives, their fortunes, and their sacred honor" in their revolutionary endeavors. Patriots that they were, they liked to think of themselves as one, while, in the face of the British threat, they needed to think of themselves as one. Paradoxically, the sons discovered that they really *were* one as they created their mutual present, but that the oneness did not prevent them from being many. The Revolution was fought in an atmosphere which included disagreement, dissension, keen bitterness and rancor, and, in short, all the manifestations of the party spirit which George Washington would later so strongly condemn. Confronted with the juxtaposition of their oneness and their manyness, the patriots more and more perceived the need for unity in their common task. Their perception generated a largely unconscious demand for a collective symbol to express and—in the process of expressing—to create and re-create their union. Because theirs was a humanocentric religion of militant history-makers who yet loved their fathers' land beyond the time and space of history, it was fitting that their collective symbol should bind the elements of their myth in a human center. It was fitting that their collective symbol should be a man—a farmer, a soldier, and, at least metaphorically, a father.

Fortunately for their situation, Americans found in George Washington an individual who met their requirements as completely as any human being could. In him, the mysterious chemistry of body and spirit provided the raw material out of which a collective representation of American personhood could be formed. Washington became a kind of superbeing who summarized the ideals of character and consciousness which patriots together understood as best, in the old Greek sense of *arete*. In retrospect, they knew that in Washington they had discovered the highest, the strongest, the most excellent way; they were heartened in their pursuit of the goal because they could contemplate it in the person of one of their own. Despite minority opposition to him as commander-in-chief and as president, almost overnight, Washington became a living "tribal" totem for an emerging nation-state. He was "good for thinking," for he helped the patriots define the good by embodying it in visible form. In this sense his person resolved the classificatory difficulties which had to be confronted before Americans could be sure of how to relate to one another and to the world. He was also "good for feeling," because in a diverse society he provided a fixed point with which people could identify, and he generated in the collective psyche a *participation mystique* which brought zest and exuberance to living.[1]

The activities of George Washington, holy man, which delighted and inspired the patriots, shed light on the values and functioning of American society. His image became a mirror that reflected the picture of the folk he represented; for, as Peter Brown has observed, "in studying both the most admired and the most detested figures in any society, we can see, as seldom through other evidence, the nature of the average man's expectations and hopes for himself. It is for the historian, therefore, to analyze this image as a product of the society around the holy man."[2] We have seen to some extent in the British and in Benedict Arnold, the traitor, the image of the very worst. In George Washington, the patriots brought into view the image of the most admired. Passing through a time of crisis in which their very existence as they knew it had been called into question, they sought a leader who would empower them in his doing and being. Collective exorcist against the demonic forces of British tyranny, "charismatic ombudsman" in the face of the centripetal tendencies of disparate personalities and states—Washington mediated between the extremes, becoming the focus for ritual exchanges for an entire community which needed its identity reaffirmed.

With the aloof and reserved demeanor which so many of his countrymen remarked in him, Washington, by remaining a sort of archetypal stranger, was able to absorb the waves of collective meaning which swept over him. He became indeed a "blessed object" even as he led, a sacramental center which at once pointed to the spiritual power of the fledgling nation and embodied it. In an uncertain time of new freedoms, he allayed anxiety by reassuring the patriots that the American manhood he stood for could be counted on. And as the language of the mythos became literary, during his very lifetime, the printed record revealed that the story of George Washington, father and founder of his country, fitted a paradigm which had much in common with the composite portrait of the great religious leaders of other cultures who, like him, had been divine men.

If Washington was a founder who expressed and reconciled the meaning of all the Founding Fathers, the establishment he left was not a "founded religion" in the sense in which Jesus was thought to have initiated Christianity or the Buddha, Buddhism. True Freemason that he was, Washington had "founded" through the symbolic activity of casting in the first spade by assuming command of the Continental Army and by presiding over the Constitutional Convention and later the new American government. His deeds had not been performed in response to a solitary confrontation with the sacred, but rather as first among equals, answering the call of patriots who required him to summarize the act of leadership which they had begun themselves. From the 1850s, according to one biographer, there had been foreshadowings of Washington's future role. Mason Weems, whose talents for feeling the national pulse were considerable, explained the Fort Necessity incident in these terms. Here, during the French and Indian War, the youthful Colonel Washington prefigured his later activity on behalf of the republic by commanding the men who built the wilderness fortification. "Soon as the lines of the entrenchments were marked off, and the men about to fall to work, Washington, seizing the hand of the first that was lifting his spade, cried out '*stop, my brave fellow! my hand must heave the first earth that is thrown up in defence of this country*.'[3]

Thus, George Washington, founder, was a curious anomaly in at least one respect: other times and other places had seen only founded religions with founders. Now though, a founder would be linked by popular acclaim to an act of mythic foundation and a sacred story of origins, historicized and self-conscious, yet, paradoxically, to a large extent unconscious of its religious import. Perhaps the need of Americans to designate one man founder at all reflects the historically oriented cast of their consciousness, of which we have already seen so much. As the central protagonist in the myth, Washington for his own and later generations was the great culture-hero and demi-god who, outside ordinary time and space, had brought the world into recognizable form. Yet, in the subtle democracy of myth, when Americans acknowledged that George Washington had founded their nation, in effect they were saying that they had founded themselves.

"Archetypal stranger" that he was, the historical Washington, like the historical Jesus, seemed almost an impossible person to characterize. Historians of every ilk have experienced the difficulty: in the late 1950s, Marcus Cunliffe concluded that it was "useless for his biographers to try to separate Washington from the myths and images surrounding him."[4] We do know that Washington happened to be the right man in the right place at the right time. His physical stature (over six feet) and stately bearing lent him an aura which could be translated, for the devout, into religious experience. His taciturnity complemented his physique in generating that sense of awe and regard which Americans felt in his presence. Military training and success in the French and Indian War gave him the necessary prerequisite for his role in the first act of the Revolution, while his involvement in Virginia politics provided sufficient background, the patriots thought, for his function in the constitutional phase which was to make the Revolution permanent. Washington's agrarian Virginia origins offered a desired balance to the dominance of Boston and Massachusetts, so that John Adams was politically astute when he suggested that Congress appoint Washington commander-in-chief. At the same time, Washington himself seemed to possess the political savvy to cultivate those qualities and demeanors which fostered the legend already growing around him. His protestations of modesty and renunciations of pay, his public attitude of putting his country ahead of himself, his slow and deliberate pace, his cultivation of Stoic dispassion and the Aristotelian mean—all combined to produce the popular image of a *theios aner*, or divine man.

The growth of the Washington legend during his own lifetime seemed the surest sign that Americans, caught between their oneness and their manyness, had made a fundamental decision in favor of unity. For the national myth continued to develop despite the fact that Washington the man was the focus for stringent criticism both in the war and in his presidency. As commander, he was sometimes hesitant and deferred to lesser officers to the detriment of the army; he became the object of disloyalty by subordinates; he fought poorly and became the butt of attempts to dislodge him. As president, he steered an unpopular neutral course between Britain and France during the war between them; he enforced an excise tax, similar to the Stamp Act, on the citizens of western Pennsylvania and threatened to suppress the resultant Whiskey Rebellion with military force; he supported John Jay's negotiations with Great Britain in the Jay Treaty, which angered southern planters and northern traders alike; he completely overlooked the implications of party in a cabinet in which Alexander Hamilton and Thomas Jefferson pitted themselves at each others' throats. During his second ad-

ministration, abuse was heaped on Washington as the press
hounded him and the public generally disregarded him, so that
he left office an unpopular man.

Yet the idolization of George Washington was stronger still.
Moreover, it did not go unnoticed by some of the other men of
the Revolution. As early as 1777, John Adams was remonstrating
on the floor of Congress against the "superstitious veneration that
is sometimes paid to General Washington."[5] Privately, he wrote
to his friend Benjamin Rush to tell him that "the idea that any
one Man alone can save us is too silly for any Body, but such
weak Men as [the Reverend Jacob] Duche, to harbour for a
Moment." "The History of our Revolution will be one continued
Lye from one end to the other," he complained again years later.
"The essence of the whole will be that *Dr. Franklins electrical
Rod, smote the Earth and out sprung General Washington*. That
Franklin electrified him with his rod—and thence forward these
two conducted all the Policy, Negotiations, Legislatures and
War."[6] Rush heartily concurred, not only to Adams but to others
as well. To William Marshall, he aired his grievance: "We have
not instituted divine honors to certain virtues in imitation of the
inhabitants of Paris, but we ascribe all the attributes of the Deity
to the name of General Washington. . . . God would cease to be
who HE is, if he did not visit us for these things."[7] It was an echo
of the anonymous letter which had circulated among the influential in the midst of the so-called Conway Cabal: "The people of
America have been guilty of idolatry in making a man their god,
and the God of heaven and earth will convince them, by woful
experience, that he is only a man. No good may be expected from
the standing army, until Baal and his worshippers are banished
from the camp."[8]

Still, while some were critical and others disgruntled, the collective acclaim would not cease. Growing while Washington
lived, it waxed in eloquence and enthusiasm at his death and, as
the nineteenth century progressed, became a deluge of overwhelming, if monotonous, testimony. Even during the Revolu-

tion, children were christened with his name, and locks of his hair were cherished. When Washington assumed charge of the army in 1775, one chaplain, who was an eyewitness, mused in his journal: "The expression 'born to command' is peculiarly applicable to him. Day before yesterday, when under the great elm in Cambridge he drew his sword and formally took command of the army of seventeen thousand men, his look and bearing impressed every one, and I could not but feel that he was reserved for some great destiny."[9] Abigail Adams, although she probably did not know it, agreed with the chaplain. She wrote to her husband extolling the general's "dignity with ease and complacency" and quoting John Dryden: "Mark his majestic fabric; he's a temple/ Sacred by birth, and built by hands divine; His soul's the deity that lodges there;/Nor is the pile unworthy of the god."[10] One American correspondent wrote back to England in early 1776, rhapsodizing, "If you do not know General Washington's person, perhaps you will be pleased to hear, that he has so much martial dignity in his deportment, that you would distinguish him to be a General and a Soldier, from among ten thousand people: there is not a King in Europe but would look like a valet de chambre by his side."[11] On Long Island, Lydia Post confided to her diary that she would "confess a womanly admiration of a noble exterior. Washington's influence and authority must be enhanced by his gallant bearing and commanding figure, as he sits his proud steed."[12]

Harvard and Yale awarded Washington honorary doctorates, and eulogies were addressed to him by actors on stage during the revolutionary years and thereafter. Meanwhile, it became fashionable to print his name in large or small capitals and to follow references with a few words of praise. For Washington's birthday in 1784, John Parke wrote the verse production, "Virginia: a Pastoral Drama," in which nymphs, shepherds, and assorted pastoral characters celebrated the joy of the homecoming of Daphnis (Washington). By February 22, 1796, Isaac Weld observed that "not one town of any importance was there in the whole union, where some meeting did not take place in honor of this day."[13] Washington's stepgrandson, George Washington Parke Custis, told how on Philadelphia's Second Street, as Washington the president walked along, "often would mothers bring their children to look on the paternal chief." The children, he added, were "taught to lisp the name of WASHINGTON."[14] Washingtonian oratory became a national pastime in an amount which William A. Bryan has called "staggering." "It seems unlikely that any other man in history, with the possible exception of Napoleon, was so widely 'orated' upon in his latter years and for more than a half century after his death . . ."[15]

Preachers joined in the ritual acclamations, and so did newspaper accounts. Washington seemed for all "the prop and glory of this western world." After the fall of Charles Cornwallis at Yorktown, he was "our illustrious Washington, who, like the meridian sun," had "dispelled those nocturnal vapors that hung around us, and put the most pleasing aspect upon our political affairs, that any era of the present war has ever beheld."[16] Songs and ballads told the British that they lived "the scorn of all our host, the slaves of Washington," hailed the commander-in-chief as the "second Alexander," and placed reliance "on Heaven and Washington."[17] David Ramsay thought in 1789 that "an attempt to draw the character of this truly great man, would look like flattery. Posterity will doubtless do it justice. His actions, especally now, while fresh in remembrance, are his amplest panegyric."[18]

Rituals of praise quickly moved beyond language to dramatic action. Ramsay told of Washington's route to army camp and noted that on the way he "was treated with the highest honours in every place through which he passed. Large detachments of volunteers, composed of private gentlemen, turned out to escort him. A committee from the Massachusetts congress received him about 100 miles from Boston, and conducted him to the army." Again, when he liberated Boston from the British, "General Washington was honoured by congress with a vote of thanks.

They also ordered a medal to be struck, with suitable devises to perpetuate the remembrance of the great event."[19] After York-town, newspaper accounts from various cities noted the liturgies of divine service, bonfires and illuminations, cannon discharges, and multitudinous toasts in which the name of Washington figured prominently. When, after the peace, the general made his way to Annapolis, then the seat of government, he was celebrated en route with processions and triumphal arches as well as the usual repertoire of cannon, songs, and addresses.

Elected president of the new republic, thus carrying the act of foundation to its completion, Washington journeyed to New York for the inauguration in what resembled the victory pro-cession of a Hellenistic divine emperor. In Philadelphia, the painter Rembrandt Peale had designed a bridge which would float across the Schuylkill River decorated like a Roman triumphal arch with laurel and other greens. As Washington crossed, the painter's daughter, dressed as a young boy, dropped a crown upon the president-elect's head. At Trenton, there was another triumphal arch which read, *"The defender of the Mothers, will also protect their Daughters."* Mason Weems described Washington's en-counter with his usual flair.

He approached the bridge on its south side, amidst the heartiest shouts of congratulating thousands, while on the north side were drawn up several hundreds of little girls, dressed in snow-white robes, with temples adorned with garlands, and baskets of flowers on their arms. Just behind them stood long rows of young virgins, whose fair faces, of sweetest red, and white, highly animated by the occasion, looked quite angelic—and, back of them, in crowds stood their venerable mothers. As Washington slowly drove off the bridge, the female voices all began, sweet as the first wakings of the Eolian harp, and thus they rolled the song. . . . While singing the last lines, they strewed the way with flowers before him.[20]

After he reached Elizabethtown, New Jersey, he crossed the bay in an "elegant barge," which Ramsay was careful to note, was rowed by "thirteen pilots."[21]

Elias Boudinot, who had been present, wrote back to Elizabeth-town describing the events which followed. Boat after boat joined the presidential party. Before they came to Bedloe's Island, a large sloop appeared from which "about 20 Gentn & Ladies rose up. and with excellent & melodious Voices sung an Eloquent Ode appropriate to the occasion. & set to the Music of 'God save the King,' welcoming their Great Chief to the Seat of Government." Thereafter, another boat sailed up and "threw in amongst us a number of Copies of another Ode. and immediately about a dozen Gentn began to sing it in parts as we passed along." Propitiously, as they approached New York harbor, "a shoal of porpoises came rising above the water & playing among the Boats, as if desirous to know the Cause of all this Joy & Gladness." On shore stood the people: "Tens of Thousands, from the Battery to the place of Landing Altho nearly half a Mile you could see little else along the Wharves in the Streets, and on board the Vessels, but heads as numerous as Ears of Corn before the Harvest." As the party arrived at the Wall Street Ferry Stairs where "a chosen detach-ment of the Militia in Elegant Uniform" waited, Boudinot noted that the stairs were "Covered with Carpeting, and the rails from the Water to the top of the warf hung with crimson hangings." Meanwhile, "the streets were lined with inhabitants as close as they could stand together, and it required all the exertions of a numerous train of City officers with their staves to make a passage for the procession."[22]

The story was similar during the presidential years. Every-where that Washington moved, spontaneous liturgies seemed to follow. When in 1796, John Adams was inaugurated to succeed him, the new president was all but forgotten. One eyewitness recollected that, as Washington tried modestly to retire, "there was a rush from the gallery to the corridor that threatened the loss of life or limb, so eager were the throng to catch a last look at one who had so long been the object of public veneration."[23] By the year of his death, Washington had been the subject of eight separate biographical accounts including, in 1795, James

Hardie's *General George Washington, the Father of His Country and the Friend of Mankind*. This was not the first time, however, that Washington had been called "father of his country" in print. In 1779, a German almanac had appeared in Lancaster, Pennsylvania, with as frontispiece a laureate medallion portrait of the general and the words, *"Der Landes Vater."*[24]

But the father of his country was only one among a number of designations which the patriots eagerly bestowed on their Washington. Their congeniality toward Graeco-Roman models led them to put the boldest face on his caution, so that, especially after the success of the New Jersey campaign at Trenton and Princeton, they dubbed him the American Fabius. Scarcely was the war finished when, in 1784, John Murray's "Jerubbaal, or, Tyranny's Grove Destroyed, and the Altar of Liberty Finished" extended a parallel between Washington and the biblical Gideon in which Gideon became the Jewish, and Washington the American Cincinnatus.[25] Historians of the Revolution mirrored the popular consciousness, and David Ramsay wrote admiringly:

To pass suddenly from the toils of the first public commission in the United States, to the care of a farm; to exchange the instruments of war for the implements of husbandry, and to become at once, the patron and example of ingenious and profitable agriculture, would to most men have been a difficult task. . . . let the commanders of armies learn from the example of general Washington, that the fame which is acquired by the sword, without guilt or ambition, may be preserved without power or splendour, in private life.[26]

The theme of the farmer-patriot who had left the sword for the ploughshare was taken up by Mason Weems and flourished in the nineteenth century, becoming linked to the American cult of innocence which, as we shall see, Washington also embodied. Schoolchildren, themselves innocent, learned from their textbooks that, as one reader put it, "the cultivator of the soil is indeed a *patriot*. . . . The very trees and rocks among which he has grown up, are objects of his affection."[27] Directly after the war, the strength of the Cincinnatus theme was expressed publicly in the formation of the Society of the Cincinnati. But its bent seemed more aristocratic and militaristic than agricultural to other patriots who, unlike Washington and his friends, were not old soldiers. They responded hostilely to the society, as if it were a church within a church.[28]

Classical themes helped the patriots to articulate what Washington meant to them, but so too did their Judaeo-Christian heritage. Alternately, Washington was Moses who had led his people from the fleshpots and slavery of Egypt to a new land of lawful liberty. Or he was Joshua who in a time of crisis had been one of the Judges Jehovah had raised up to save Israel. Washington, the American Joshua, became an increasingly familiar designation, probably because of the founder's warrior status and later because of Timothy Dwight's long epic poem, *The Conquest of Canaan* (1785). Already in the year of peace, George Duffield was sermonizing the "ILLUSTRIOUS WASHINGTON, the Joshua of the day and admiration of the age," while Ezra Stiles expressed the opinion that posterity and the world would acknowledge that "this American Joshua was raised up by God, and divinely formed, by a peculiar influence of the Sovereign of the universe."[29]

Although Dwight later denied a connection between the Joshua of his epic and the father of his country, he had written to Washington in early 1778 asking for permission to dedicate the uncompleted work to him. At least one scholar of the poem, Kenneth Silverman, has concluded that "Dwight probably did intend writing a patriotic allegory."[30] Indeed it was not difficult to read the "illustrious Washington" into the "Chief divine," who was Joshua in the epic. For despite the mighty presence of Jehovah who conducted affairs from the eaves, Joshua moved as a divine man, charged with power. "To Joshua's hand he gave the destin'd sway, / A chief divine! with every virtue crown'd, / In combat glorious, and in peace renown'd." Joshua of the "voice divine" lived up to the commission he had been handed, and in battle he was fierce to behold.

> The Hero view'd, and tow'rd the fainting throng,
> Swift as a rapid whirlwind, rush'd along;
> As 'gainst a mound, when tempests ride the gale,
> The raging river foams along the vale;
> Down the wall crumbles, and with dreadful reign
> Sweeps a wild deluge on the wasted plain.
> Bursting upon the dark embodied throng
> Thus the wide ruin Joshua drove along;
> Around his course increas'd the piles of dead,
> The brave sunk fighting, and the coward fled.[31]

Savior and deliverer that he was, Washington had had his "misfortunes." Even these became grist for the patriot mill, since misfortunes were those alien forces which constituted him a Suffering Servant or Innocent One in the midst of corruption and cabal. In the innocence of the father, Americans recognized their own innocence. The historians and biographers of the father reflected public sentiment as they portrayed the hero. Washington had been a maligned martyr—as colonel and commander in the French and Indian War, as Revolutionary War general, and as president: each situation generated its share of plotters and schemers who obligingly provided a foil for the virtue of the saint. The righteous one aided the process, as his letter acknowledging his awareness of the plan to put General Charles Lee at the head of the army made clear.

So soon as the public gets dissatisfied with my services, or a person is found better qualified to answer her expectation, I shall quit the helm with as much content, as ever the wearied pilgrim felt upon his safe arrival at the holy land, or haven of hope; and shall wish most devoutly, that those who come after may meet with more prosperous gales than I have done, and less difficulty.[32]

It was the more sober biographers who were particularly adept at presenting Washington as Innocent One. Their decisions to operate within the canons of historical credibility meant that they were limited in the range of apocryphal tales and miraculous events they could present, unlike some of the less scholarly ac-

counts. Hence, the *interpretation* of events to reveal their hidden
insights into the character of Washington became an important
route into the high country of religion which others had reached
by the road of imagination. Thus, John Marshall's five-volume
work began, even in the French and Indian War, to depict the
inner meaning of outer truth. Washington's long-suffering heroism could only be enhanced by Marshall's factual account of how
"colonel Washington was seized with a raging fever, which absolutely disabled him from riding on horseback. Persisting, however,
in his refusal to remain behind the troops, he was conveyed with
them in a covered waggon." Similarly, when Marshall recounted
the Thomas Conway–Horatio Gates innuendoes against Washington, the commander-in-chief was characterized by "patriotism,"
"apprehension for his country," and "purity of mind" rather than
"wounded pride." Washington's desire to remain at his post issued "from the conviction that his retaining that station would be
useful to his country." Later, the "schism" in Washington's cabinet
between the secretary of state and the secretary of the treasury,
widely reported in the press of the period, was "a subject of extreme mortification to the president." American neutrality toward
England and France meant that "these publications, in the first
instance sufficiently bitter, quickly assumed a highly increased
degree of acrimony."[33] Through it all, Washington endured and
remained for the nation a model of wounded innocence.

  For Jared Sparks in the 1830s, the theme of persecution of the
saint provided a standard mode of interpretation, beginning as
with Marshall, in the French and Indian War. As early as 1756,
while Washington remained at his Winchester headquarters:

Rumors were circulated to the disparagement of the Army, charging
the officers with gross irregularities and neglect of duty, and indirectly throwing the blame upon the commander. A malicious person
filled a gazette with tales of this sort, which seemed for the moment
to receive public countenance. Conscious of having acted with the
utmost vigilance, knowing the falsehood and wickedness of these
slanders, and indignant at so base a manoeuvre to stain his character,

it was his first impulse to retire from a station, in which patriotism, the purest intentions, hardships, and sacrifice, were rewarded only with calumny and reproach.

Throughout the course of the Revolution, Congress functioned as a collective foil against which the virtue of Washington shone more brilliantly. Inconsistent, temporizing, and unwise, it continually endangered the good of revolution it wished to accomplish. Washington, by contrast, moving with power and serenity, patiently sought to enlighten his less perceptive brethren as to the true condition of the army, the real difficulties in invading Canada, or whatever. During Washington's presidency, the press assumed the previous role of Congress and, more strikingly than in the Marshall account, magnified it. The Jay Treaty, leaked to the press, was

dissected, criticized, and condemned in a tone of passionate and violent declamation, which could scarcely have been exceeded, if the instrument had reduced the United States to their former colonial dependence on England. The merits of the treaty were studiously kept out of sight, and all its objectionable parts were thrust forward, exaggerated, and censured as disgraceful and humiliating to the nation.[34]

Two decades later, Washington Irving was playing upon the same themes as his predecessors. General Edward Braddock, on his deathbed in the French and Indian War, apologized to Washington for "the petulance with which he rejected his advice" and bequeathed to him "his favorite charger and his faithful servant, Bishop, who had helped to convey him from the field." At the end of operations for 1777, in an atmosphere of cabal and intrigue, Washington was "painfully aware" of the machinations against him.

Yet in no part of the war did he more thoroughly evince that magnanimity which was his grand characteristic, than in the last scenes of this campaign, where he rose above the tauntings of the public, the suggestions of some of his friends, and the throbbing impulses of his own courageous heart, and adhered to that Fabian policy which he considered essential to the safety of the cause. To dare is often the impulse of selfish ambition or harebrained valor: to forbear is at times the proof of real greatness.

The Whiskey Rebellion brought forward the "paternal care with which Washington watched, at all times, over the welfare of the country." At the time of the Jay Treaty, when vituperation reached such heights that impeachment was publicly suggested, Washington maintained the dignity and calm which accompanied righteousness. All told, he "possessed fewer inequalities, and a rarer union of virtues than perhaps ever fell to the lot of one man. Prudence, firmness, sagacity, moderation, an overruling judgment, an immovable justice, courage that never faltered, patience that never wearied, truth that disdained all artifice, magnanimity without alloy."[35]

Washington's yeoman background stood him in good stead for the role he had played. As the innocent American set amid the purifying influence of the land, he had been a sign of contradiction for European and domestic variants of corruption. The fact that Washington had been "wholly clothed in American manufactures" for his inauguration had not been lost on his countrymen, for whom the wearing of homespun had become a national sacramental. Even members of the patriot army had worn hunting shirts, not only because they terrified the British, but also because they evoked the wilderness theme the patriots loved. But it had been above all in his person that Washington had celebrated his innocence, and grateful Americans could learn who they were as they watched him.

Innocence though led beyond itself and beyond the double consciousness of classical and Christian traits, for perceptions of innocence deepened and widened to become perceptions of divinity. In classical antiquity, innocence had been transmuted into power and had overcome the world in the *theios aner*. In the Christian tradition, there had been only one truly Innocent Man before Washington, and that man was Jesus. Washington absorbed and unified the elements from the classical and Christian past, becom-

ing for Americans a divine man, one who embodied godly presence in a world from which the Governor was taking his leave.
Particularly after Washington's death, while Congress and the
citizenry wore crepe and public buildings were draped in black,
oratory began to dwell on his divine status. At least 440 funeral
elegies within three months provided ample opportunity for the
trend to develop. At Harvard College, Washington was numbered among the "gods upon earth," while, more subtly, Phillips
Payson did not recollect "ever hearing of a single instance of mis-
take, error, or blame, that was ever justly charged upon him."[36]
"Well may he be ranked," preached David Tappan, "among
Earthly Gods, who, to other great accomplishments united a
'humble,' yet near resemblance of HIM, who is the standard of
human perfection and the EXPRESS IMAGE of divine glory."[37]
Washington Benevolent Societies sprang up and continued poetic
tributes were written. One European traveler of the period observed that "every American considers it his sacred duty to have
a likeness of Washington in his home, just as we have the images
of God's saints."[38]

Veneration of the name and memory of the divine Washington
continued throughout the nineteenth century. Lord Erskine was
not atypical when he recalled how, as a young boy in 1790, he
had seen "the serene, the benign, the god-like expression of the
countenance of that man of men."

As Washington passed near the spot where I stood, his mild, clear,
blue eye fell upon me, and it seemed as though his very glance was a
benediction. Though high deeds and noble acts, fame, death, a nation's worship and tears, have since in the deep places of my heart
consecrated his name above every other name of earth, yet even then,
boy as I was, the glance thrilled me through and through; my eyes
fell beneath it, and my hand was involuntarily raised to uncover my
head as that august personage passed by.[39]

Even Mercy Warren, who was inclined more than others to be
critical, admitted that "an exclusive claim to the summit of human
excellence, had been yielded as a kind of prescriptive right, to

this worthy and justly venerated citizen, from affection, from gratitude, and from the real services rendered his country."[40] Mason Weems, by contrast, was unabashed in his tributes to the "Godlike Washington."

Following the path on which Weems had led, nineteenth-century textbooks took up the cause of the *theios aner*. Ruth Miller Elson has observed that in all of these books Washington bore "more resemblance to Jesus Christ than to any human being. As Christ came from heaven to bring divine salvation to human souls, so Washington was sent by the Deity to bring liberty to man. His character as a man is swallowed up in his messianic function."[41] "Godlike" became a standard epithet, while one reader appropriately confessed: "We forget for a moment that he was a man. We regard him as some propitious divinity, sent from a better world, than this, to take America by the hand, and lead her to independence, freedom and happiness."[42] Another, revealing the dramatic flair of the patriots, thought that an American should be "penetrated with astonishment, and kindled into thanksgiving when he reflects that our globe had existed 6000 years before a Washington appeared on the theatre of the world."[43] Sometimes, the father possessed magical powers which, as with the Hellenistic divine man who displayed his prowess through miracles, aided his mission. One reader noted confidentially that "*Insurrection* was so struck at his countenance, that it fled from the *shock of his aim*." Another ventured that if Washington had met Napoleon, "a single flash of justice from the countenance of Washington" would have been "sufficient to strike dead every laurel on his brow."[44] Divinity evidently had extended Washington's native talents considerably, for a number of the lists of American artists included his name.

Patriot parents of children who used these texts were reinforced in their own perceptions of Washington's divine nature as literature and oratory perpetuated the message. Joel Barlow's *Columbiad* repeated the utterance of Hesper, Guardian Genius of the West, before the Revolution: "And see bright Washington behind thee rise, / Thy following sun to gild our morning skies, / O'er shadowy climes to pour enlivening flame, / The charm of freedom and the fire of fame." Yorktown, they were reminded, was the place where "still dread Washington directs his way, / And seas and continents his voice obey;/ While brave Cornwallis, mid the gathering host. / Perceives his glories gone, his promised empire lost."[45] Similarly, Daniel Webster had discovered that the Son of the fathers was also a Sun: "Our own firmament now shines brightly upon our path. WASHINGTON is in the clear, upper sky."[46]

The centennial celebration of Washington's birth in 1832 and the fiftieth jubilee of the United States Constitution in 1839 both inspired orators to new rhetorical heights. The latter prompted John Quincy Adams to describe a dream in which, on the night before his inauguration, Washington was visited by his guardian angel "in the venerated form of his mother." The apparition "delivered to him a suit of celestial armour—"

a helmet, consisting of the principles of piety, of justice, of honour, of benevolence, . . . a spear, studded with the self-evident truths of the Declaration of Independence—a sword, the same with which he had led the armies of his country through the war of freedom to the summit of the triumphal arch of independence—a corslet and cuishes of long experience and habitual intercourse in peace and war with the world of mankind, . . . and last of all, the Constitution of the United States, a SHIELD embossed by heavenly hands, with the future history of his country.[47]

He was a veritable warlord of the spirit, the epitome of the warrior religion of Americans who knew that in their democratic faith they had donned the helmet of salvation and were wearing the sword of the spirit. Yet Washington could also imitate the serene composure of Nature's God. Francis Gray in 1832 saw him on top of the mountain.

The eye of posterity therefore, in looking back on the pyramid of a nation's glory, less to scrutinize its structure, than to contemplate its lofty grandeur, will always involuntarily rest upon its summit. And if

it behold there, not a gigantic phantom, gifted with power and genius
indeed, yet distorted by ambition, or polluted by crimes;—but a majestic form, erect and serene; of exact proportions and severe simplicity; without a fault for censure, an extravagance for ridicule, or a
blemish for regret;—on that it will delight to linger, to that it will
direct the admiration of mankind.[48]

The lives of Washington, as mid-century approached, continued the theme. James K. Paulding was representative as he too
contemplated the *theios aner* upon the mountain. "As in ascending
the lofty peaks of the Andes, we at length arrive at a line where
vegetation ceases, and the principle of life seems extinct; so in the
gradations of human character, there is an elevation which is
never attained by mortal man. A few have approached it, and
none nearer than Washington."[49] Walter Marshall McGill's epic
poem *The Western World* used language still more graphic as it
depicted ghosts, angels, and supernatural voices which accompanied Washington during the battles of the Revolution. Youthful
politicians such as Abraham Lincoln in 1842 found that "to add
brightness to the sun or glory to the name of Washington is alike
impossible. Let none attempt it. In solemn awe pronounce the
name, and in its naked deathless splendor leave it shining on."[50]
Horatio Hastings Weld told readers of the *Pictorial Life of
George Washington* that "the first word of infancy should be
mother, the second, father, the third, WASHINGTON," while Nathaniel Hawthorne asked, "Did anybody ever see Washington
nude?" and pronounced the notion "inconceivable." Washington
must obviously have been "born with his clothes on, and his hair
powdered, and made a stately bow on his first appearance in the
world."[51]

As Americans remembered Washington, they were confronted
with a kind of hierophany, a form of experience which the
founder had evoked in so many of his contemporaries. David
Ramsay's 1814 edition of *The Life of George Washington* visual-
ized the appearance of the sacred in its frontispiece. There a huge
boulder, redundantly labeled "WASHINGTON," was being struck

by lightning and storm and lashed by waves, while below the legend read, "Firm as the Surge-Repelling Rock."[52] For the Washington Centennial, the Massachusetts legislature in a poetic tribute recollected a night long ago on Dorchester Heights.

> There, like an angel form,
> Sent down to still a storm,
>   Stood WASHINGTON—
> Clouds broke and rolled away;
> Foes fled in pale dismay;
> Wreathed were his brows with bay,
> When war was done.[53]

Catharine Maria Sedgwick, the author, owned confidentially that "whenever the writer has mentioned Washington, she has felt a sentiment resembling the awe of the pious Israelite when he approached the ark of the Lord." On the other hand, Caroline Kirkland unawares challenged Hegel's vision of Napoleon on his horse with her picture of Washington assuming command of the Continental Army: "As they approached the line the eye sought and easily recognized him in whose bearing should shine forth the right to rule. At the same moment the central figure galloped forward, and wheeling his charger beneath the Great Elm which still adorns the spot, drew his sword, and, flashing it in the air, took command, in form, of the armies of the United Colonies."[54]

When piety came again into fashion in the nineteenth century, Washington became pious. Edward G. McGuire's *The Religious Opinions and Character of Washington* (1836) obligingly supplied the public demand for knowledge of his praying habits. Religious bodies embroidered their recollections of Washington's relationship to their denomination to provide for themselves abundant evidences of his devotion. The father of his country was discovered in prayer at Valley Forge, in libraries, and in private rooms. He could be identified in Congress because he was *"the gentleman who kneels down"* and, at the Constitutional Convention, because of the flash of his indignant eye at one who opposed Franklin's suggestion for prayer. He appeared at Morristown at the communion table of the Presbyterian church and else-where quite regularly disappeared *"at a certain hour for the de-votion of the closet."*[55]

Since morality had never gone out of fashion, Washington con-tinued to function as an exemplar of moral rectitude. G. W. P. Custis recalled the anecdote of General Charles Scott, an invet-erate swearer, who had been asked if Washington ever swore.

Yes, once. It was at Monmouth, and on a day that would have made any man swear. Yes, sir, he swore on that day, till the leaves shook on the trees, charming, delightful. Never have I enjoyed such swear-ing before, or since. Sir, on that ever-memorable day he swore like an angel from Heaven.[56]

Washington, in short, had no blemishes, or if he did, they were microscopic. "If we estimate him by the examples recorded in history," wrote James K. Paulding, "he stands without a parallel in the virtues he exhibited, and the vast, unprecedented conse-quences resulting from their exercise." Francis Gray owned that history "demands the whole truth, and will ask if he had no fail-ings. If he had any, for he was a man, they have left no trace in the annals of his country, and no speck upon his own bright fame."[57] Washington engaged in *useful* learning and "never learned a syllable of Latin." He rescued a debtor who owed him money from jail, paid to have bread regularly supplied to the poor, declined a sizable gift of shares of stock, and adamantly re-fused to eat an extravagant shad which had cost his steward three dollars. An early riser, he spent one to two hours before dawn in his library in winter and arrived there at daybreak in summer. Significantly, although gout was hereditary in his family, he never showed signs of the disease.[58] As a child he had been a model of filial obedience, and in adulthood he continued to reverence au-thority in his obedience to Congress and later to the Constitution.

It was this last, Washington's bond with the Constitution, which especially occupied the attention of the new sons when they looked toward the generation of their father to support their own fragile union. The meaning of Washington seemed irrevocably linked to the Constitution which, they all believed, had established and preserved the Revolution for ages to come. The patriots made it clear that they remembered the farewell prayer of the president in 1796, "that your union and brotherly affection may be perpetual—that the free constitution, which is the work of your hands, may be sacredly maintained."[59] Daniel Webster told Americans in 1832 that Washington's domestic policy had "found its pole-star in the avowed objects of the Constitution itself" and that "the Union was the great object of his thoughts."[60] In similar fashion, John Quincy Adams later found that, although the Constitution's longevity was a function of its own soundness, "we may, without superstition or fanaticism, believe that a super-intending Providence had adapted to the character and principles of this institution, those of the man by whom it was to be first administered."[61] The "eloquence" that carried the Constitution, for Francis Gray, was the eloquence of George Washington's life, and "no one man had so much influence in establishing and secur-ing [it], as GEORGE WASHINGTON."[62] The motif of union was, in sum, entwined with Washington's name and person. Here his title and role as Innocent One in the midst of party strife greatly aided his cause. In the growing tension which preceded the Civil War, more and more, Washington, just as the Bible, would become the authority to which differing parties turned to justify their posi-tions. "When controversy arose, both sides agreed in using his name as a charm against sectional turmoil and disunion."[63]

More unconsciously, the patriots found in Washington a hero who epitomized the military values they embraced. From the be-ginning, the histories and biographies painted a vivid portrait of Washington the soldier and general, a portrait in fact so vivid that it far eclipsed the treatments of his political involvement and his presidency. It was as if, even in the early years of the myth, Americans found a purifying and regenerative spectacle in the shedding of the nation's blood for a lofty cause. In the political arena, by contrast, the ambiguities of human interaction did not lend themselves to easy glorification and pointed instead toward human corruptibility. John Marshall's life of Washington in the first decade of the nineteenth century presented Americans with a history of the colonies in which all events led up to the climactic years of the Revolution. Washington did not appear until the second volume, and thereafter, more space was devoted to the revolutionary years than to all the rest of the hero's life. The founder was preeminently *General* Washington, the man who was preserved "from the fate all around him" in the French and Indian War by the "superintending care of Providence," who had "had two horses killed under him, and four balls through his coat; but to the astonishment of all, escaped unhurt, while every other officer on horseback was either killed or wounded."[64] David Ramsay's life of the hero was simply another version of his *History of the American Revolution* with huge excerpts from the earlier work reprinted in the new narrative. Washington dominated the battles as the paradigmatic soldier whose "composition was all nerve; full of correct and manly ideas, which were expressed in precise and forcible language."[65]

Popular biographies likewise allocated huge portions of their narratives to the Revolutionary War years and described the train of events with ardor. Thus, James K. Paulding's accounts of battles, in 1835, came close to being ecstasies. Princeton was an example. Here events came together at fever pitch, for "the cause of freedom now quivered on the brink of a precipice, from which, if it fell, it might never rise again." But at the critical moment, Washington, "seeing at a single glance that all was now at stake, and all would be lost by defeat, . . . became inspired with that sublime spirit which always most animates courage and genius in the hour of greatest peril. He snatched a standard, and calling on his soldiers to come to the rescue of their country, dashed into the midst of the enemy." Some time later, patriots were once again able to hold up their heads.

Thus once more did the heart of all America throb at the news that light had come out of darkness, and hope sprung up with renewed vigour from the regions of despair. . . . The genius of liberty again held up her head amid the gloom that surrounded her, and flapped her wings for joy. Her votaries, who had partaken in her despair, shared in her rejoicings, and now, for the first time since the catalogue of disasters, which, one after the other, had depressed the very souls of the stoutest advocates and defenders of freedom, did their awake in the bosoms of all a noble prophetic consciousness, that the land which had determined to be independent was capable of achieving the boon. In ten days, Washington had changed the whole aspect of affairs, and given to his country a respite, if not a deliverance.[66]

Caroline Kirkland's biography (1857), written, she emphasized, for the instruction and edification of the young, included fifteen chapters on the Revolution, twenty on the early life of the hero, and five on the events after 1783. Her style was representative of much of the material which had appeared on the father of his country, for Kirkland deplored war but at the same time presented hierophanies of war. From youth, she told her readers, Washington had displayed a "military turn." "By some strange prophetic instinct—though indeed prophecy often works its own fulfillment—it was his pride to form his schoolmates into military companies, with cornstalks for muskets and calabashes for drums, and to drill and exercise them, to command them and lead them to sham battle."[67]

The case continued to be similar, with Washington Irving begging his subscribers to hold him excused when his three-volume projected life of the hero extended into a fourth and fifth volume. He explained the reason: "To present a familiar and truthful picture of the Revolution and the personages concerned in it, required much detail and copious citations, that the scenes might be placed in a proper light, and the characters introduced might speak for themselves, and have space in which to play their parts."[68] When the Reverend John Norton thought that Washington the Christian was being neglected at the expense of Washington the soldier, he endeavored to correct the situation in a work which devoted nearly as much space to the war years as the remainder of the general's life.[69] George Washington Parke Custis delighted in accounts of battles and waxed eloquent in his descriptions of such scenes as Princeton, Germantown, Monmouth, and Yorktown.

While recitation of the myth made Washington present through the power of language, the relics of the divine man evoked his presence by sacramental sign. Speedily and effectively, they had become religious treasures, venerated with awe and charged in some mysterious fashion with the power of George Washington and the might of America he represented. Some of these relics were secondary—physical objects which had been in Washington's possession or sacred sites where major events in his life had occurred. Such for example were Washington's sword which had stood him and the nation in such good service during the Revolution and his Bible on which he had sworn the oath of office as president. Such too was the spot where Washington was born and where, in 1815, a "First Stone" was placed, enveloped in the "star-stangled banner" and "borne to its resting-place in the arms of the descendants of four revolutionary patriots and soldiers," while bricks from the chimney which had been the hearth of the Washington house formed a "rude kind of pedestal" and a cannon fired.[70]

But Washington's physical remains were the relics of primary rank. As Daniel Boorstin has observed, "The struggle over the possession and proper location of the bodily remains of the Hero, if not equaling that over the Holy Grail, expressed a not dissimilar cultic spirit."[71] Horatio Hasting Weld's *Pictorial Life of George Washington* illustrated the mid-century involvement of Americans in the question. Quoting an earlier account, Weld took his youthful readers on a detailed tour of the tomb and sarcophagus which enclosed "the sacred dust of the Great Founder," including a description of its removal in 1837 from an older to a new marble coffin. The sketch culminated with the decision of Major Lawrence Lewis, executor of Washington's will, to view the sacred remains, after it was discovered that the soldered joints of the old coffin had partially given way.

At the request of Major Lewis this fractured part was turned over on the lower part of the lid, exposing to view a head and breast of large dimensions, which appeared, by the dim light of the candles, to have suffered but little from the effects of time. The eye-sockets were large and deep, and the breadth across the temples, together with the forehead, appeared of unusual size. There was no appearance of grave-clothes; the chest was broad; the colour was dark, and had the appearance of dried flesh and skin adhering closely to the bones. We saw no hair, nor was there any offensive odour from the body, but we observed, when the coffin had been removed to the outside of the vault, the dripping down of a yellow liquid, which stained the marble of the Sarcophagus. A hand was laid upon the head and instantly removed; the lead of the lid was restored to its place; the body, raised by six men, was carried and laid in the marble coffin, and the ponderous cover being put on and set in cement, it was sealed from our sight on Saturday, the 7th day of October, 1837.[72]

Interest in the location of the tomb had been present since Martha Washington had given her reluctant consent to John Adams and the American Congress for the removal of the body to a place of honor in the nation's capital. As the Centennial of Washington's birth approached, it had grown in an atmosphere of heightened tension between Congress, on the one hand, and the Washington family, Virginia, and the rest of the south on the other. At one point, there had even been suggestions for the removal of the body to Richmond, capital of Virginia, but in the end, Mount Vernon, the ancestral home, had prevailed. Yet the politics of the tomb were simply one manifestation of a deep religious instinct which had gripped the American people. It was important where the divine man lay because, whatever the site, it would unalterably become a center of sacred power. While some argued for the newness of the federal city as the best context for the power which Washington embodied, others looked to the soil from which he had sprung. It was the soil to which the farmer-patriot had returned again and again after he had loyally served his country. It seemed sacrilegious to disturb the sleep of the dead. When, in 1858, J. A. Wineberger published his *Tomb*

of Washington at Mount Vernon, "embracing a full and accurate
description of Mount Vernon, as well as of the Birthplace, Genealogy, Character, Marriage and last Illness of Washington. Together with Incidents pertaining to the Burial of Washington,
removal from the old Family Vault, and his being placed in a new
Tomb in a marble Sarcophagus," he was performing a religious
exercise for equally religiously minded patriots, who in the latter
days, wanted to remember.[73]

Beyond the domain of these physical relics of the father, there
had been a living human relic in the Marquis de Lafayette, the
beloved and "adopted" son of Washington. As an old man in
1824, Lafayette visited the United States, and his presence occasioned a heightened sense of mythic awareness on the part of the
natural sons. It was a case of the hero blessed by the father return-
ing to represent the father among men.[74] The "Nation's Guest,"
by being once more in the land he had helped to liberate, performed sacramental functions for Americans who yearned, amid
the anxieties of the age of progress, to tap the power of the events
of their foundation. The identification that had grown up over
the years between Washington and Lafayette meant that the
father really *was* present again, to comfort and to save. There had
been signs and portents to testify to the truth, as for instance the
rainbow which attended both Lafayette's arrival and his departure
on board ship, and the eagle that had been sighted flying over the
tomb of Washington when Lafayette had entered it. Lafayette's
descent into the tomb of the dead father seemed a collective ritual
of initiation in which the patriots reimmersed themselves in the
meaning of the Revolution in order to be born anew as sons. Fred
Somkin captured the mood of Americans and its religious import
when he called Lafayette's visit a "ritual of mass reconciliation."
Somkin observed that "at a time when the possibility of Lafayette's brand of virtue, the virtue attributed to the life-giving
Fathers, seemed problematical, the communal entertainment of
Lafayette, by allowing an imaginative re-entry into a virtuous
past, provided the ritual substitute for a desired republican

grace."[75] In myth and in ritual, the patriots rediscovered the reality of themselves which transcended the world of every day, and they drew strength for the present from the encounter.

Members of George Washington's family did not escape canonization as well. Thus, Mary the mother of Washington came to be treated in terms which suggested Mary the mother of Jesus. For the patriots, there was, as Rufus Griswold said, "no fame in the world more pure than that of the mother of Washington, and no woman since the Mother of Christ has left a better claim to the affectionate reverence of mankind."[76] The perception grew stronger as the nineteenth century grew older and its cult of motherhood, more encompassing. Already, in the Mason Weems account, George Washington in his fifteenth year, like Jesus in the temple, heeded the pain he was causing his mother and turned away from the career he was about to begin as a midshipman. "But when he came to take leave of his mother, she wept bitterly, and told him *she felt that her heart would break if he left her.* George immediately got his trunk ashore! as he could not, for a moment, bear the idea of inflicting a wound on that dear life which had so long and so fondly sustained his own."[77] Jared Sparks repeated the story, citing the authority of Washington's mother "to which nature gave a claim"; but Sparks had been preceded in his veneration by President Andrew Jackson. On May 7, 1833, Jackson laid the cornerstone of a marble obelisk dedicated to the mother and prayed: "When the American pilgrim shall, in after ages, come up to this high and holy place, and lay his hand upon this sacred column, may he recall the virtues of her who sleeps beneath, and depart with his affections purified, and his piety strengthened, while he invokes blessings upon the memory of the mother of Washington."[78]

Likewise, Martha Dandridge, Washington's "spiritual partner," laid claim to her share of veneration. For as a divine man in a Protestant nation, Washington was no celibate but the model of fulfilled and fulfilling family life. As early as January 1776, a Massachusetts child had been given Martha's name in baptism, the baby girl "dressed in buff and blue, with a sprig of evergreen on its head, emblematic of his Excellency's glory and provincial affection."[79] David Ramsay had interrupted his history of the Revolution to pay tribute to "the feelings and character of the amiable partner of [Washington's] conjugal happiness." It was clear for Ramsay that "she deserved this tide of unparalled [sic] female honour and felicity, for she loved her country, and bore with more than Roman—with christian patience and fortitude, the pains to which his long absence, and the perils of his health and life had exposed her."[80] Caroline Kirkland in the 1850s hailed Martha as a positive and virtuous contrast to the wife of Benedict Arnold: "When she was in the highest position in the nation, [Martha] wore gowns spun under her own roof; and she always took care, in her conversation with the ladies about her, to exalt domestic employments, and to represent them as belonging to the duty of woman in any station."[81] She was for all concerned the "bright saint," whom Mason Weems had affirmed earlier in the century. Her beauty "was not the shallow boast of a fine skin, which time so quickly tarnished, nor of those short-lived roses, which sometimes wither almost as soon as blown." Her beauty instead sprang "from the HEART—from the *divine* and *benevolent affections*." It was fitting for Martha Dandridge and George Washington, "two such *kindred souls* to love."[82]

Kindred as was the soul of the father of his country to his wife, it had proved to be far more closely interfused with the structures of meaning and value of his countrymen. Washington, as *theios aner*, had become a grand collective representation, a tribal totem, among these sophisticated nineteenth-century sons. Founder and father, the divine man had knit together the divergent themes from Christian and classical sources and exemplified at every turn the qualities which Americans most admired in themselves. Like the god-hero that he was, George Washington existed in a realm beyond the idiosyncratic limitations of individual personality. He towered above the particular in transcendental remoteness, and for this reason drama and fiction found it difficult to portray him.

James Fenimore Cooper's novel *The Spy* was typical, with Washington as a great off-stage presence, continually alluded to in his guise as Mr. Harper, but appearing in person only three times throughout the tale. Similarly, in nineteenth-century schoolbooks, Washington's role as the "monumental framework on which to hang all the heroic virtues to be indoctrinated" meant that individual presence was lost.[83]

Biographies of Washington experienced the difficulty too. William Bryan concluded after his study of Washingtonian literature that "if one were to read only the biographies written before 1855, he would think Washington a demigod who descended to earth (his character already fully developed and flawless even in childhood), freed his people from oppression, steered their government for a few years, and then returned to heaven."[84] The more serious biographers sensed that they had a problem and understood it as a function of the epic sweep of Washington's life, which made it impossible to write about him without writing the history of America. Thus, Jared Sparks observed that "whoever would understand the character of Washington, in all its compass and grandeur, must learn it from his own writings, and from a complete history of his country during the long period in which he was the most prominent actor."[85] Washington Irving confessed unabashedly that his biography was "essentially historic."

Washington, in fact, had very little private life, but was eminently a public character. All his actions and concerns almost from boyhood were connected with the history of his country. In writing his biography, therefore, I am obliged to take glances over collateral history, as seen from his point of view and influencing his plans, and to narrate distant transactions apparently disconnected with his concerns, but eventually bearing upon the great drama in which he was the principal actor.[86]

If biography became history with George Washington, history was essentially myth, the sacred story of the divine man and his heroic friends who had, in a mighty act of power, effected the

foundation of the republic. Given the place that Washington occupied in the minds and hearts of his countrymen, it was not surprising that these historical myths were not completely factual.
Myth told the truth, a truth which in America was understood to
occur in the time and space of the public arena. But the truth of
the myth was an inner truth nonetheless that required measure-
ment for authenticity by inner criteria. So the biographies, which
were histories, which were myths, although they ranged along a
continuum from the more contained and sophisticated to the
more exuberant and innocent, were all paradigmatic tales. A divine man, foretold by prophetic signs, grew to manhood, encountered transforming power, plunged into the task of saving
his people, accompanied the while by the miraculous protection
of supernatural forces, and finally passed on through death to
glory.[87] What was revelatory about these sacred histories, or
aretalogies, was their disclosure of the underlying structure of
American consciousness: it conformed to perceptions of charismatic religious leaders in other times and places. Jesus, Buddha,
Appolonios of Tyana, even Socrates had been the subjects of
adulatory biographies which had much in common with these
lives of Washington.

All of them began with the factual structure of external reality;
unconsciously selected from it that which conformed to the paradigm of a holy man; sometimes invented, sometimes embroidered,
to fill in what history had left blank; and presented their finished
accounts to eager audiences of Americans. The Mason Weems
biography, going through nine printings in six years and reaching
fifty-nine editions before 1850, was an early and alltime success
within the context of the genre. While scholars have given
Weems low marks for scholarship and high marks for imagination and fantasy, as an aretalogist, he had written a classical text
which touched the core of the inner truth Americans shared.
Every popular biography which followed was, despite some authors' conscious intentions to the contrary, modeled after the pro-
totype Weems had exhibited. The more sophisticated lives by

John Marshall, Jared Sparks, and Washington Irving revealed that
they too had been captured by the paradigm which, though
weaker, was nonetheless still discernible. Weems had indeed not
been the source for their works—an observation particularly true
for the John Marshall biography—but the archetypal quality of
the American perception of Washington had informed their consciousness so deeply that, at once shapers and reflectors of the
myth, they complied with it. Generally, they departed most from
the pattern in avoiding involvement with the childhood of the
hero, while the popular accounts gloried in the young Washington and constructed a life which in childhood had been replete
with the signs and portents of future greatness.

In the Weems version, the *theios aner*, unlike Jesus or Buddha
or Apollonios, gave no hints of his divine call and mission during
his mother's pregnancy and his birth. But when he was five years
old, matters quickly righted themselves, as aretalogy came into its
own. Mary the mother of Washington at this time had a prophetic dream in which she heard "a kind of roaring noise on the
eastern side of the house" and discovered to her horror a "dreadful sheet of fire bursting from the roof." Her husband and servants were paralyzed by shock, but "in this most distressing
state," she remembered, "the image of my little son came."
Screaming, she called him, and little George came running.

He looked up and saw the house all on fire: but instead of bursting
out a crying, as might have been expected from a child, he instantly
brightened up and seemed ready to fly to extinguish it. But first looking at me with great tenderness, he said, *"Oh, Ma! don't be afraid:
God Almighty will help us, and we shall soon put it out."* . . . A ladder
was presently brought, on which, as I saw in my dream, he ran up
with the nimbleness of a squirrel; and the servants supplied him with
water, which he threw on the fire from an *American gourd.* . . . For
a long time the contest appeared very doubtful; but at length a venerable old man, with a tall cap and iron rod in his hand, like a lightning
rod, reached out to him a curious little trough, like a *wooden shoe!*
On receiving this, he redoubled his exertions, and soon extinguished
the fire. . . . Then I saw in my dream that after some time spent as

in deep thought, he called out with much joy, "*Well, Ma! now if you and the family will but consent, we can make a far better roof than this ever was*; a roof of such a *quality*, that, if well *kept together*, it will last for ever; but if you take it apart, you will make the house ten thousand times worse than it was before.[88]

With less than two decades since the "new roof" of the Federal Constitution had been paraded through the center of Philadelphia in the Grand Constitutional Procession, it seemed unnecessary to interpret, but Weems obligingly did so, pointing to the symbolic meanings of the house, the east, the American gourd, the old man with his iron rod (Benjamin Franklin), the wooden shoe (French aid), and finally the roof.

Parson Weems had been privy to other signs as well. He had seen the angels which protected the young hero, who "with their roseate wings, fanned his glowing cheeks, and kissed his lips of innocence." He knew of the divine child's physical, mental, and moral prowess; how in running, "the swift-eyed Achilles could scarcely have matched his speed," while in throwing, one eye-witness had seen him cast a stone "across Rappahannock, at the lower ferry of Fredericksburg"—no easy matter for a grown man, as Weems was careful to point out. It was Weems who noted that it was not Latin but useful knowledge, which Washington eagerly imbibed, and Weems who hailed his integrity in confessing to his father that he had barked the cherry tree. Washington's "*zeal for unblemished character, his love of truth, and detestation of whatever was false and base*," the Parson assured Americans, won him the love and confidence of his schoolmates. Weems celebrated the hero's courage in reproving his youthful peers when they would begin to fight. Significantly, even the smallpox to which the youthful George succumbed "marked him rather agreeably than otherwise." Meanwhile, he had already given prophetic indications of the future as he organized his comrades for war-games.[89]

As a young man, Washington entered upon a period of preparation and subsequent withdrawal before his call and mission would claim him. The French and Indian War provided a training ground for future military virtue, and Washington acquitted himself in a manner which portended greatness. His prowess was evidenced by his journey for Governor Robert Dinwiddie across the wild country of Pennsylvania to the French commander on the Ohio, a task that led to a threat of drowning or perishing in the ice, which Washington survived, and being "way-laid and shot at by an Indian, . . . not fifteen paces distant," which Washington also survived. Later, the hero's sage advice to General Edward Braddock on military techniques in the wilderness went unheeded, but though Braddock and his men were seriously defeated, Washington emerged unscathed.

A famous Indian warrior, who acted a leading part in that bloody tragedy, was often heard to swear, that *"Washington was not born to be killed by a bullet! For,"* continued he, *"I had seventeen fair fires at him with my rifle, and after all could not bring him to the ground!"* And indeed whoever considers that a good rifle, levelled by a proper marksman, hardly ever misses its aim, will readily enough conclude with this unlettered savage, that there was some invisible hand, which turned aside his bullets.[90]

Interestingly, Jared Sparks would support Mason Weems in this account of the Battle of Monongahela, and with G. W. P. Custis would link the authenticity of the event to the testimony of Washington's personal physician.[91] The patriots reverenced the historical fact, and those who at once shaped and expressed their myth were sensitive to that condition. It was for this reason that Weems and others, such as Horatio H. Weld, snatched up a statement by Samuel Davies in a sermon on religion and patriotism. In a footnote on "martial fire," Davies had surveyed events in 1755 and noted the endeavors of the young Washington with admiration: "I may point out to the public that heroic youth, Col. Washington, whom I cannot but hope Providence has hitherto preserved, in so signal a manner, for some important service to his country."[92]

Meanwhile, with prophecy ringing, the parson conducted his youthful prodigy through a phase of withdrawal, and the hero retired to his farm. Even here, however, cultic homage was not lacking, for it "always waited upon him, though always un-courted." At the same time, political involvement in the state legislature was training him for another future role. The motif of preparation and withdrawal would be repeated as Washington approached each major phase of his destiny, so that structurally his final retirement from public life became a last period of readying before he encountered sacred reality for a climactic and eternal union with it. But in 1775, Washington heard the transcendent call for the first time, "for in the midst of his favourite labours, of the plough and pruning-hook, covering his extensive farms with all the varied delights of delicious fruits and golden grain, of lowing herds and snowy flocks, he was suddenly called on by his *country*, to turn his plough-share into the sword, and go forth to meet a torrent of evils which threatened her."[93] Weems had appropriately emphasized "country," for the call had come, not in the voice of God, but in the voice of John Adams who had proposed Washington's name to Congress. What followed was an account of the founder's virtues and his exploits, his temptations and his traumas. He prayed; he was godly; his Innocence had its perfect foil in the treachery of Benedict Arnold who, Judas-like, was "very willing to be filled up with English guineas. English guineas, to the tune of ten thousand, with the rank and pay of Brigadier General, are offered; and Arnold agrees, Oh! shocking to humanity! Arnold agrees to sacrifice Washington."[94]

When toward the end the troops would have mutinied and made Washington their king, "happily for America, the voice of Washington still sounded in their ear as the voice of a father." He defied temptation and turned the very tempters around, "an angel orator, animating poor mortals to the sublime of god-like deeds." Then, "having won the great prize for which he contended, he returns to his plough."[95] He had been, for Parson Weems and for those who followed after him in the paradigm, a man of power, a superb general, militarily brilliant and hampered on every side by obstacles not of his making. Those who transcribed the feats of the divine man were very far from the consciousness of historians who would later declare the father of his country an uninspired general; who would claim that Trenton and Princeton involved luck and a redeeming moment; who would point to the presence of more Frenchmen than Americans at the great battle of Yorktown; who would resurrect the tensions between Washington and Congress over military drafts and troop payments, the loss of morale over deflated and worthless currency, the spate of mutinies. That part of the *other* truth which later scholars would see, if it surfaced at all, surfaced in the aretalogies only to show Washington, the serene and Innocent One, who labored under extraordinary difficulties and emerged above them all.

Washington entered the presidential phase of his mission and took upon himself the institutionalization of the Revolution in answer to another call which was again a human version of the voice of God. After over five years at Mount Vernon, *"the call to the magistracy was the most unwelcome he had ever heard,"* but Washington heeded the collective voice of Congress and hastened to New York, hailed en route by the homage of throngs of patriots, as we have already seen. Again, there were the great deeds, this time of the statesman, and again, Washington could do no wrong. Yet the Weems description and the others were truncated, for deeds of war and glory displayed more fittingly the virtue of a god-hero which overcame all obstacles. In fact, the short shrift which the presidency of Washington received seemed almost a function of the paradigm which had captured the minds and imaginations of American writers and their audiences. Thus, after an interval of statesmanship, the aretalogies swept the hero on to the final phase of his withdrawal which culminated in death and ascension. "Feeling that the hour of his departure out of this world was at hand," uttered the believing Weems, "he desired that every body should quit the room." "There, by himself, like Moses alone on the top of Pisgah, he seeks the face of God."[96]

Alone with God, the Jesus-Moses of his generation, whose most intimate thoughts Weems was able to read, remembered his country and its "beloved children" he had "so often sought to gather, even as a hen gathereth her chickens under her wings." He saw them "now spread abroad like flocks in goodly pastures; like favoured Israel in the land of promise." At last came the moment of severance, when "the silver chord of life" was 'loosing," and Washington correctly closed his eyes and folded his arms "decently on his breast." Then, "breathing out *Father of mercies! take me to thyself,'*—he fell asleep." But death was merely a prelude to ultimate bliss. Weems summoned all his powers to recount what followed, admitting soberly to the patriots that he heard/saw it only *"in Fancy's ear."*

Swift on angels' wings the brightening saint ascended; while voices more than human were heard (*in Fancy's ear*) warbling through the happy regions, and hymning the great procession towards the gates of heaven. His glorious coming was seen far off, and myriads of mighty angels hastened forth, with golden harps, to welcome the honoured stranger. High in front of the shouting hosts, were seen the beauteous forms of FRANKLIN, WARREN, MERCER, SCAMMEL, and of him who fell at Quebec, with all the virtuous patriots, who, on the side of Columbia, toiled or bled for *liberty* and *truth*.[97]

Others would shy away from the spectacular death account arranged by Weems, but the Tobias Lear version which they substituted, while far more restrained and carrying the authenticating stamp of an eyewitness, portrayed Washington as a divine man in the manner of Socrates. The hero was stern and beyond reproach in the face of the inevitable: he told his physicians, *"Doctors I die hard,"* and intrepidly inquired of Dr. Craik, *"Doctor, what is the clock? How long am I to continue in this situation?"* "The doctor answered, *'Not long sir.'* He then rejoined, with the firmest countenance imaginable, *'I have no fear, doctor, to die.'* " As a practical American as well as a Socratic disciple, he had already told Colonel Lear: "Have me decently buried, and do not let my body be put into the vault in less than two days after I am dead."[98]

Americans, as they contemplated their Washington, had been seized by an archetype. While they skewed it to their own horizontal religious sense and the historical pattern of Washington's life, they saw their leader as a *theios aner* in the pattern of a charismatic founder. They had been ambivalent about what ancient models had shaped his identity, but the ambivalence was an expression of their ambivalence about themselves. If the Washington of Weems and the others seemed a two-in-one, with Christian and classical motifs interfused, it was because that was the way Americans perceived the ideal which they sought for imitation. Americans moved between their role as soldiers in the army of Jehovah and as builders with the square and compass of the Architect who was Nature's God.

It was clear though that the Washington who had left his army for the last time, weeping because "nature stirred all the father within him," who after the war "with a father's joy . . . could look around on the thick-settled-country," and who died as the "shepherd father" to the "sons and daughters of Columbia" had in life and in memory performed a sacral function.[99] The sons of the fathers had become fathers themselves, but George Washington towered above them as Father to the fathers. He had added to his fatherhood his role as founder, for America had become the center of a new dispensation which Washington, as first among equals, had established.

Chapter 6

A New Covenant
We Give Ourselves

Q. What are the exact measurements of the originals of the Declaration of Independence and of the Constitution of the United States?

A. The Declaration of Independence: 19 7/8 in. by 24 7/16 in.; The Constitution: four sheets, approximately 28 3/4 in. by 23 5/8 in. each.

Q. How many words are there in the texts . . . and how long does it take to read them?

A. The Constitution has 4,543 words, including the signatures but not the certificate on the interlineations; and takes about half an hour to read. The Amendments have 2,214 words and they can be read in about half the time the Constitution takes. The Declaration of Independence has 1,458 words, with the signatures, but is slower reading, as it takes about ten minutes.[1]

This carefully researched piece of enlightenment for American schoolchildren of 1937 was indicative. Beyond displaying a concern for factual precision, it was evidence of a more basic orientation which informed succeeding generations of patriots as they contemplated the documents testifying to their foundation. Knowledge was key, for by controlling the measurements and statistics of the documents, Americans could control their materiality and thereby gain access to power. In other words, the documents were *sacraments*, signs of power which at the same time *were* the realities toward which they pointed. Knowing every penstroke and every correction was important because it brought the patriots in touch with the actuality of events in the beginning by means of contact with the documents. In effect, when Americans learned about how many inches and how many words there were in the Declaration and Constitution, they were learning the answers to questions which, emerging from the context of patriotic remembrance, were religious.

But the Declaration and the Constitution grew to be sacraments because they once had played a part in the revolutionary scenario. They did not possess nearly the sacramental power for their own time that they did in the subsequent history of the republic. For in the time of origins, they were simply part of the stream of events which told the tale of religious meanings discovered in the midst of action.

This was especially true of the Declaration, which, when it was enacted, was one ritual sign among many. For those who were involved, the *act* of separation from England seemed far more meaningful than the document which recorded the act. John Adams, as an example, had the religious but not the sacramental sense of later Americans when, after Congress had declared the colonies independent on July 2, 1776, he told Abigail that "the second day of July, 1776, will be the most memorable epocha in the history of America. I am apt to believe that it will be celebrated by succeeding generations as the great anniversary festival."[2] Thomas Jefferson, until at least 1800, was casual about his role in the composition of the Declaration and his possession of a manuscript draft. In the twentieth century, Margaret Willard's study of colonial letters appearing in British newspapers from 1774 to 1776 turned up so few which mentioned the document that she commented it was "surprising" and decided that the Declaration was "evidently considered but the formal statement of a foregone conclusion."[3]

Yet the evidence for sacramentality was not all negative. Thomas Paine had adumbrated the sacramental significance of the Declaration even before the actual document had been conceived and had suggested correct ritual behavior: "Let a day be solemnly set a part for proclaiming the Charter; let it be brought forth placed on the Divine Law, the Word of God; let a crown be placed thereon, by which the world may know, that so far as we

approve of monarchy, that in America THE LAW IS KING."[4] Moreover, in the case of the Constitution it was almost overnight that
it took on its sacramental character. From the time of separation
from England, thus, the patriots were caught in a dialectic between living the event in the absoluteness of the moment of
origins and enshrining it for future ages, as the historically conscious people they were. Paine and others were attempting the
establishment of the deed of the patriots as an absolute event
which would guarantee their unity because it would supply their
collective will in place of king or pope. Yet because of their self-
consciousness, establishment and canonization were occurring almost together. The patriots were giving themselves a new covenant.

Declaration and Constitution quickly assumed the aura of sacrality which that understanding elicited. These documents, fusing
event with memorialization, pointed to a human past grounded
on human acts rather than either divine events in the lives of the
gods or divine events occasioned by a God who acted in history.
The twin texts bent their Christian past to an affirmation of the
novus ordo saeclorum in which the novelty came from the pri-
macy of human action.

In the revolutionary era, the Declaration (which symbolized
the act of Revolution) and the Constitution (which symbolized
its institutionalization) were signposts for a living history which
unfolded in between. The chief interpreters of events and con-
trollers of sacred signs were the leaders among the patriots who
had come together in Congress. For as the delegates to the Continental Congress went about conducting the business of government, they also seemed to be running a national church, with
themselves the self-appointed keepers of the keys. Here was another anomaly: an act of foundation which became a myth of
origins, closely tied to the evolution of a divine man who had
founded, yet not founded the republic, now revealing at its center
a hierarchy of leaders who served as national priests. The congressional hierophants were held in honor and esteem, yet they

never received the adulation offered to the founder who, in his presidency, later assumed the role of great high priest to the nation, a role which American presidents after him would continue to enact. Among the hierarchy in the Continental Congress, meanwhile, there was again the quality of self-consciousness at the very heart of patriotic endeavor. There was besides an understanding of government which seemed to emerge from the old Puritan theocratic ideal and buttress the priestly functions of the members of Congress. In sum, the patriots did not demand consistency of themselves in their appropriation of religious forms but adopted what was useful. They shaped for their own and later times a myth which had been bent to the needs of history-makers who were literate and enterprising men.

In the beginning, however, was the *event*. That the patriots had to argue "simultaneously for rebellion and legitimacy" explained to some extent the absoluteness of their Declaration. They had to convince both themselves and the rest of the world of the justice of their cause. Yet their words were true not because they conformed to natural rights philosophy. Rather, as Carl Becker said, the efficacy of language brought their actions "into harmony with a rightly ordered universe" and enabled them to think of themselves as "having withdrawn from a corrupt world in order to serve God or Humanity or a force that makes for the highest good."[5] Partly aware and partly unaware of the pragmatic nature of the absolute they had fashioned, the patriots nonetheless recognized that they had done something extraordinary. Although, as John Adams recalled years later, there was "not an idea in it but what [had] been hackneyed in Congress for two years before," in 1776 he was less nonchalant. Then he had been "surprised at the suddenness as well as greatness of this revolution," and he had warned Abigail she would think him "transported with enthusiasm," though he declared he was not.[6] "The Declaration was yesterday published and proclaimed from that awful stage in the State-house yard," Adams wrote to Samuel Chase about a week later. "Three cheers rended the welkin. The battalions paraded on the Common, and gave us the *feu de joie*, notwithstanding the scarcity of powder. The bells rang all day and almost all night. Even the chimers chimed away."[7] In the evening, added the *Constitutional Gazette*, "our late king's coat of arms was brought from the hall in the State House, where the said king's courts were formerly held, and burned amidst the acclamations of a crowd of spectators."[8]

It was the same throughout the colonies. Everywhere, as the Declaration was ceremonially read, statues of George the Third tumbled in the dust, if they survived at all, while jubilant celebrations ensued. In New York, the *Pennsylvania Journal* announced, "the lead wherewith the monument was made is to be run into bullets, to assimilate with the brains of our infatuated adversaries, who, to gain a pepper-corn, have lost an empire." The newspaper called the event the "ominous fall of leaden majesty" and likened it to the fall of Lucifer: "If thou be'st he! But ah, how fallen! how changed!" At Savannah there was an official procession to the liberty pole where the Declaration was read and the Georgia batallion fired their weapons. Evening brought a "very solemn funeral procession, attended by the grenadier and light infantry companies, and other militia, with their drums muffled, and fifes, and a greater number of people than ever appeared on any occasion before, in that province, when George the Third was interred before the court-house."[9] The celebration at Fort Stanwix, New Jersey, was typical. Here, "after the Declaration had been read, cannons fired, and huzzas given, the battalion was formed in a circle with three barrels of grog in the center. The Colonel took a cup and drank to the toast—'God bless the United States of America.' The other officers followed, drinking the same toast as did afterwards the battalion, accompanied by loud hurrahs, shouting, and other signals of approbation."[10]

The unabridged Declaration was printed on the front page of newspapers and on broadsides, and before the month was out at least one child in East Windsor, Connecticut, had been baptized Independence. Benjamin Rush wrote to Charles Lee to tell him that the document had "produced a new era in this part of America. The militia of Pennsylvania seem to be actuated with a spirit more than Roman. Near 2000 citizens of Philadelphia have lately marched towards New-York."[11] Meanwhile, in Boston, Abigail Adams recorded that the Declaration had been "read from the pulpit by order of Council." Charles Chauncy had not been displeased, for "the good man after reading it, lifted his eyes and hands to heaven. 'God bless the United States of America, and let all the people say Amen.' "[12] In Virginia, the Convention had resolved almost immediately that references to the king and royal family be omitted from church services and litanies.

Gradually and imperceptibly, more attention began to focus on the document which had memorialized the act of the patriots. On July 19, after receiving official notice that New York had subscribed to it, Congress had the text committed to parchment as "The Unanimous Declaration of the Thirteen United States of America." The following January, it ordered that an authenticated copy be sent to each of the states. As Congress moved the seat of government during the war and thereafter, the Declaration moved with it, carried with other official papers and without ceremony from place to place, and in the War of 1812, it was spirited away to Leesburg, Virginia, before the British burned Washington. It was only after the war, when Americans felt secure in their land and their government, that a surge of patriotism swept through the nation and the Declaration gained greater symbolic power. When two separate attempts to produce a decorative facsimile led to a publishers' quarrel, Americans became still more aware of their own growing veneration for the document, until by 1824, John Quincy Adams, as secretary of state, was reporting to the Senate that "an exact facsimile, engraved on copperplate, has been made by direction of this department, of the original copy of the Declaration of Independence, engrossed on parchment." "Two hundred copies," he added, "have been struck off from this plate."[13] Now even the desk on which Thomas Jefferson wrote the Declaration became an object of special honor. Presented by him to Joseph Coolidge, Jr., of the State Department Library, it remained there after 1825.

Before mid-century, the Declaration was reposing in the Patent Office Exhibition Hall of the United States. After a Centennial which generated a flood of interest and facsimiles when it was exhibited at Independence Hall in Philadelphia, the Declaration journeyed to the Department of State. At first in a cabinet in the Library and afterwards in a steel safe because the light was fading the ink, it eventually reached the Library of Congress in 1921, visited Fort Knox during World War II, and returned to the Library of Congress in 1944, where Army, Navy, and Marine soldiers guarded it in rotation. But the ultimate reverence had not yet been attained. With the Constitution, which had joined it, the Declaration was moved in 1952 to a new shrine in the National Archives Building. The historian Dumas Malone has detailed the liturgy in which "it was borne down the steps by guards from all the armed services, transported in a tank which breathed defiance against all foreign and domestic enemies, and escorted by service men and women." At the new shrine, the chairman of the Joint Congressional Committee on the Library performed the unveiling, while the chief justice of the Supreme Court presided and the president of the United States spoke. Not inappropriately, Malone has observed that the "present shrine may be regarded as a sarcophagus within which it lies embalmed."[14] In a helium-filled case with special protective glass, the Declaration, with the Constitution, rises each day from a steel vault below where it is guarded by tons of metal.

American historians early acclaimed the power of the Declaration. "From the promulgation of this declaration," David Ramsay wrote, "every thing assumed a new form."[15] Mercy Warren thought it a "celebrated paper" which would "be admired in the annals of every historian" and which "ought to be frequently read by the rising youth of the American states, as a palladium of which they should never lose sight, so long as they wish to continue a free and independent people."[16] Later in the nineteenth century, for George Bancroft the Declaration involved the "reform of the British Parliament, the emancipation of Ireland, the disinthralment of the people of France, the awakening of the nations of Europe. Even Hungary stretched forward to hear from the distance the gladsome sound; the Italians recalled their days of unity and might."[17]

American schoolbooks supported the panegyric by understanding liberty as an undefined and mystical entity which had been central gift of the Declaration. The composition of the document had been the "supreme event in the history of man." The fit response of later generations of schoolchildren was reverence rather than analytical observation.[18] Meanwhile, Moses Coit Tyler, the literary historian, called the Declaration "a kind of war-song," "a stately and passionate chant of human freedom," and "a prose lyric of civil and military heroism." In the early twentieth century, John H. Hazelton's *Declaration of Independence*, with its painstaking almost hour-by-hour scrutiny of the history of the document, was itself indicative of the religious veneration the Declaration inspired.[19] Hazelton and the others had in fact been "historians against history."[20] They were reciting, not a matter-of-fact account of a chronological event, but a sacred history which demanded solemn and serious consideration.

If the document of the Declaration was sacred, so too was the time in which the separation from Britain had occurred and consequently the text had been promulgated. John Adams had predicted the natural liturgy of religious remembrance that would follow the anniversary of the act of separation—"pomp and parades, . . . shows, games, sports, guns, bells, bonfires, and illuminations, from one end of the continent to the other, from this time forward forevermore."[21] The Fourth of July took shape as an annual event during which one left the profane time of ordinary activity and participated in a reality which had happened *in illo tempore*. The Fourth stood outside the ordinary sequence of days and hours because it was sacred time in which the rememberers of the great proclamation no longer merely recollected, but lived the event in its own moment with all the power which the moment unleashed. There were spontaneous celebrations in various places on the first anniversary. The *Pennsylvania Gazette*'s account of festivities (typical) was illuminating, since the ritual imitated in many ways the behavior of citizens in 1776. After armed ships and galleys were drawn up, there was a "discharge of thirteen cannon from each of the ships, and one from each of the thirteen gallies, in honour of the thirteen United States." A Hessian band and *feux de joie* by British deserters combined with toasts, artillery, and music. "The glorious fourth of July was reiterated three times, accompanied with triple discharges of cannon and small arms, and loud huzzas that resounded from street to street throughout the city." There was bell-ringing and a "grand exhibition of fireworks" at night as the day ended with the firing of thirteen rockets.[22]

By the following year, Congress had made Fourth of July celebrations official and in 1779 ordered that "the chaplains of Congress be requested to prepare sermons suitable to the occasion."[23] David Ramsay took note of the new holy day in 1789 by observing that "the anniversary of the day on which this great event took place, has ever since been consecrated by the Americans to religious gratitude, and social pleasures. It is considered by them as the birth day of their freedom."[24] The orations which chaplains and other patriotic Americans preached with "religious gratitude" quickly assumed similar structural characteristics. They opened with a ceremonial recall of the history of the Revolution and tributes to George Washington and the soldiers he had led, then progressed to the main body of the text in which some problem of the union, some point at which corruption was beginning to tarnish the brand-newness, became the focus. One of the chief uses of history for the patriots was the moral lessons it inculcated. Indeed, there was something of the jeremiad in the confident yet tremulous way the Fourth of July sermons embraced the future. There would be a national millennium, provided the patriots lived wholesome lives and did not tamper with government: for they might disturb the fragile structure of liberty which had been completed once and for all in the Revolution. The Declaration was to be contemplated in mythic remembrance, not used to effect change in the present.

Daniel Webster's mid-century eulogy at a Fourth of July ceremony was representative. The Declaration of Independence had now "stood for seventy-five years," and still stood. "It was sealed in blood." The lesson to be learned from its past was that "now, to-day, raising its august form higher than the clouds, twenty millions of people contemplate it with hallowed love, and the world beholds it, and the consequences which have followed from it, with profound admiration." Webster drew his listeners on to the moment of re-creation as he conjured forth the "venerable form" of the father of his country, "dignified and grave," but with "concern and anxiety" which seemed to "soften the lineaments of his countenance." In a climactic prayer to Washington, Webster addressed him:

We cannot, we dare not, we will not, betray our sacred trust. We will not filch from posterity the treasure placed in our hands to be transmitted to other generations. The bow that gilds the clouds in the heavens, the pillars that uphold the firmament, may disappear and fall away in the hour appointed by the will of God; but until that day comes, or so long as our lives may last, no ruthless hand shall undermine that bright arch of Union and Liberty which spans the continent from Washington to California.[25]

Twenty-five years earlier, the patriots had been greeted by a clear sign from Heaven when John Adams and Thomas Jefferson had died within a few hours of each other on the Fourth of July. That Providence should so mark the fiftieth jubilee of the document was an event not to be taken lightly by sons of the men of the Revolution. It was true that Adams and Jefferson had been leaders of contending parties and had been reconciled only in old age, but this fact did not jar the sense of the marvellous, for, if noticed at all, it only underlined the union which had been a sure foundation even when patriots disagreed. The "most prominent act" in the lives of the two, Daniel Webster had declared, had been "their participation in the DECLARATION OF INDEPENDENCE." "ADAMS and JEFFERSON are no more," he told Americans, as any disunion between the two men was lost and forgotten. "On our fiftieth anniversary, the great day of national jubilee, in the very hour of public rejoicing, in the midst of echoing and reëchoing voices of thanksgiving, while their own names were on all tongues, they took their flight together to the world of spirits."[26] It was not surprising that nineteenth-century textbooks followed the interpretive path of Webster and so many others, understanding that the mutual death of these two original patriots on the anniversary of the Declaration of Independence was a certain indication of divine blessing.

Providence had spoken. So long as Americans remained true to the ideals which Adams and Jefferson had enunciated with the other patriots in the Declaration of Independence, a future of unending progress lay ahead. The rhetorical questions of John Quincy Adams on another Fourth of July were only an anagogical step away.

Is it not that, in the chain of human events, the birth-day of the nation is indissolubly linked with the birth-day of the Saviour? That it forms a leading event in the progress of the gospel dispensation? Is it not that the Declaration of Independence first organized the social compact on the foundation of the Redeemer's mission upon earth? That it laid the cornerstone of human government upon the first precepts of Christianity, and gave to the world the first irrevocable pledge of the fulfilment of the prophecies, announced directly from Heaven at the birth of the Saviour and predicted by the greatest of the Hebrew prophets six hundred years before?[27]

As their fathers before them, nineteenth-century patriots, caught in the ambiguity of their religious center, embraced at once their Christian and revolutionary sacred histories and simultaneously tried to grasp the past and the future. But their fathers' generation had known another ambiguity as well, for the men of the Revolution had received the Declaration in the context of a dissolution of forms which would precede the new creation. Event more than sacrament, it tooks its existence from that body of individuals who provided a semblance of structure while the world turned upside down. Before the Declaration had come to be, there had been other acts and men who acted in the Continental Congress. Like the leadership of a national church, Congress had been at work, and it would continue to be at work after the Declaration had been promulgated. The national priests were performing the functions appropriate to authority in an ecclesiastical situation: teaching and preaching, governing and celebrating. In a real sense, the sacraments of American civil religion were the offspring of this hierarchy which guarded the myth even as it was being lived at the center of a social universe. The action of Congress, for the most part spanning the years between the Declaration and the Constitution, returns us to the side of the revolutionary dialectic in which events were primary.

The patriots recognized their priests and gave them the veneration that was fitting. When delegates from Massachusetts Bay and Connecticut arrived in New York on their way to Philadelphia to attend the Continental Congress, "the roads were lined with a greater number of people than were ever known on any occasion before. Their arrival was announced by the ringing of bells, and other demonstrations of joy."[28] The *Virginia Gazette* reported that the "eastern delegates" who reached Philadelphia were "met about six miles out by the officers of all the companies in the city, and by many other gentlemen on horseback, in all amounting to five hundred."

When they came within two miles of the city they were met by the company of riflemen, and a company of infantry, with a band of music, who conducted them through the most public streets of the city to their lodgings, amidst the acclamations of near fifteen thousand spectators.[29]

Peyton Randolph, "late president of the Grand Continental Congress," journeyed home from the congressional city with similar acclaim. The newspaper told how he was escorted from Ruffin's

Ferry to Williamsburg by detachments of cavalry and infantry.
When Randolph and the military arrived about sunset,

the bells began to ring as our worthy delegate entered the city, and
the unfeigned joy of the inhabitants, on this occasion, was visible in
every countenance; there were illuminations in the evening, and the
volunteers, with many other respectable gentlemen, assembled at the
Raleigh, spent an hour or two in harmony and cheerfulness, and drank
several patriotic toasts.[30]

Recipient of the collective reverence, Congress quickly assumed
a theological function and began interpreting events in religious
terms and exhorting other patriots on doctrine and morality. Edward F. Humphrey was well aware of the role which Congress
had appropriated when he wrote in 1924:

The proclamations and other state papers of Continental Congress are
so filled with Biblical phrases as to resemble Old Testament ecclesias-
tical documents. They unabashedly exhibit a belief in a Protestant
Christianity and they invoke, as a sanction for their acts, the name of
"God," "Almighty God," "God of Armies," "Lord of Hosts," "His
Goodness," "God's Superintending Providence," "Providence of God,"
"Providence," "Supreme and Universal Providence," "Overruling
Providence of God," "Creator of All," "Indulgent Creator," "Great
Governor of the World," "The Divinity," "Supreme Judge of Religion," "Jesus Christ," "God and the Constitution," and "Free Prot-
estant Colonies." *Their extreme insistence upon the religious sanction
may be explained in part by the fact that the Government was without
definite legislative authority*; this deficiency could be remedied in no
other way so well as by a reliance upon religion.[31]

One need only casually peruse the Journals of Congress to corrob-
orate the Humphrey assessment. Particularly in 1774, Congress
seemed to do little besides issuing resolutions and proclamations
which stated colonial grievances and rights as they stood under
the eye of God. But as the early years faded and the years of the
war began to pass, Congress made progressively fewer pronouncements which required any reference to the foundation of things
in God and busied itself more and more with mundane affairs
such as the disposition and pay of the Continental Army. Aware

of a transcendent otherness in their collective endeavor, the patriots unconsciously turned less and less for support to God.

Yet the shift was decidedly gradual. Throughout the war years,
Congress continued in its self-appointed task of providing a nu-
cleus for a civil and national church understood in Christian
terms. For its own edification—and no doubt that of other patriots too—it sought regular chaplains and prayer at its sessions.
Only a day after its initial meeting on September 5, 1774, the Continental Congress was resolving that "the reverend Mr. Duche be
desired to open the Congress to-morrow morning with prayers,
at the Carpenter's Hall at nine o'clock."[32] Similarly, Congress appointed army chaplains, paid them, and granted bounties after
military service. It encouraged the general religious efforts of the
chaplains during their tours of duty and their special observances
for congressionally inspired days of fast and thanksgiving as well.

Congressmen edified the general public and one another in the
rituals they honored. It was unthinkable for Congress to meet on
the sabbath. Should one of their number die, Congress issued its
standard resolution that members "in a body, attend the funeral
this evening, at six o'clock, as mourners, with a crape round the
left arm" and "continue in mourning for the space of one
month."[33] When the interruption of regular commerce with Britain led to a scarcity of Bibles in America, Congress gravely appointed a committee. In 1777, its members reported that "the use
of the Bible is so universal, and its importance so great" that Congress should "order the Committee of Commerce to import 20,000
Bibles from Holland, Scotland, or elsewhere, into the different
parts of the States of the Union."[34] But there were difficulties in
such a course. Four years later, the Reverend Robert Aitken was
seeking congressional aid to print an American edition of the
Bible.

Whereupon, *Resolved*, That the United States, in Congress assembled,
highly approve of the pious and laudable undertaking of Mr. Aitken,
as subserviant to the interests of religion, as well as an instance of the
progress of the fine arts in this country; and, being satisfied . . . of

his care and accuracy in the execution of the work, they recommend this edition of the Bible to the inhabitants of the United States, and hereby authorize him to publish this recommendation in the manner he shall think proper.[35]

Not only did Congress encourage doctrinal and moral edification indirectly, but it also involved itself in the restraint of extravagance and the moral purification of community life. Certainly, there had been precedent for the congressional concern: the Massachusetts House of Representatives, with the Puritan theocratic ideal as backdrop, had found nothing unusual in passing resolves for the "suppression of Extravagance, Idleness and Vice and promoting Industry, Economy and good morals also to discountenance the use of foreign superfluities." Quaker Philadelphia had likewise tried to restrain the expenses of funerals after the Stamp Act went into effect by inspiring such deeds of patriotic abnegation as burial in an oaken coffin with iron handles or interment without a pall or mourning-dress.[36] The impulse for such moral rigor came from ascetic instinct as much as economic boycott. Six weeks after their convocation, the members of the Continental Congress were acting like the collected sons of thunder, blending moral fervor with economic need, as they resolved to

encourage frugality, economy, and industry, and promote agriculture, arts and the manufactures of this country, especially that of wool; and . . . discountenance and discourage every species of extravagance and dissipation, especially all horse-racing, and all kinds of gaming, cockfighting, exhibitions of shews, plays, and other expensive diversions and entertainments; and on the death of any relation or friend, none of us, or any of our families, will go into any further mourning-dress, than a black crape or ribbon on the arm or hat, for gentlemen, and a black ribbon and necklace for ladies, and we will discontinue the giving of gloves and scarves at funerals.[37]

Since the army was also a congressional responsibility, the members obliged with disciplinary pronouncements for the soldiers, whose virtue, Congress was determined, would be preserved. No "suttler" would "be permitted to sell any kind of liquors or victuals, or to keep their houses or shops open, for the entertainment of soldiers, after nine at night, or before the beating of the reveilles, or upon Sundays, during divine service or sermon, on the penalty of being dismissed from all future suttling."[38] Congress took itself seriously, for in 1778 when the Marquis de Lafayette invited the president of Congress to accompany him to a play, Henry Laurens of South Carolina politely excused himself. Pressed by the marquis, Laurens informed him that "Congress having that day passed a resolution, recommending to the several States to enact laws for the suppression of theatrical amusements, he could not possibly do himself the honor of waiting upon him to the play."[39]

The religious vocation of Congress reached its theocratic heights, however, in the proclamations of days of fast and thanksgiving which fostered moral regeneration and at the same time the collective identification of patriots. Winthrop Hudson has traced the custom of the fast days from Puritan to English roots and has stressed the Deuteronomic understanding of history which accompanied them by calling Thanksgiving the American Sukkoth, and fasts the American Days of Atonement.[40] With such a history, fasts and thanksgivings were well suited to a people who invoked Jehovah, God of Battles. The congressional keepers of the keys took up the practices of their Christian past and used them to articulate the meanings of their own evolving civil religion. Beginning in July 1775 with "Congress Sunday," the leaders of the patriots generally declared a fast day each spring and a thanksgiving each fall, following the New England tradition. Predictably, it was "recommended to Christians, of all denominations, to assemble for public worship, and to abstain from servile labour and recreation on said day."[41]

Americans took the declarations of the Continental Congress at their word. Writing from Philadelphia, John Adams assessed that Congress Sunday "was observed here with a decorum and solemnity never before seen on a Sabbath. The clergy of all denominations here preached upon politics and war in a manner that I never heard in New England. They are a flame of fire."[42] The Presbyterian Synod of New York and Philadelphia, which had appointed its own fast day for the end of June 1775, had made provision that if there should be a congressional fast, it should "be observed in preference to the day appointed by themselves, provided that it is not more than four weeks distant from the last Thursday of June; if at a greater distance, they have ordered both days to be kept."[43] Those who violated fasts or thanksgivings by engaging in social frivolity were decried by the press and frowned upon by their more serious brethren. At the same time, most experienced no conflict between the exhortations of Congress and their traditional Christianity.

Yet a few were not so sanguine. At least Eleazar Wheelock, the president of Dartmouth, refused to keep a congressional thanksgiving proclaimed at Exeter after he had already observed one. "I had ever been from the first steadily and firmly attached to the constitutional rights and liberties of the Colonies," he wrote in his own defense, "but the making such a solemn offering to God as had been proposed, purely and only out of respect and obedience to the advice of Congress, would be an open affront to the King of Zion unprecedented in America, and expressive of a principle abhorred by all protestants."[44]

Wheelock was a purist, but most of the patriots, not so rigorously inclined, preferred to unite the need for moral purity to the usefulness of a grand collective ritual in which they could experience their oneness. This did not mean that the patriots and their leaders had "secular" motives for their religiosity but rather that, with the liminal awareness they possessed, they were yoking the symbols of traditional religion to the emerging religion of the Revolution. And, as we have seen, value was a kind of ultimate for Americans, an ultimate which was expressed in the material order by utility. To say that Americans engaged in ritual exchanges on days of fast and thanksgiving because they were socially and psychologically useful was not to question the religious significance of these days, for utility existed at the core of patriotic religion. The record of congressional proclamation argued in the same direction. Days of fast and thanksgiving were regularly solemnized during the war, while in 1783, the year of victory and peace, there was only a thanksgiving, and in succeeding years neither fasts nor thanksgivings.[45] Just as Jehovah, God of Battles, had disappeared in the centrality of deeds of war, the God of Congress receded in the reality of national success and the humdrum of the ordinary tasks of legislation.

During the Revolution, however, Congress kept the Christian ritual trappings, yet more and more adapted them to the emerging humanocentric religion by, for example, proclaiming memorials for military and diplomatic victories gained in the war. Thus, after the victory over Cornwallis, Congress "determined to go in solemn procession to the Dutch Lutheran church, to return thanks to Almighty God, for crowning the allied arms with success by the surrender of the whole British army." Declaring the customary thanksgiving, Congress also resolved that "a marble column should be erected at Yorktown in Virginia with emblems of the alliance between the United States and his most christian majesty, and inscribed with a succinct narrative of the surrender of Earl Cornwallis to his excellency general Washington."[46]

The commander-in-chief and Americans generally needed no prodding for such civil celebrations. Washington, after the victory of Horatio Gates at Saratoga, had issued orders that "every face brighten, and every heart expand with grateful Joy and praise to the supreme disposer of all events, who has granted us this signal success." Army chaplains were to "prepare short discourses, suited to the joyful occasion to deliver to their several corps," while at Cambridge there were spontaneous demonstrations with bonfires and illuminations, toasts and the discharge of ceremonial cannons.[47] Newspapers in early 1779 carried reports of popular celebrations of the anniversary of the French alliance. The birthday of King Louis XVI was commemorated that August with union flags decorating the ships in the Philadelphia harbor, bells ringing, fireworks exploding, and rounds of ammunition fired.[48] Congress had blessed the spontaneity and provided for its regular recurrence through a series of reminders such as the marble column which it planned to erect at Yorktown. Medals were awarded to the "heroes" in successful military encounters. As early as the spring of 1776, a special medal was struck and distributed by order of Congress among the officers in the Continental Army. The *Middlesex Journal* reported that one side bore the imprint of "two vases swimming on the water, with the motto, *Frangimur si Collidimur* [we will break if we collide]," while on the other side was "an emblematical device: four hands clinched together, and a dove over them; beneath them . . . a serpent cut in pieces."[49]

Meanwhile, the flag which had flown over Continental Army camps merged its identity in 1777 with a flag of congressional resolution, "thirteen stripes, alternate red and white," and the union symbolized by "thirteen stars white in a blue field, representing a new constellation."[50] The patriots had striven earnestly for symbolic precision as though, by pinning their symbol to an almost logical consistency, they could guarantee the purity and vigor of their newness. One member of the Continental Congress recalled the fervor of detail which accompanied the emergence of the national flag.

The stars of the new flag represent the new constellation of States rising in the West. The idea was taken from the constellation Lyra, which in the hand of Orpheus signifies harmony. The blue in the field was taken from the edges of the Covenanters' banner in Scotland, significant of the league and covenant of the United Colonies against oppression, incidentally involving the virtues of vigilance, perseverance, and justice. The stars were in a circle, symbolizing the perpetuity of the Union—the ring, like the circling serpent of the Egyptians, signifying eternity. The thirteen stripes showed, with the stars, the number of the United Colonies, and denoted the subordination of the States of the Union, as well as equality among themselves. The whole was the blending of the various flags previous to the Union flag, viz.: the red flags of the army and the white of the floating batteries. The red color, which in Roman days was the signal of defiance, denotes daring; and the white, purity.[51]

In similar fashion, seals were created for various governmental departments such as the treasury, the navy, and the admiralty. But the search for symbolic exactness was nowhere more evident than in the creation of the Great Seal of the United States. Significantly, Congress had appointed a committee to design a seal on July 4, 1776. It was a prestigious group—Benjamin Franklin, John Adams, and Thomas Jefferson—which met and reported to the full congressional body in late August, and the divisions among committee members were indicative of the ambivalence of Americans about their own religious identity. John Adams explained to Abigail what the discussions of the committee had produced for Congress to consider.

Dr. F. proposes a device for a seal: Moses lifting up his wand and dividing the Red Sea, and Pharaoh in his chariot overwhelmed with the waters. This motto, "Rebellion to tyrants is obedience to God."

Mr. Jefferson proposed the children of Israel in the wilderness, led by a cloud by day and a pillar of fire by night; and on the other side, Hengist and Horsa, the Saxon chiefs from whom we claim the honor of being descended, and whose political principles and form of government we have assumed.

I proposed the choice of Hercules, as engraved by Gribelin, in some editions of Lord Shaftesbury's works. The hero resting on his club. Virtue pointing to her rugged mountain on one hand, and persuading him to ascend. Sloth, glancing at her flowery paths of pleasure, wantonly reclining on the ground, displaying the charms both of her eloquence and person, to seduce him into vice.[52]

With such diversity from leading men of the Revolution, it was not surprising that the report of the committee was tabled. New committees took up the work of designing the seal in 1780 and 1782. By the time the committee of 1780 had reported, Moses, the children of Israel, and Hercules had all disappeared to be replaced by "the Figure of Liberty seated in a chair holding the staff and cap."[53] The committee of 1782 was at last successful in persuading Congress to adopt its design: the familiar eagle with olive branch and thirteen arrows announcing "E pluribus Unum," while on the back, an unfinished pyramid was surmounted by an undesignated Eye.[54] *Novus ordo saeclorum* had begun, and the patriots had perhaps unconsciously made some fundamental decisions concerning their own religious orientation. Natural and humanocentric religion had won an edge over the new Israel, although it would be clear as the future of the republic unfolded that a chosen people was still, though in thisworldly fashion, pursuing its errand into the wilderness.

As the congressional hierarchy dealt in monuments and medals, in flags and seals for national identification, it was engaged in the task of inventing sacramental signs. Religiously, the most profound problem with their endeavor was the fact of invention, since sacraments had always been discovered and encountered in their otherness which pointed beyond themselves to power. They had emerged without control from subjective and unconscious centers, quite literally possessing a life of their own. But the new sacraments which had come into being by congressional and committee fiat were the creations of their masters, so that as sacramental centers they seemed deficient. Still, what the Continental Congress could not give to these symbols, the people would be able to confer if they should adopt them as their own, charging them with the energy which came from their affirmation of themselves as a nation. This process occurred most perceptibly in the case of the Constitution of the United States, the greatest sacramental sign of the new republic, one which issued only indirectly from Congress and which at the same time indicated with strongest clarity the anthropocentric direction of the new civil religion.

There is an old anecdote which reflected what had happened at the Constitutional Convention.

It is said that, after the convention had adjourned, Rev. Dr. Miller, a distinguished professor in Princeton College, met Alexander Hamilton in the streets of Philadelphia, and said, "Mr. Hamilton, we are greatly grieved that the Constitution has no recognition of God or the Christian religion." "I declare," said Hamilton, "we forgot it!"[55]

The Hamilton remark was symptomatic. Although it may have been true that, as Benjamin Rush wrote to Richard Price, "the same enthusiasm *now* pervades all classes in favor of *government* that actuated us in favor of *liberty* in the years 1774 and 1775," there were also some significant differences.[56] For one, even Nature's God had been relegated to nongoverning bliss, while the natural law, which disclosed in unalienable rights and reason the workings of his general providence, had all but disappeared. Throughout the debates of the Convention, there was little discussion of natural rights and the consent of the governed. As Roger Sherman understood it, the question was, "not what rights naturally belong to man, but how they may be most equally and effectually guarded in society." "Experience," John Dickinson thought, "must be our only guide. Reason may mislead us. It was not reason that discovered the singular and admirable mechanism of the English constitution."[57]

Nature's God was not governing, but Jehovah had also been repudiated. Luther Martin remarked that when it was decided that there should be no religious test for the holding of any federal office, there were some few members "*so unfashionable* as to think that a *belief of the existence of a Deity*, and of a *state of future rewards and punishments* would be some security for the good conduct of our rulers."[58] Just how unfashionable the affirmation of the deity had become grew evident when, after the delegates had been stymied for some time over the question of representation in Congress, Benjamin Franklin asked rhetorically, "How has it happened . . . that we have not hitherto once thought of humbly applying to the Father of lights to illuminate our understandings?" Franklin went on to recall the frequent recourse to prayer which had characterized the patriots during the Revolution and to affirm "*that God Governs in the affairs of men*." "And if a sparrow cannot fall to the ground without his notice,

is it probable that an empire can rise without his aid?" He concluded with a request for official prayer by the clergy in the
assembly each morning, an appeal which in the context seemed a
further confirmation of the pragmatism of Franklin's own religious orientation. Yet the response of Franklin's fellow-delegates
was more pragmatic still. Alexander Hamilton and others voiced
their objection that such a course might "lead the public to believe that the embarrassments and dissensions within the Convention, had suggested this measure." Significantly, Edmund Randolph tried to break the impasse by proposing "that a sermon be
preached at the request of the convention on *4th of July, the anniversary of Independence;* & thenceforward prayers be used in yᵉ
Convention every morning." Yet even this compromise in the direction of civil religion did not sit well with the erstwhile followers of Jehovah, and the session adjourned without any vote
having been taken.[59]

The delegates to the Federal Convention remained within the
protective structure of their mythic worldview, however, even
though they were willing to consign the Almighty to oblivion.
They knew that perfection had been theirs in the newness of
Revolution and feared the ever-present danger of a fall from grace
as they grew further away from the strength of the time of origins. Gouverneur Morris, George Mason, and James Wilson had
all expressed their apprehension concerning "cabal and corruption" in the mode of electing a president. Mason had in addition
"moved without success for a power to make sumptuary regulations."

After descanting on the extravagance of our manners, the excessive
consumption of foreign superfluities, and the necessity of restricting it,
as well with economical as republican views, he moved that a committee be appointed to report articles of association for encouraging,
by the advice, the influence, and the example, of the members of the
Convention, economy, frugality, and American manufactures.[60]

The frequent discussion of the need for checks and balances in
government issued from the same suspicion of the corruptibility

of latter-day patriots. James Madison captured the delegates' fears when he judged that "democratic communities may be unsteady, and be led to action by the impulse of the moment.—Like individuals they may be sensible of their own weakness, and may desire the counsels and checks of friends to guard them against the turbulency and weakness of unruly passions."[61]

Thus, an important consideration throughout the debates of the Convention was how to preserve liberty in its revolutionary purity and at the same time create a reservoir of power from which "energy in government" could flow. There was perhaps a lingering, though unconscious, perception of original sin as the delegates pondered, and a simultaneous willingness to take the risks which the consolidation of power involved. Power had always been an ambivalent reality: the person or persons who dealt with it had to be strong enough for the encounter with forces which were equally capable of enhancing or destroying human life. The delegates understood the dangers and saw, as Bernard Bailyn has observed, that power was the natural enemy of liberty and yet could be properly channeled in a government of checks and balances.[62] Thus, the Constitution became understood as an arrangement for handling the two-edged sword of power. For the final word of the patriots, as they presented their document for public consideration and ratification, was that the people could regulate themselves and trust their representatives with the temptations of governmental power.

The ambiguities which were interwoven with American structures of consciousness had reached social and political expression in the Constitution, but here the patriots thought that at last they had reconciled them. John Dickinson, advocating the particular checks he deemed most useful, grew eloquent in his belief that "a government thus established would harmonize the whole, and like the planetary system, the national council like the sun, would illuminate the whole—the planets revolving round it in perfect order."[63] Others were in substantial agreement with Dickinson. While the last members were signing the finished document, Benjamin Franklin remarked that he was finally certain that the sun which had been painted behind the president's chair was "a rising, and not a setting sun."[64] The American Revolution was not over. As Benjamin Rush had said in 1787, the Revolution had just begun.

There is nothing more common, than to confound the terms of *American Revolution* with those of *the late American war*. The American war is over; but this is far from being the case with the American revolution. On the contrary, nothing but the first act of the great drama is closed. It remains yet to establish and perfect our new forms of government; and to prepare the principles, morals, and manners of our citizens, for these forms of government, after they are established and brought to perfection.[65]

What the patriots were groping to express was their sense that the Constitution would insure the continual regeneration of the republic. "If the new Constitution be examined with accuracy and candor," James Madison wrote in *The Federalist Papers*, "it will be found that the change which it proposes consists much less in the addition of NEW POWERS to the Union, than in the invigoration of its ORIGINAL POWERS."[66] The Articles of Confederation had mediated these original powers by pledging the states to "perpetual union," but the powers themselves had issued from the people in the act of revolution. More and more, Americans had looked for a way to guarantee that they could tap the energy of their act in each successive stage of their history. They had come to regard the work of the convention as the task of making the power of the new creation accessible to the future. The foundation they were institutionalizing had become manifest as what John Adams had called in 1766 "*stamina vitae*, or essentials and fundamentals of the constitution; parts, without which, life itself cannot be preserved a moment."[67]

This "roots-of life" understanding of the Constitution was part of the novelty of the *novus ordo saeclorum*. Traditionally, *constitution* had been a term which designated a general collection of laws, customs, and institutions required in the governance of the state. It was the child of whatever legislators happened to believe or desire, and far from setting a limit to their arbitrariness, it could be the result. The British did not *create* a constitution, nor did they transcribe it in a single document. Their "constitution" existed only in retrospect through the force of tradition. But in the prerevolutionary era, Americans had begun to shift away from this inherited understanding and had started to develop a conceptualization in which a constitution became an absolute which could limit a lawmaking body.

The patriots recognized the newness of their proposition. According to James Madison, "The important distinction so well understood in America between a Constitution established by the government and alterable by the government, seems to have been little understood and less observed in any other country." Even in England, Madison reminded his fellow-citizens, Parliament had been "transcendent and uncontrollable."[68] The American Constitution, by contrast, was to be the new covenant of the people whose collective action had generated it as the "roots of life." Their deed of revolution had given strength to their word of government. Now that word would become a ground for all future decision and action.

It was true that the new covenant had first to make its way among all the covenanters. There was intense disagreement concerning the merits of the proposed document when it was initially communicated to patriots-at-large. Delegates Elbridge Gerry, George Mason, and Edmund Randolph had perhaps already indicated that there would be problems by their own refusal to sign. Later, opposition in some quarters—such as the Massachusetts circle of Mercy Otis Warren—was bitter, while even individuals like James Monroe voiced their objections in milder terms.[69] Indeed, Warren would later assure readers of her history that Franklin had signed the new Constitution "with tears, and apologized for doing it at all, from the doubts and apprehensions he felt, that his countrymen might not be able to do better, even if they called a new convention."[70] Mordecai Myers recalled in his memoirs the protests against ratification in New York where "mobs and riots were common, the Democratic printing office of [Thomas] Greenleaf was attacked, and the type scattered in the street."[71] Earlier, there had been much ill feeling over the secrecy of the Convention, "lest," as Mercy Warren complained, "their consultations and debates should be viewed by the scrutinizing eye of a free people." "We the People of the United States," who according to the Preamble had ordained and established "this Constitution for the United States of America," had in fact done so mostly because of the decision of the Committee of Style. Finally, after pressure was exerted by a number of the states at the time of ratification, the decision came to amend the Constitution immediately with a Bill of Rights.[72]

But New Hampshire and Virginia had no sooner fallen into line with their ratification votes—which insured that the Constitution was now the law of the land—than ranks closed among the patriots, disagreement ceased, and almost overnight, worship of the document began. "Opposition to the Constitution as a constitution, and even hostile criticism of its provisions, ceased almost immediately upon its adoption," wrote Woodrow Wilson, "and not only ceased, but gave place to an undiscriminating and almost blind worship of its principles, and of that delicate dual system of sovereignty, and that complicated scheme of double administration which it established."[73]

The power that had come from the people in their act of revolution had come from the collective strength and will of the people *united*. As we have seen, protestations of oneness seemed to be made most strenuously when the greatest threats of division and fragmentation were present. Even as the natural rights philosophy was growing less fashionable, the atomistic social and governmental cosmology which supported it continued. There was in American society a clear and frank avowal of individualism; as the patriots pulled hard in one direction, they seemed to tug with equal fervor on the opposite side. Reconciliation, if it came at all, arose from a theoretical vision of the monads in a political universe which harmoniously circled the center without collision, at once serving themselves and serving the whole. "Society is composed of individuals," Enos Hitchcock declaimed in an oration celebrating both the Fourth of July and the ratification of the Constitution. "They are parts of the whole,—and when each one moves in his own orb, and fills his own station, the system will be complete."[74]

Hence, precisely because of their manyness, the patriots worked hard to celebrate their oneness around the Constitution. The adulation with which they speedily began to praise the work of their leaders was an exercise not only in national self-congratulation but also in the need for unity. And the adulation was everywhere forthcoming. Jonathan Boucher, the Loyalist, dourly commented from England that he was "conscious that the only very strong point in the present Constitution of these States is in the attachment and partiality of their people for it." Americans, he grumbled, were "blind" and "commendably blind" to "the defects of their present system."[75]

Newspapers of the period were an apt illustration of Boucher's point. While the former Virginia clergyman was marking the defects, the *Connecticut Gazette* was anticipating "the praise with which the new federal government will be viewed by the friends of liberty and mankind in Europe." With millennial exuberance, it noted that "the philosophers will no longer consider a republic as an impracticable form of government; and pious men of all denominations will thank God for having provided in our Federal Constitution an ark, for the preservation of the justice and liberties of the world."[76] The *New York Packet* had expressed equal confidence that "the cloud which gathers in the European hemisphere serves as a foil, to set off the luster of the prospect that opens upon America. While the ancient establishments of the world are rent with civil discord and national contention, this infant empire deliberately examines her present wants and weaknesses, in order to provide for her future strength and glory."[77]

In the atmosphere of collective euphoria, the word *federal* quickly assumed a symbolic import which made it a standard invocation to bless any project. By 1788, this addition to American popular vocabulary appeared on the masthead of a spate of news-papers such as *The Federal Herald* of Albany, *The Federal Gazette, and the Philadelphia Evening Post*, and *The Federal Post* of Trenton. A *Federal Almanack* appeared for the year 1789, a *Federal Harmony* for voice, and a *New Constitution March and Federal Minuet* for "pianoforte, Violin and German Flute."[78]

Orators began to hail the federal document with millenary zeal. Aaron Hall of New Hampshire celebrated that state's ratification of the Constitution in 1788 by telling his fellow-patriots that "the frame of government now adopted for the United States of America, gives her citizens rank, if not superiority among the nations of the earth." "Till this period," he continued, "the revolution in America, has never appeared to me to be completed; but this is laying on the cap-stone of the great American Empire." It was "a very critical moment with America," he warned, for "the eyes of Europe, and the world, are upon us."[79] In New Haven at a Fourth of July oration the same year, Simeon Baldwin echoed Hall's message: "A part of the debt which the citizen owes to the soldier and to his country, is, to complete the revolution and to secure its blessings, by a liberal, free, and efficacious government. In vain have we struggled against the grasp of despotism, if we degenerate into licentiousness and anarchy." Perhaps the Constitution was "not the best possible," he said with a bow toward modesty. "But we boldly assert that in theory it appears to be the best form of government that has ever been offered to the world. . . . Language cannot praise it more." Baldwin ran through the scale of American achievements and then pulled out all stops: "If such effusions of genius distinguish the infancy of this nation, what may we expect when she [*sic*] shall ripen into manhood! . . . It would not require the warmth of enthusiasm to embellish the piece."[80]

In Providence, Enos Hitchcock's oration was similar in content and tone as he told his listeners that "a revolution can never be considered as complete till government is firmly established—and without this independency would be a curse instead of a blessing—

These jointly were the great object of the American revolution."
It was clear that America would be recorded in history without
peer, for "after ages of fruitless attempts in other countries, this
country affords the first instance of an entire revolution in policy
and government, the most important that ever marked the progress of human society, without the effusion of human blood, without force, fraud or surprize." With such a deed as warrant, Hitchcock's vision was classical.

The vast tracts of uncultivated lands, and their rapid population, present us with the most extensive theatre for human action, and the
most magnificent empire on which the sun ever shone. Hither shall
the oppressed of all nations flee for safety, and find a refuge from the
encroachments of restless ambition!—The hand of industry shall
change the haunts of wild beasts into fruitful fields—the wilderness
shall blossom as a rose—the desert become vocal with the praises of
God. The friendly bosom of the earth shall nourish and unfold to her
noble lord, the illustrious farmer, her inexhaustible sources of support
and wealth—and pour forth her blessings, through the extended chan-
nels of trade and commerce, to all quarters of the globe.[81]

As ratification of the Constitution proceeded, rituals of accla-
mation spread from state to state. In Georgia, the fourth state to
indicate approval, there was "a salute of thirteen guns in token of
faith that every state would accede to the new bonds of union."
In Boston, after Massachusetts ratified, wrote George Bancroft,
"the bells and artillery announced the glad news to every part of
town." "The Boston people," exclaimed one correspondent, "have
lost the senses with joy." Bancroft noted that "with the declaration of the vote, every symptom of persistent opposition vanished.
No person even wished for a protest." New York celebrated as
men "hoisted the pine tree flag with an appropriate inscription.
Six states had ratified, and six salutes, each of thirteen guns, were
fired."[82] Mordecai Myers remembered the procession which followed, organized by various civic and trade groups throughout
the city and coordinated under a central corporation.

The governor, both branches of the legislature, the judges, the members of the bar, the officers of the courts, officers of the army and

navy, the mayor and corporation, and other city officers, took part in the procession. All the mechanical trades were represented by men engaged at their respective occupations in cars mounted on trucks. The ship carpenters contributed a miniature frigate of thirty-six guns, completely rigged, armed, and manned. She was called the "United States," and commanded by Commodore Francis Nicholson. Her crew consisted of young lads dressed as sailors, her sails were loosed and sheeted home, and her guns were loaded and fired. This attracted great attention. During the day, the streets were crowded with people, and the houses were decorated with flags.

Nighttime brought "extensive fireworks" with "all places of amusement . . . opened and thronged. Most of the houses and public buildings were illuminated. It was near morning before the streets were again quiet."[83]

New York was typical, for as David Ramsay recorded, the ratification of the Constitution was "celebrated in most of the capitals of the states with elegant processions, which far exceeded any thing of the kind ever before exhibited in America."[84] Probably the most memorable procession occurred in Philadelphia on the Fourth of July 1788 in a spectacle which combined at their height the elaborate stage-managing of the planners and the spontaneous enthusiasm of the people. It was liturgy in the fullest sense. Francis Hopkinson, who had chaired the Grand Federal Procession, issued a complete report.

Sunrise had been greeted by a "full peal" of bells from the steeple of Christ Church, while in the harbor, ten vessels for the ten states which by that time had ratified the Constitution sailed into view, each bearing a white flag with the name of a state engraved in gold. On the city streets, companies of soldiers, tradesmen, and professionals were already marching to the place where they would meet to form one great procession.

The order of march was a masterpiece of studied symbolic detail as eighty-eight divisions extended in a line that was about a mile and a half long. First came "twelve axe-men, dressed in white frocks, with black girdles round their waists, and ornamented caps," followed by a troop of dragoons and a man on horseback, "bearing the staff and cap of liberty; under the cap, a silk flag with the words *fourth of July*, 1776,' in large gold letters." There was a division of artillery behind which Thomas Fitzsimmons rode, carrying a white flag with three fleurs-de-lys and thirteen stars in union over the words "sixth of February, 1778." A corps of light infantry preceded another horseman with a staff in hand, decorated with olive and laurel and bearing the legend, "third of September, 1783." Now came Colonel John Shea on horseback, his flag with a blue field on which the olive and laurel stood over the words which had been inscribed in silver: "Washington, the friend of his country." Further along, Richard Bache on his horse played the part of a herald whose trumpet displayed hanging from its staff the golden words "new era." The thirteenth division was titled THE CONSTITUTION, and three judges including the chief justice wore their official robes, sitting "in a lofty ornamental car, in the form of a large eagle, drawn by six horses, bearing the constitution, framed, and fixed on a staff, crowned with the cap of liberty. The words, *the people*,' in gold letters, on one staff, immediately under the constitution."

Consuls and foreign dignitaries walked in the parade along with officials who carried symbolic reminders of their functions. A citizen and an Indian chief sat in procession "in a carriage, smoking the calumet of peace together." They were followed by what must have been the most celebrated exhibit.

The new roof, or grand federal edifice, on a carriage drawn by ten white horses; the dome supported by thirteen Corinthian columns, raised on pedestals proper to that order; the frieze decorated with thirteen stars; ten of the columns complete, and three left unfinished: on the pedestals of the columns were inscribed, in ornamental cyphers, the initials of the thirteen American states. On the top of the dome, a handsome cupola, surmounted by a figure of Plenty, bearing her cornucopiae, and other emblems of her character.

Around the pedestal were the words, "In union the fabric stands firm." Appropriately, after the "new roof" marched architects and house-carpenters, followed by saw-makers and file-cutters.

On the floor of the building, ten symbolic "citizens" who had ratified the Constitution sat on chairs.

"The federal ship Union" seemed the only adequate competition for the float. Thirty-three feet long and mounted on a carriage drawn by ten horses, it boasted a canvas "scene" tacked around it and painted to represent the sea. Behind it came the pilots of the port with their own ship, "the Federal Pilot," and every conceivable trade and profession. There were ship carpenters and boat builders; sail makers and ship joiners; rope makers and ship chandlers. Merchants and traders joined cordwainers and coach painters. Cabinet and chair-makers carried signs inscribed "Federal cabinet and chair-shop," while brick-makers bore aloft a flag with a federal city building and the inscription, "It was found hard in Egypt, But this prospect makes it easy." Porters carried sacks of "federal flour," and coach-makers announced "no tax on American carriages." The tallow chandlers carried a flag imprinted with a chandelier of thirteen branches and thirteen silver stars in a half circle, proclaiming "the stars of America, a light to the world." Meanwhile, printers, bookbinders, and stationers walked beside a "federal printing press." An ode, which Francis Hopkinson had composed for the occasion, was distributed to spectators by Mercury, the messenger of the gods, while "pidgeons" flew from his cap to the ten states. In the midst, marching together in one division were "the clergy of the different christian denominations, with the rabbi of the Jews, walking arm in arm."[85] Benjamin Rush, commenting on this clerical contingent in an enthusiastic letter to a friend, told him that "pains were taken to connect ministers of the most dissimilar religious principles together, thereby to show the influence of a free government in promoting Christian charity."[86]

Unconsciously, Rush had said considerably more than he might have been comfortable with in the form of reasoned argument: the Procession was an elaborate and dramatic sermon on the true source of union among Americans. Representatives of traditional religious bodies had quietly taken their place among the rank and file of the parade, all innocent variations on the grand theme of a unity which had its ultimate ground in the religion of the republic and the Constitution, its most cherished sacrament. Hopkinson delivered the message clearly and noted with satisfaction that "universal love and harmony prevailed, and every countenance appeared to be the index of a heart glowing with urbanity and rational joy." Since he estimated that about five thousand had marched and seventeen thousand had gathered in Union Green, the destination of the Procession, with "the footways, the windows and roofs of the houses . . . crouded with spectators" along the way, Hopkinson had cause to be pleased.[87]

Benjamin Rush only underscored Hopkinson's account when he remarked, "Never upon any occasion during the late war did I see such deep-seated joy in every countenance." "The order of the procession was regular," he wrote approvingly, "and begat correspondent order in all classes of spectators. A solemn silence reigned both in the streets and at the windows of the houses." He had understood the visual logic of the liturgy with its interconnection of independence, the French alliance, the peace, George Washington, and the new Constitution. The floats and exhibits of these events were narrative recollections calculated "to unite the most remarkable transports of the mind which were felt during the war with the great event of the day, and to produce such a tide of joy as has seldom been felt in any age or country." "Political joy," he added suggestively, "is one of the strongest emotions of the human mind."[88]

In this context, the ringing constitutional oratory of James Wilson's address to the crowds seemed only ordinary. As evening drew on, people were impressed by the aurora borealis which was surely a sign of divine approval. The fact that, with their hasty construction, no accident marred the display of the huge floats led many to remark that "Heaven was on the federal side of the question." Benjamin Rush concurred with attempted modesty and confessed that he did not "believe that the Constitution was the offspring of inspiration" but was "as perfectly satisfied that the

Union of the States, in its *form* and *adoption*, is as much the work
of a Divine Providence as any of the miracles recorded in the Old
and New Testament, were the effects of a divine power."[89]

If, as Rush said, the Grand Federal Procession had succeeded
in making *federal* and *union* household words, it had also succeeded beyond measure in at once creating and expressing meaning in the civil religion. With all the contrived spontaneity which
the spectacle suggested, it indicated too that there was an authentic and unforced response from the people. As the makers of the
Constitution had so assiduously preached, power lay with the
people; that is, the people united. Hence, by fostering unity, the
Procession was fostering the popular power which could bring
"energy in government" to the United States. At the same time,
the Procession was simply allowing a unity which was already
there to manifest itself publicly. Finally, with its emphasis on
building and constructing in every trade and profession and its
central symbols of the "new roof" and the "ship of state," the
Procession had spoken eloquently on the side of the Grand Architect and the Great Governor. It was human beings who would
build America. Their only requirement for the deity seemed a
benevolent retirement.

It was clear that the Constitution had become sacrosanct. As
the power of the Revolution which it institutionalized, it provided
an absolute which stood in judgment of future persons and times.
The Constitution was regarded, as Alexander Hamilton had confessed, as a "prodigy." It seemed analogous to the Bible in the
mind not only of Benjamin Rush but of many of his fellow-
patriots as well. *The Federalist Papers*, as an apologetic for the
document, were not unlike a defense of the biblical text. James
Madison, in fact, saw the problem of language in constitution-
writing as parallel to that in the Bible. Just as the "cloudy me-
dium" of human language had "rendered dim and doubtful" the
language of the Almighty, so the language of the Constitution had
not been able to capture precisely the pure essence of its framers'
thought in human words. And just as generations of scholarly

exegesis had illuminated the Bible, judges, thought Hamilton, should be "faithful guardians of the Constitution."[90]

Although Chief Justice John Marshall articulated the full doctrine of judicial exegesis in the early nineteenth century, prior to his era there was, as Louis Pollak has documented, a "widespread assumption" that it was the task of the judiciary to pass on the constitutionality of legislation.[91] As early as 1761, James Otis had grounded his argument in the Writs of Assistance case on the idea of judicial review. In addition, there was a precedent of court authority in a number of the colonies before 1787. While the Court took well over a decade to assert its prerogative, in the celebrated *Marbury v. Madison* case of 1803, Marshall propounded what Americans had less formally assumed: "The particular phraseology of the Constitution of the United States confirms and strengthens the principle, supposed to be essential to all written constitutions, that a law repugnant to the Constitution is void; and that *courts*, as well as other departments, are bound by that instrument." But in 1815, in *McCulloch v. Maryland*, Marshall and his court dropped the other shoe and propelled the judiciary into the business of interpretation. Implied powers, they agreed, stemmed from the enumerated powers in the Constitution, for its nature required that "only its great outlines should be marked, its important objects designated, and the minor ingredients which compose those objects be deduced from the nature of the objects themselves." "That this idea was entertained by the framers of the Constitution" was "not only inferred from the nature of the instrument, but from the language."[92] Marshall was talking about what was, in religious terms, a "deposit of faith" from which the "development of doctrine" could deduce norms of living for the present. Throughout the evolving history of the judiciary in America, there was evidence of the normative status of the Constitution for court decisions.

In fact, the most severe anathema which the Supreme Court could pronounce was to declare a law or an action unconstitutional, a condemnation which grew progressively more weighty as the United States grew further away from the time of its foundation. In such an atmosphere of constitutional absolutism with its accompanying fear of deviance, it seemed natural that the Supreme Court should become, in the words of Daniel Boorstin, "a kind of secular papacy" and the "Great Remembrancer of our foundations."[93] For although popular will and political exigency subtly shaped the manner in which each generation read the fundamental law of the Constitution, Americans preferred not to allude to the fact but sought instead to blunt the rough edge of change by cloaking it in the mantle of the Constitution.

Thus, nineteenth-century Americans eagerly joined the Supreme Court justices in remembrancing the document which had insured the durability of their foundation. The federal judges, who were legal cousins to the justices on the Court, rode circuit with the gospel of the civil religion and preached sermons in which the Constitution, its virtue and its promise, figured prominently. Schoolchildren learned to discuss "our glorious Constitution" which represented "the collected patriotism of ages ripened to maturity." It had been put forward by "the wisest men of the country," whose disagreements had been painlessly buried in the forgotten past.[94] In 1825, Joel Barlow's *Columbiad* celebrated the "holy triad" of "EQUALITY," "FREE ELECTION," and the "FEDERAL BAND," which would be the model for all of humankind: "Each land shall imitate, each nation join/ The well based brotherhood, the league divine,/ Extend its empire with the circling sun,/ And band the peopled globe within its federal zone."[95]

Barlow's contemporary, Jedidiah Morse, eulogized a federal system which could not be "too highly appreciated: too sacredly venerated"; which was "the palladium of our safety, of our union, of our national strength, our prosperity, and of all the political and social blessings which we enjoy."[96] For John Quincy Adams in 1839, the act of establishing the Constitution had been a "complement to the Declaration of Independence," while "the revolution itself was a work of thirteen years." The Declaration was the

ark of the American covenant; the Constitution, its Mount Geri-
zim, or place of blessing.

Lay up these principles, then, in your hearts, and in your souls—bind
them for signs upon your hands, that they may be as frontlets between
your eyes—teach them to your children, speaking of them when
sitting in your houses, when walking by the way, when lying down
and when rising up—write them upon the doorplates of your houses,
and upon your gates—cling to them as to the issues of life—adhere to
them as to the cords of your eternal salvation.[97]

George Bancroft hailed the framers of the Constitution who
had "moulded their design by a creative power of their own," yet
introduced nothing "that did not already exist, or was not a natural development of a well-known principle." For Bancroft, the
Constitution meant that "the tree of union was firmly planted,"
and he prayed with fervor: "Never may its trunk be riven by the
lightning; nor its branches crash each other in the maddening
storm; nor its beauty wither; nor its root decay."[98] The Constitution, in short, was Liberty Tree reborn in a form to endure
through time.

Unlike the Liberty Trees which the British soldiers had cut
down, this one was preserved and protected with what care the
young republic could muster. As the Declaration of Independence, the Constitution followed the Continental Congress to
New York in 1787 and eventually was given into the custody of
the State Department. In the War of 1812, it was removed from
the path of the British who invaded Washington. Yet curiously,
unlike the Declaration, it was never exhibited until it was moved
to a special shrine in the Library of Congress where, beginning in
1924, it could be viewed under conditions which prevented any
further deterioration. Its later history, we have already seen, was
lived in concert with the Declaration, a situation which bears
testimony to the continuing sense of many Americans that these
two, Declaration and Constitution, were the Alpha and Omega of
the time of foundation.

The sons of the fathers, as Bancroft had concluded, had used the past in their creation of a living present. Yet they had done so with a drive and passion which meant that, both literally and metaphorically, they had not sprung organically from the soil. As their fathers before them, they had seized the land by force.[99] The "unconscious" self-consciousness had led them to know and not know that they had contrived their myth of origins intelligently and wilfully, that their innocence was a complicated one, and their sonship and fatherhood even more complex. The new covenant, a pledge to one another that they might remain in the innocence of the new world, was a sign of their complicity. The Revolution which the sons had perpetrated had not been simply against the homeland of their fathers, but against the fathers too. By reciting the language of veneration long and loudly enough, they had disguised the evidence of their innovation and continued apace. In their human activity, the men of the Revolution had sealed the promise at the center of a civil religion for the sons and daughters of a new America.

Epilogue

Did the Revolution of the patriots succeed? Did they really, however unwillingly in their own minds, leave the world of the fathers and replace it with a new one? This was the final two-in-one, for, like all the others, the answer lay in ambiguity. The mythic truth about America was juxtaposed between yes and no in a present of self-confident uncertainty and a past in which the new creation lived beside the provisos of the ancients. The truth never stood still for the patriots of the eighteenth century. It continued to move with the dynamic of American history. God's New Israel in the tradition of the fathers and a Brave New World in the charisma of the sons, America has never known quite what to make of itself despite its willingness to declare its identity anyway. The sons of every generation have continued to be sons even as they succeeded in being fathers. Between their guilt and their exultation, the United States of America became a nation.

Yet the purpose of the book has been, not to arbitrate the question of patriotic success or failure, but rather to understand the deep structures from which patriotic action in the world emerged. From this perspective, the very process of making history set up the tension the patriots experienced, driven as they were from the pole of their guilt to the opposite pole of their exultation. Making history made the patriots new, but being new made them rootless as well. Because they opted for meaning almost exclusively in the human project, it was difficult for them to meet the nature of their "natural" religion in other than pragmatic terms. The naked sons of the wilderness wanted to be regenerated through the determination of their own carefully controlled violence.[1] They had not arisen effortlessly from a native soil, and now they had even cut the political ties that bound them to the traditions of British history which might have provided a surrogate continuity. It is not surprising, therefore, that the patriots internalized their anxiety as a basic structure of consciousness.

Mircea Eliade has written that the passion for history from a religious point of view "signifies the proximity of Death."[2] Such a statement in its own terms is logical, or more, mytho-logical. The rootless situation, with its ever widening rift from the natural ground which nourishes, leads to a form of collective starvation. Culture requires the sustenance of nature in order to remain alive. Perhaps this is why the wilderness motif has played so large a role in the development of the republic. Whether in Thomas Jefferson's mitigated version as the agrarian dream, in Transcendental poetry and communes, in the Daniel Boones and Davy Crocketts of the frontier, in the conservation movement, or, more recently, its ecological counterpart, Americans have continued to look to the redemptive powers of nature. In the progressive growth of culture away from this sustenance, there is a compelling need to create artificial roots in the story of the human community. Hence, in other moments, Americans have returned to the historical myth of Revolution which we have been scrutinizing, or they have inverted it in periodic outbursts of millennial expectation. The intensity of both processes is telling: a people who are new and rootless must expend huge amounts of energy in maintaining their identity. Since energy dissipates as it is used, there is a need for an ever-charging supply—a supply which comes, as Eliade has observed, from cosmogony or eschatology.[3]

In other words, the myth provides fuel for its own fire. It is only with some difficulty that Americans can emerge from the interpretive circle of the myth of Revolution to reflect on who they are and what that identity means when seen from the somewhat different perspective provided by other categories. The historians of the American dream, like Frederick Jackson Turner, who epitomized their consociation, have been "historians against history," as we have earlier remarked. The enduring national consciousness has been so colored by a sense of collective uniqueness that even interpreters of the American experience have been caught in the vision of destiny. Discontinuity has been favored over continuity; the catalog of outer deeds which made history over the record of inner experience with its ambiguities and ambivalences, its uncertainties and contradictions.

One indication of the vigor of the myth in the present has been the scholarship concerning civil religion on which the present essay rests. It is a commonplace to note that the study of civil religion has loomed larger and larger in recent years, but the focus of the discussion on the present manifestations of the phenomenon and, even more, on its moral valuation, has gone unremarked. Yet if, wearing the glasses which different categories provide, we view the body of scholarly work which has delineated the religion of the republic, much of it appears as woven of the same thread as the myth of Revolution. Is civil religion good and to be fostered, or idolatrous and to be decried? is its underlying question. Rising out of this construction, the answer moves from celebration to rebuke. Or, in a variation, the answer praises the good that once was at the time of Revolution and laments the American fall from glory. Thus, the moral concern which has stamped its imprint on scholarship is a hermeneutical circle which insures that those who seek to understand do so from the vantage of a mythic worldview. It acclaims a world over and over again created anew by making history which equals or rivals the tale of the fathers. On the other hand, it deplores a world winding itself down and becoming waste.

In seeking to understand the *origins* of American civil religion, this study has had to confront the suggestion that although the myth of Revolution, as any powerful myth, has spoken the truth, the myth of Revolution is also an *invention*. Because it is a narrative symbol, composed of words which are the elements of lan-

guage, the myth of Revolution is fictive, "made up." It is as arbitrary as the human linguistic constructions which shape and mold
it. To acknowledge the fictitious quality of the sacred story of-
fers the possibility of leaving its orbit in order to view it from the
interpretive stance which other categories, also true and also
"made up," can offer. It means that the categories of the history-
makers can make room for alternate structures with which judgment may likewise be rendered.

What has taken shape here as a result is a kind of inner history
of mainstream national consciousness lived under the canopy of
the myth of Revolution. While "plain" history announced its
presence on the external surfaces of American life with its significant deeds and remarkable events, below those surfaces the
interior life was going on. By naming these inner experiences, it
becomes clear that the patriots, quite simply, were human too.
There is a religious ground for speaking of the continuity between these Americans and other peoples: a common humanity
undergirds the experience of those who know they are chosen and
those who do not. If we may borrow a phrase from the Declaration of the myth of Revolution, all are "created equal." Such observations may at first appear trite, but in the context of much of
the religious and "secular" historiography in this country—and the
implications of its categorical pursuit of an American uniqueness,
ex grege—they are not.

The attempt to decipher the underlying structures of American
religion in the Revolution, therefore, has had methodological significance. Traditional historiography has had to take less tried
paths by merging with the form-comparative approach of history
of religions, the awareness of context of the sociology of knowledge, and the interest in the language of the Revolution of some
literary interpreters. The result has illuminated the story of the
Revolution in a way which I hope will serve a useful purpose for
the study of religion in America. The categories which inform
this essay suggest that in the Revolution Americans had found a
kind of "invisible" religion, that God was not so much the center

of it as themselves, and that secularism was in fact one description of this religion. The categories, in short, question traditional understandings of the relationship between religion and culture in the modern west and lead to an understanding of religion as a system of meaning-making which may or may not center on the life of God.

To come full circle, the structures of thinking used here present us with a different mode of analysis. They enable us to look at America with a perception that makes it appear as at once our own and yet other. The nature of these categories suggests that there may be still more and invites a mental pluralism which echoes the social and geographical pluralism of the United States. The categories hint that there are ways which we yet do not know to dream the religiousness of America.

Notes

Introduction

1. Millard E. Crane, Letter to the Editor, *Time*, April 14, 1975, p. 4; Henry Kissinger to the Boston World Affairs Council, ibid., March 22, 1976, p. 6.

2. J. Paul Williams, *What Americans Believe and How They Worship*, 3d ed. (New York: Harper & Row, 1969), pp. 477–78.

3. Ibid.

4. Robert N. Bellah, "Civil Religion in America," *Daedalus* 96, no. 1 (Winter 1967): 1–19. The concept goes back to Jean-Jacques Rousseau. See "Of Civil Religion," in *The Social Contract*, ed. Ernest Barker (New York: Oxford University Press, 1960), book 4, chap. 8.

5. Joseph Galloway, *Historical and Political Reflections on the Rise and Progress of the American Rebellion* (London: G. Wilkie, 1780), pp. 45–46.

6. See, for example, Sidney E. Mead, *The Lively Experiment: The Shaping of Christianity in America* (New York: Harper & Row, 1963); Will Herberg, *Protestant—Catholic—Jew*, rev. ed. (Garden City, N.Y.: Doubleday, 1960); William Lloyd Warner, *The Living and the Dead* (New Haven: Yale University Press, 1959); Martin E. Marty, *The New Shape of American Religion* (New York: Harper & Bros., 1958). A more recent volume, Russell E. Richey and Donald G. Jones, eds., *American Civil Religion* (New York: Harper & Row, 1974), contains Sidney Mead's "The 'Nation with the Soul of a Church'" (*Church History* 36, no. 3 [September 1967]); an excerpt from Lloyd Warner's *American Life: Dream and Reality* (Chicago: University of Chicago Press, 1953); and new statements by Will Herberg, Martin Marty, and Robert Bellah.

7. Mead, "American Protestantism during the Revolutionary Epoch" and "Thomas Jefferson's 'Fair Experiment'—Religious Freedom," in *Lively Experiment*, pp. 38–71; Alan Heimert, *Religion and the American Mind* (Cambridge, Mass.: Harvard University Press, 1966); Carl Bridenbaugh, *Mitre and Sceptre: Transatlantic Faiths, Ideas, Personalities, and Politics, 1689–1775* (New York: Oxford University Press, 1962); Winthrop Hudson,

"Fast Days and Civil Religion," in *Theology in Sixteenth and Seventeenth Century England* (Los Angeles: William Andrews Clark Memorial Library, University of California, 1971), pp. 3–24, and *Nationalism and Religion in America: Concepts of American Identity and Mission* (New York: Harper & Row, 1970); Conrad Cherry, ed., *God's New Israel: Religious Interpretations of American Destiny* (Englewood Cliffs, N.J.: Prentice-Hall, 1971); Cushing Strout, *The New Heavens and New Earth: Political Religion in America* (New York: Harper & Row, 1974); Robert N. Bellah, *The Broken Covenant: American Civil Religion in Time of Trial* (New York: Seabury Press, 1975).

8. Claude Lévi-Strauss, *The Savage Mind* (Chicago: University of Chicago Press, 1966) and *Totemism* (Boston: Beacon Press, 1963) are perhaps the best discussions in English for purposes of comparison.

9. Benjamin Rush to James Rush, Philadelphia, November 23, 1801, in *Letters of Benjamin Rush*, ed. L. H. Butterfield, 2 vols. (Princeton: Princeton University Press, 1951), 2:839.

10. My understanding of myth follows Mircea Eliade here. For a good discussion, see Mircea Eliade, *Patterns in Comparative Religion* (Cleveland: Meridian Books, 1963), especially pp. 410–36, and *Myth and Reality* (New York: Harper & Row, 1963). It is from Eliade that I take the phrase *in illo tempore* to refer to the sacred time of origins.

11. *Pennsylvania Packet*, April 22, 1776, quoted by Arthur M. Schlesinger, Jr., *Prelude to Independence: The Newspaper War on Britain, 1764–1776* (New York: Alfred A. Knopf, 1958), p. 275.

12. Arthur M. Schlesinger, Jr., has noted that an examination of the relative frequency of signatures as compared with other identifying marks on official documents shows that by 1700 illiterates in Massachusetts and in Connecticut were one in twenty. In Virginia, an investigation of wills from the first half of the eighteenth century revealed that only one person in four was illiterate. See Arthur Schlesinger, Jr., *The Birth of the Nation: A Portrait of the American People on the Eve of Independence* (New York: Alfred A. Knopf, 1968), pp. 156–57. Philip Davidson has estimated, more generally, that about one-half of the men and one-quarter of the women in the colonies could read, although they could not all be characterized as a "reading public" (*Propaganda and the American Revolution, 1763–1783* [Chapel Hill, N.C.: University of North Carolina Press, 1941], p. 209).

13. David Ramsay. *The History of the American Revolution* (1789), 2 vols. (Lexington, Ky.: Downing and Phillips, 1815), 1:43.

14. Schlesinger, *Birth of the Nation*, p. 167. Interestingly, there was only one new book title per ten thousand Americans in 1965, according to Schlesinger.

15. For discussion of newspaper publication in the colonies, see Schlesinger, *Birth of the Nation*, pp. 160–61, and *Prelude to Independence*, pp. 303–4; Davidson, *Propaganda and the American Revolution*, p. 225; Milton M. Klein, ed., *The Independent Reflector; or, Weekly Essays on Important*

Subjects . . . by William Livingston and Others (Cambridge, Mass.: Harvard University Press, Belknap Press, 1963), p. 29; and Bernard Bailyn, ed., *Pamphlets of the American Revolution, 1750–1776* (Cambridge, Mass.: Harvard University Press, 1965), 1:3. Bailyn estimated that there were thirty-eight newspapers on the American mainland by 1775.

16. "A Friend to Decency," *Freeman's Journal* (Portsmouth), November 12, 1776, quoted by Schlesinger, *Prelude to Independence*, p. 285.

17. Davidson, *Propaganda and the American Revolution*, p. 17. Peter Oliver seems to have coined the phrase "black regiment," in *Origin and Progress of the American Rebellion: A Tory View* (1781), ed. Douglass Adair and John A. Schutz (San Marino, Calif.: The Huntington Library, 1961). Classic studies of the role of the clergy include Joel T. Headley, *The Chaplains and Clergy of the Revolution* (New York: C. Scribner, 1864), and Alice Baldwin, *The New England Clergy and the American Revolution* (1928; New York: Frederick Ungar Publishing Co., 1958).

18. Jonathan Boucher, *Reminiscences of an American Loyalist, 1738–1789* (1925; New York: Kennikat Press, 1967), pp. 118–19.

19. Davidson, *Propaganda and the American Revolution*, p. 31. The Davidson study is the most important work to offer this interpretation.

20. Ibid., p. 410.

21. Boucher, *Reminiscences of an American Loyalist*, p. 121; James Wilson, June 16, 1787, as recorded by James Madison, *Journal of the Federal Convention* (1840), ed. E. H. Scott, 2 vols. (reprint ed., Chicago: Scott, Foresman and Co., 1898), 1:171; John Adams to Thomas McKean, Quincy, August 31, 1813, in *The Works of John Adams the Second President of the United States*, ed. Charles F. Adams, 10 vols. (Boston: Little, Brown and Company, 1850–56), 10:63; John Adams to Mrs. Mercy Warren, Quincy, February 2, 1814, in *Correspondence between John Adams and Mercy Warren* (1878), ed. Charles F. Adams (New York: Arno Press, 1972), p. 506. Arthur Schlesinger's contemporary assessment is representative: one-third patriot, one-third neutral, one-third Loyalist (*Birth of the Nation*, p. 243).

22. Nathaniel Whitaker, "An Antidote against Toryism; or, The Curse of Meroz," in *The Patriot Preachers of the American Revolution*, ed. Frank Moore (New York: Charles T. Evans, 1862), p. 197.

23. Ernest Lee Tuveson, *Redeemer Nation* (Chicago: University of Chicago Press, 1968).

Chapter 1

1. John Adams, *The Works of John Adams the Second President of the United States*, ed. Charles F. Adams, 10 vols. (Boston: Little, Brown and Company, 1850–56), 10:133.

2. Carl Bridenbaugh, *Mitre and Sceptre: Transatlantic Faiths, Ideas, Personalities, and Politics, 1689–1775* (New York: Oxford University Press, 1962), p. 174.

3. Quoted by Wesley Frank Craven, *The Legend of the Founding Fathers* (New York: New York University Press, 1956), p. 34.

4. Thomas Hutchinson, *The History of the Province of Massachusetts Bay*, 3 vols. (Cambridge, Mass.: Harvard University Press, 1936), 1:407.

5. Quoted by Craven, *Legend of the Founding Fathers*, p. 30.

6. Ibid., pp. 53–54.

7. Samuel Cooke, Election Sermon, May 30, 1770, in *The Pulpit of the American Revolution*, ed. John Wingate Thornton (1860; reprint ed., New York: Da Capo Press, 1970), pp. 174, 186.

8. Samuel West, Election Sermon, May 29, 1776, in ibid., p. 310.

9. George Duffield, Sermon, March 17, 1776, in *Christian Life and Character of the Civil Institutions of the United States*, by Benjamin F. Morris (Philadelphia: George W. Childs, 1864), pp. 356–57.

10. Letter from Boston, June 26, 1775, *Morning Post and Daily Advertiser*, July 30, 1775, in *Letters on the American Revolution, 1774–1776* ed. Margaret W. Willard, (1925; Port Washington, N.Y.: Kennikat Press, 1968), p. 149.

11. Benjamin Rush to Granville Sharp, Philadelphia, July 9, 1774, in "The Correspondence of Benjamin Rush and Granville Sharp 1773–1809," ed. John A. Woods, *Journal of American Studies*, 1, no. 1 (April 1967):9.

12. Letter from Boston, May 26, 1775, *Farley's Bristol Journal*, July 8, 1775, in *Letters on the American Revolution*, ed. Willard, p. 120; and Letter from Boston, November 20, 1774, *Gazetteer and New Daily Advertiser*, January 19, 1775, in ibid., p. 12.

13. From Broadside no. 2042, "Two Favorite New Songs at the American Camp," in *Broadsides, Ballads, &c. Printed in Massachusetts 1639–1800*, ed. Worthington C. Ford (Boston: Massachusetts Historical Society, 1922), p. 281.

14. A Son of Liberty [Silas Downer], *A Discourse Delivered in Providence . . . at the Dedication of the Tree of Liberty* (Providence, R.I.: John Waterman, 1768), p. 14. I use the term *ritual* to mean a performatory event, either spontaneous or planned, which communicates the myth and transforms people in the direction of mutual identification and action while expressing and reinforcing already existing identification patterns. Since both transformative and conservative movements occur in these patriotic collective events, I have used "ritual" interchangeably with "celebration" to describe the happenings. See Victor Turner, *The Forest of Symbols: Aspects of Ndembu Ritual* (Ithaca, N.Y.: Cornell University Press, 1967), pp. 94 ff. for a discussion of ritual which is germane to the understanding offered here, although Turner places more stress on the element of transition.

15. Joseph Warren, Boston Massacre Oration, March 5, 1772, in *Principles and Acts of the Revolution in America*, ed. Hezekiah Niles (Baltimore: William Ogden Niles, 1822), p. 8.

16. Joseph Warren, Boston Massacre Oration, March 6, 1775, in ibid., p. 18.

17. Thornton, ed., *Pulpit of the American Revolution*, p. 308.

18. September 17, 1774, *Journals of Congress*, 13 vols. (Philadelphia: Folwell's Press, 1800), 1:15.

19. William Billings, "A Hymn" (1778), in *Songs and Ballads of the American Revolution*, ed. Frank Moore (New York: D. Appleton & Co., 1856), p. 241.

20. Thornton, ed., *Pulpit of the American Revolution*, p. 191.

21. Petition of Congress to the King, October 26, 1774, *Journals of Congress*, 1:65.

22. Broadside of the Massachusetts House of Representatives, April 19, 1776, in "Early American Broadsides, 1680–1800," by Nathaniel Paine, *Proceedings of the American Antiquarian Society*, n. s. 11 (April 1896–April 1897: 494.

23. Arthur M. Schlesinger, Jr., *The Birth of the Nation: A Portrait of the American People on the Eve of Independence* (New York: Knopf, 1968), p. 236.

24. Samuel Langdon, "Government Corrupted by Vice" (Election Sermon, May 31, 1775), in *The Patriot Preachers of the American Revolution*, ed. Frank Moore (New York: Charles T. Evans, 1862), p. 57.

25. Nathaniel Whitaker, "An Antidote against Toryism; or, The Curse of Meroz," in ibid., p. 201.

26. Phillips Payson, Election Sermon, May 27, 1778, in *Pulpit of the American Revolution*, ed. Thornton, p. 353.

27. Mercy Otis Warren, *History of the Rise, Progress and Termination of the American Revolution, Interspersed with Biographical, Political and Moral Observations*, 3 vols. (Boston: E. Larkin, 1805), 3:298. The work was begun in 1775, the first two volumes were mostly completed by 1791, and the bulk of the third was finished after 1800. I am indebted for this information to Charles H. Lippy, in his manuscript, "The Latter-Day Puritan as Historian: Mercy Otis Warren Remembers the Revolution," p. 2.

28. Warren, *History of the Rise*, pp. 435–36.

29. John Adams to Nathan Webb, Worcester, ca. October 12, 1755, in *Old Family Letters: Copied from the Originals for Alexander Biddle*, series A (Philadelphia: M. B. Lippincott, 1892), 1:5–6.

30. Michael Kammen has used the language of "biformities" in characterizing the American experience throughout the history of the United States. See *People of Paradox: An Inquiry concerning the Origins of American Civilization* (New York: Alfred A. Knopf, 1972).

31. [Downer], *A Discourse Delivered in Providence*, p. 4.

32. Payson, Election Sermon, p. 349.

33. John Witherspoon, "The Dominion of Providence over the Passions of Men" (May 1776), in *The Works of the Rev. John Witherspoon*, 4 vols. (Philadelphia: William W. Woodward, 1802), 3:41.

34. Adams, Diary, December 20, 1770, in *Works*, 2:250–51.

35. Quoted by Morris, *Christian Life*, p. 287.

36. Warren, *History of the Rise*, 1:17–18.

37. David Tappan, "A Discourse Delivered in the Third Parish in New-bury, Massachusetts, on the 1st of May, 1783," in *Patriot Preachers*, ed. Moore, pp. 305–6.

38. Whitaker, "An Antidote against Toryism," in ibid., pp. 218–20; Langdon, "Government Corrupted by Vice," in ibid., pp. 60, 65.

39. Broadside of the Provincial Congress, Watertown, June 16, 1775, in "Early American Broadsides,'" by Paine, pp. 489–90.

40. Broadside, 1777, in *American Broadside Verse from Imprints of the Seventeenth and Eighteenth Centuries*, by Ola Elizabeth Winslow (New Haven: Yale University Press, 1930), p. 189.

41. Benjamin Rush to John Adams, Morristown, August 8, 1777, in *Letters of Benjamin Rush*, ed. L. H. Butterfield, 2 vols. (Princeton: Princeton University Press, 1951), 1:152.

42. For a good discussion, see Perry Miller, *Errand into the Wilderness* (New York: Harper & Row, 1964), especially pp. 7–9. See also *The New England Mind: From Colony to Province* (1953; Boston: Beacon Press, 1961), pp. 27–39.

43. Joel Barlow, *The Columbiad* (Washington City: Joseph Milligan, Georgetown, 1825), 4:331–42, in *The Works of Joel Barlow*, 2 vols. (Gainesville, Fla.: Scholars' Facsimiles & Reprints, 1970), vol. 2. An earlier version of the poem, "The Vision of Columbus: A Poem in Nine Books," appeared in 1787, significantly during the age of foundation. My understanding of the identical structure of the time of origins and the time of the eschaton is derived largely from Mircea Eliade. See "Eschatology and Cosmogony," in *Myth and Reality* (New York: Harper & Row, 1963), pp. 54–74.

44. Richard L. Merritt, *Symbols of American Community, 1735–1775* (New Haven: Yale University Press, 1966), p. 140.

45. James W. Jones, *The Shattered Synthesis: New England Puritanism before the Great Awakening* (New Haven: Yale University Press, 1973), p. 169.

46. Ibid., p. 31.

47. Ibid., p. 87.

48. Quoted by Morris, in *Christian Life*, p. 341.

49. John Wise, *The Vindication of the Government of the New England Churches* (1717) (Gainesville, Fla.: Scholars' Facsimiles & Reprints, 1958), pp. 3–5, 10.

50. Ibid., pp. 30, 31–32.

51. Quoted by Jones, *Shattered Synthesis*, p. 139.

52. Ibid., p. 132.

53. Joseph Galloway, *Historical and Political Reflections on the Rise and Progress of the American Rebellion* (London: G. Wilkie, 1780), pp. 25–26.

54. Peter Oliver, *Origin and Progress of the American Rebellion: A Tory View* (1781), ed. Douglass Adair and John A. Schutz (San Marino, Calif.: The Huntington Library, 1961), pp. 42–43.

55. *Rivington's Gazette*, March 9, 1775, in *The Diary of the American Revolution: From Newspapers and Original Documents*, comp. Frank Moore, 2 vols. (New York: Charles Scribner, 1860), 1:43–44.

56. David Ramsay, *The History of the American Revolution* (1789), 2 vols. (Lexington, Ky.: Downing and Phillips, 1815), 1:243.

57. Samuel Davies, *Religion and Public Spirit* (New York: James Parker & Co., 1761), pp. 4–6.

58. Charles W. Akers, *Called unto Liberty: A Life of Jonathan Mayhew* (Cambridge, Mass.: Harvard University Press, 1964), p. 228.

59. Jones, *Shattered Synthesis*, p. 160.

60. Jonathan Mayhew, *Sermons* (Boston, 1755), p. 103; quoted in ibid., p. 148.

61. Quoted in Akers, *Called unto Liberty*, p. 74.

62. Jonathan Mayhew, *A Discourse concerning Unlimited Submission and Non-Resistance to the Higher Powers* (Boston, 1750), pp. 42–43; quoted in ibid., p. 87.

63. Jonathan Mayhew, "The Snare Broken: A Thanksgiving Discourse" (May 23, 1766), in *Patriot Preachers*, ed. Moore, pp. 39–40.

64. Jones, *Shattered Synthesis*, p. 177.

65. Ibid., p. 181. Charles H. Lippy argues persuasively for Chauncy's traditionalism in his support of the Revolution. See Charles H. Lippy, "Restoring a Lost Ideal: Charles Chauncy and the American Revolution," *Religion in Life*: 44, no. 4 (Winter 1975), 491–502.

66. [Downer], *A Discourse Delivered in Providence*, p. 6.

67. Samuel Stillman, "A Sermon Preached before the Honorable Council, and Honorable House of Representatives of the State of Massachusetts Bay" (May 26, 1779), in *Patriot Preachers*, ed. Moore, p. 265.

68. See Miller, *Errand into the Wilderness*, pp. 159–62, for a discussion of the public ritual of "owning the covenant" and its democratic implications. Elsewhere, Miller argued that the "basic fact is that the Revolution had been preached to the masses as a religious revival, and had the astounding fortune to succeed" ("From the Covenant to the Revival," in *The Shaping of American Religion*, ed. James W. Smith and A. Leland Jamison, Religion in American Life [Princeton: Princeton University Press, 1961], p. 353). Miller's *New England Mind* contains a lengthy analysis of the covenant theme.

69. Here I follow Claude Lévi-Strauss in his structural interpretation of myth. The best short introduction to the method of Lévi-Strauss is his article "The Story of Asdiwal" (ca. 1958). See Edmund Leach, ed., *The Structural Study of Myth and Totemism* (London: Tavistock Publications, 1967), pp. 1–47.

70. Perry Miller has cogently addressed himself to this aspect of the new republic. See Miller, "From the Covenant to the Revival," pp. 322–68.

71. John Marshall, *The Life of George Washington, Commander in Chief of the American Forces, during the War Which Established the Inde-*

pendence of His Country, and First President of the United States, 5 vols. (Philadelphia: C. P. Wayne, 1804–7), 2:168–69.

72. Town of Plainfield, New Hampshire, July 28, 1774, in *A History of Dartmouth College and the Town of Hanover, New Hampshire* (1891), by Frederick Chase, and ed. John K. Lord, 2 vols., 2d ed. (Brattleboro, Vt.: Vermont Printing Co., 1913–28), 1:320.

73. Wise, *Vindication of the Government*, pp. 44–45.

74. Thomas Jefferson, Fair Copy of the "Declaration of the Causes and Necessity for Taking Up Arms," in *The Papers of Thomas Jefferson*, ed. Julian P. Boyd, 19 vols. to date (Princeton: Princeton University Press, 1950–   ), 1:199.

75. The Reverend Dr. Ladd, "An Oration Delivered before His Excellency the Governor of South Carolina" (July 4, 1785), in *Principles and Acts*, ed. Niles, p. 399.

Chapter 2

1. J. G. A. Pocock, *Politics, Language and Time: Essays on Political Thought and History* (New York: Atheneum, 1971), p. 243.

2. Claude Lévi-Strauss conceived myth-making as a form of intellectual *bricolage* in *The Savage Mind* (Chicago: University of Chicago Press, 1966), pp. 16–33. Although the French word *bricoleur* has no exact equivalent in English, it refers to a kind of handyman or jack-of-all-trades who uses ad hoc materials to mend whatever broken object requires his skills. Similarly, the myth-maker works with unsystematic and heterogeneous elements in the structure of events which comprise his story. My understanding of the social construction of reality, here and elsewhere in this study, utilizes the categories of Peter L. Berger in *The Sacred Canopy: Elements of a Sociological Theory of Religion* (Garden City, N.Y.: Doubleday, Anchor Books, 1969), pp. 4 ff. See also Peter L. Berger and Thomas Luckmann, *The Social Construction of Reality: A Treatise in the Sociology of Knowledge* (Garden City, N.Y.: Doubleday, Anchor Books, 1967).

3. Victor Turner enunciated his understanding of *communitas* in *The Ritual Process: Structure and Anti-Structure* (Chicago: Aldine Publishing Company, 1969), especially pp. 94–165.

4. Hermon Husband, *An Impartial Relation*, in *Some Eighteenth Century Tracts concerning North Carolina*, ed. William K. Boyd, Publications of the North Carolina Historical Commission (Raleigh, N.C.: Edwards & Broughton Co., 1927), 18:268.

5. Mercy Otis Warren, *History of the Rise, Progress and Termination of the American Revolution, Interspersed with Biographical, Political and Moral Observations*, 3 vols. (Boston: E. Larkin, 1805), 1:358–59.

6. David Ramsay, *The History of the American Revolution* (1789), 2 vols. (Lexington, Ky.: Downing and Phillips, 1815), 1:79. Ramsay was referring to the Resolutions of Virginia, May 28, 1765.

7. Peter Oliver, *Origin and Progress of the American Rebellion: A Tory View* (1781), ed. Douglass Adair and John A. Schutz (San Marino, Calif.: The Huntington Library, 1961), pp. 51, 53, 63–64.

8. Instructions from the town of Boston to their representatives, May 15, 1770, quoted by Thomas Hutchinson, *The History of the Province of Massachusetts Bay*, 3 vols. (Cambridge, Mass.: Harvard University Press, 1936), 3:376–77.

9. Warren, *History of the Rise*, 1:109–10; John Adams, *The Works of John Adams the Second President of the United States*, ed. Charles F. Adams, 10 vols. (Boston: Little, Brown and Company, 1850–56), 2:328.

10. Ramsay, *History of the American Revolution*, 1:180.

11. Letter from Boston, November 15, 1774, *Bristol Gazette*, January 12, 1775, in *Letters on the American Revolution, 1774–1776*, ed. Margaret W. Willard (1925; Port Washington, N.Y.: Kennikat Press, 1968 [1925]), p. 8.

12. Letter from New York, n.d., *Morning Post and Daily Advertiser*, July 18, 1775, in ibid., p. 106.

13. Simeon Howard, Election Sermon, May 27, 1778, in *The Pulpit of the American Revolution*, ed. John Wingate Thornton (1860; reprint ed.: New York: Da Capo Press, 1970), p. 362; Samuel Cooke, Election Sermon, May 30, 1770, in ibid., pp. 158–59.

14. Charles Woodmason, *The Carolina Backcountry on the Eve of the Revolution: The Journals and Other Writings of Charles Woodmason, Anglican Itinerant*, ed. R. J. Hooker (Chapel Hill, N.C.: University of North Carolina Press, 1953), p. 15.

15. Notes of debates of First Continental Congress, in Adams, *Works*, 2:366–67.

16. Warren, *History of the Rise*, 1:145–46.

17. Richard Bland, *An Inquiry into the Rights of the British Colonies* (Williamsburg, Va., 1766), in *Tracts of the American Revolution, 1763–1776*, ed. Merrill Jensen (Indianapolis: Bobbs-Merrill Company, 1967), p. 114.

18. Henry Laurens, *Extracts from the Proceedings of the Court of Vice-Admiralty* (Charleston, 1769), in ibid., p. 202.

19. Samuel Langdon, "Government Corrupted by Vice" (Election Sermon, May 31, 1775), in *The Patriot Preachers of the American Revolution* ed. Frank Moore (New York: Charles T. Evans, 1862), p. 55.

20. Adams, *Works*, 4:43.

21. John Adams to Abigail Adams, Boston, May 12, 1774, in *Familiar Letters of John Adams and His Wife Abigail Adams, during the Revolution* ed. Charles Francis Adams (1875; Boston: Houghton, Mifflin and Company, 1898), p. 2.

22. Jonathan Boucher, *A View of the Causes and the Consequences of the American Revolution* (1797) (New York: Russell & Russell, 1967), p. lxvi; Oliver, *Origin and Progress*, p. 9.

23. Letter from Philadelphia, December 24, 1774, *London Chronicle*, April 25–27, 1775, in *Letters on the American Revolution*, ed. Willard, p. 41.

24. Enos Hitchcock, *An Oration: Delivered July 4, 1788, at the Request of the Inhabitants of the Town of Providence, in Celebration of the Anniversary of American Independence, and of the Accession of Nine States to the Federal Constitution* (Providence, R.I.: Bennett Wheeler, 1788), p. 12.

25. Warren, *History of the Rise*, 1:216.

26. Richard L. Merritt, *Symbols of American Community, 1735–1775* (New Haven: Yale University Press, 1966), p. 128.

27. Ibid., p. 181.

28. Jonathan Mayhew to James Otis, Boston, June 8, 1766, in Warren, *History of the Rise*, 1:415–16.

29. Warren, *History of the Rise*, 1:51.

30. John Adams to Jedidiah Morse, Quincy, December 5, 1815, in *Annals of the American Revolution; Or, A Record of Their Causes and Events*, by Jedidiah Morse (Hartford, Conn.: Oliver D. Cooke & Sons, 1824), pp. 201–2.

31. John Adams to Abigail Adams, Philadelphia, May 27, 1776, in *Familiar Letters*, p. 177.

32. Benjamin Rush to Granville Sharp, Philadelphia, April 7, 1783, in "The Correspondence of Benjamin Rush and Granville Sharp 1773–1809," ed. John A Woods, *Journal of American Studies* 1, no. 1 (April 1967):17.

33. *New-York Gazette and Post-Boy*, April 11, 1768, quoted by Arthur M. Schlesinger, Jr., *The Birth of the Nation: A Portrait of the American People on the Eve of Independence* (New York: Alfred A. Knopf, 1968), p. 237.

34. "The Present Age," *New Hampshire Gazette* (1779) in *Songs and Ballads of the American Revolution*, ed. Frank Moore (New York: D. Appleton & Co., 1856), p. 257.

35. Howard Mumford Jones, *O Strange New World; American Culture: The Formative Years* (1952; New York: Viking Press, 1967), pp. 251–65.

36. Joel Barlow, *The Columbiad* (Washington City: Joseph Milligan, Georgetown, 1825), 8:151–54, in *The Works of Joel Barlow*, 2 vols. (Gainesville, Fla.: Scholars' Facsimiles & Reprints, 1970), vol. 2.

37. Ibid., 9:301–4.

38. Joseph Galloway, *Historical and Political Reflections on the Rise and Progress of the American Rebellion* (London: G. Wilkie, 1780), p. 112.

39. Extract of a letter from a member of the Virginia Convention, *New York Packet*, April 3, 1776, in *The Diary of the American Revolution: From Newspapers and Original Documents*, comp. Frank Moore, 2 vols. (New York: Charles Scribner, 1860), 1:204–5.

40. Hezekiah Niles, ed., *Principles and Acts of the Revolution in America* (Baltimore: William Ogden Niles, 1822), p. iv.

41. Arthur M. Schlesinger, Jr., *Prelude to Independence: The Newspaper War on Britain, 1764–1776* (New York: Alfred A. Knopf, 1958), p. 28.

42. Adams, Diary (August 14, 1769), *Works*, 2:218.

43. Elbridge H. Goss, *The Life of Colonel Paul Revere* (1891), 3 vols., 3d ed. (Boston: H. W. Spurr, 1898), 1:113–14. Goss cited James Kimball, who, in the *Historical Collections of the Essex Institute* 12:204, had quoted from a manuscript (1850) by Colonel John Russell, the son of one of the "Sons." It was Russell who had originally described the medal.

44. Ramsay, *History of the American Revolution*, 1:83–84. A good short account of the history of Liberty Tree is contained in Arthur M. Schlesinger, "Liberty Tree: A Genealogy," *New England Quarterly* 25 (1952): 435–58.

45. Mircea Eliade has discussed the structure and various manifestations of the cosmic tree in *Patterns in Comparative Religion* (Cleveland: Meridian Books, 1963), pp. 265–78.

46. Hutchinson, *History of the Province of Massachusetts Bay*, 3:98, 101.

47. Goss, *Life of Colonel Paul Revere*, 1:39–45. The obelisk unfortunately burned before it could be used.

48. Hutchinson, *History of the Province of Massachusetts Bay*, 3:146.

49. Adams, Diary (ca. February 26, 1770), *Works*, 2:227–28.

50. *Essex Gazette*, August 31, 1775, quoted by Benson J. Lossing, *Pictorial Fieldbook on the American Revolution*, 2 vols. (New York: Harper & Brothers, 1860), 1:467.

51. Lossing, *Pictorial Fieldbook*, 1:599.

52. William Gordon, *The History of the Rise, Progress, and Establishment of the Independence of the United States of America*, 3 vols. (New York: Hodge, Allen, and Campbell, 1789), 1:211. Gordon's history first appeared in 1788.

53. Letter from Boston, August 20, 1775, *Morning Chronicle and London Advertiser*, October 31, 1775, in *Letters on the American Revolution*, ed. Willard, p. 198.

54. *Rivington's Gazette*, March 2, 1775, in *Diary of the American Revolution*, comp. Moore, 1:23–24.

55. *Holt's Journal*, April 6, 1775, in ibid., p. 55.

56. Lossing, *Pictorial Fieldbook*, 2:584–85.

57. Charles Warren, *Jacobin and Junto; or, Early American Politics As Viewed in the Diary of Dr. Nathaniel Ames, 1758–1822* (Cambridge, Mass.: Harvard University Press, 1931), pp. 33–34.

58. Oliver, *Origin and Progress*, p. 54.

59. Letter from South Carolina, n.d., *Gazetteer and New Daily Advertiser*, February 1, 1775, in *Letters on the American Revolution*, ed. Willard, p. 21.

60. A Son of Liberty [Silas Downer], *A Discourse Delivered in Providence . . . at the Dedication of the Tree of Liberty* (Providence, R.I.: John Waterman, 1768), pp. 15–16.

61. Francis Hopkinson, *A Prophecy* (Philadelphia, 1776), quoted by Moses Coit Tyler, in *The Literary History of the American Revolution*, 2

vols. (New York: G. P. Putnam's Sons, 1897), 1:490.

62. Hutchinson, *History of the Province of Massachusetts Bay*, 3:143.

63. Michel de Chevalier, *Society, Manners, and Politics in the United States: Letters on North America* (1839) (Gloucester, Mass.: Peter Smith, 1967), p. 306.

64. Thomas Paine, "Liberty Tree," in *The Life and Works of Thomas Paine*, ed. William M. Van der Weyde, 10 vols. (New Rochelle, N.Y.: Thomas Paine National Historical Association, 1925), 10:312.

65. "A Voyage to Boston" (1775), quoted by Lossing, *Pictorial Fieldbook*, 1:467 n.

66. Frank Moore's *Songs and Ballads of the American Revolution* contains a number of examples of parodies which refer to Liberty Tree; among them, "The Parody Parodised" (1768) and "A New Song to an Old Tune" (1775). John Dickinson's "Liberty Song" celebrated "the Tree their own hands had to Liberty rear'd," while one broadside from 1765 bore a representation of a Liberty Tree, and another, a poem which began, "A stately elm appear'd before my eyes." See Moore, ed., *Songs and Ballads of the American Revolution*, pp. 45, 107, 38; Worthington C. Ford, ed., *Broadsides, Ballads, &c. Printed in Massachusetts 1639–1800* (Boston: Massachusetts Historical Society, 1922), p. 181; Ola Elizabeth Winslow, *American Broadside Verse from Imprints of the Seventeenth and Eighteenth Centuries* (New Haven: Yale University Press, 1930), p. 185.

67. Hutchinson, *The History of the Province of Massachusetts Bay*, 3:135.

68. Jonathan Mayhew, "The Snare Broken: A Thanksgiving Discourse" (May 23, 1766), in *The Patriot Preachers of the American Revolution*, ed. Frank Moore (New York: Charles T. Evans, 1862), p. 42.

69. John Dickinson, *Letters from a Farmer in Pennsylvania to the Inhabitants of the British Colonies* (Philadelphia, 1768), in *Tracts of the American Revolution*, ed. Jensen, p. 147.

70. Samuel Adams [?], *A Statement of the Rights of the Colonists* (1772), in ibid., p. 254.

71. "Massachusetts" [Daniel Leonard], *Massachusetts Gazette and Boston Post-Boy*, January 1, 1775, quoted by Schlesinger, *Prelude to Independence*, p. vii.

72. *Constitutional Gazette*, September 9, 1775, in *Diary of the American Revolution*, comp. Moore, 1:131–32.

73. Thomas Jefferson, "A Declaration on the Necessity of Taking Up Arms" (1775), in *The Papers of Thomas Jefferson*, ed. Julian P. Boyd, 19 vols. to date (Princeton: Princeton University Press, 1950–   ), 1:201. (The final draft of the Declaration owed more to John Dickinson.)

74. Thomas Jefferson to William Stephens Smith, Paris, November 13, 1787, in ibid., 12:356.

75. Hitchcock, *Oration*, p. 6.

76. Caleb Bingham, *The American Preceptor* (1796), quoted by Ruth Miller Elson, *Guardians of Tradition: American Schoolbooks of the Nineteenth Century* (Lincoln: University of Nebraska Press, 1964), p. 261.

77. Daniel Webster, "A Discourse in Commemoration of the Lives and

Services of John Adams and Thomas Jefferson" (August 2, 1826), in *The Works of Daniel Webster*, 6 vols. (Boston: Charles C. Little and James Brown, 1851), 1:116.

78. Ramsay, *History of the American Revolution*, 1:90.

79. Adams, Diary (December 18, 1865), in *Works*, 2:154.

80. Gordon, *History*, 1:141. It was obvious that Gordon, Ramsay, and Warren had all read the same war reports, because their descriptions and even their language were strikingly similar.

81. Ramsay, *History of the American Revolution*, 1:89–90.

82. Adams, Diary (January 16, 1766), in *Works*, 2:179.

83. Mayhew, "Snare Broken," p. 21.

84. Lossing, *Pictorial Fieldbook*, 1:473–74.

85. Ibid., 2:53.

86. John Adams to Jedidiah Morse, Quincy, January 5, 1816, in *Works*, 10:203. There had been forty-five Boston Masacre Anniversary Orations by the time Adams wrote.

87. Oliver, *Origin and Progress*, p. 91.

88. Hutchinson, *History of the Province of Massachusetts Bay*, 3:241.

89. Ibid.

90. Adams, Diary (March 5, 1774), Works, 2:332.

91. See Schlesinger, *Prelude to Independence*, pp. 29–30, for a description of tableaux. Examples of broadsides may be found in Ford, ed., *Broadsides, Ballads, &c.*, pp. 217–18; Nathaniel Paine, "Early American Broadsides, 1680–1800," *Proceedings of the American Antiquarian Society*, n. s. 11 (April 1896–April 1897), p. 476; Winslow, *American Broadside Verse*, pp. 44, 97.

92. *Boston Gazette*, May 28, 1770, quoted by Philip Davidson, *Propaganda and the American Revolution, 1763–1783* (Chapel Hill, N.C.: University of North Carolina Press, 1941), p. 150.

93. Joseph Warren, Boston Massacre Oration, March 5, 1772, in *Principles and Acts*, ed. Niles, p. 6.

94. Joseph Warren, Boston Massacre Oration, March 6, 1775, in ibid., p. 20.

95. Benjamin Church, Boston Massacre Oration, March 5, 1773, in ibid., p. 12; John Hancock, Boston Massacre Oration, March 5, 1774, in ibid., p. 15.

96. Warren, *History of the Rise*, 1:107.

97. Adams, Diary (December 17, 1773), in *Works*, 2:323.

98. See Ford, *Broadsides, Ballads, &c.*, p. 221, and Moore, ed., *Songs and Ballads of the American Revolution*, pp. 56–57.

99. *The First Book of the American Chronicles of the Times* (1774–75), quoted by Tyler, in *Literary History*, 1:259.

100. Gordon, *History*, 1:249.

101. Warren, *History of the Rise*, 1:133.

102. Ramsay, *History of the American Revolution*, 1:152.

103. Thomas Jefferson, quoted by Benjamin F. Morris, in *Christian Life and Character of the Civil Institutions of the United States* (Philadelphia: George W. Childs, 1864), p. 526. Morris does not share this assessment of self-consciousness and pragmatism.

104. First Provincial Congress of Massachusetts, October 22, 1774, quoted in *Pulpit of the American Revolution*, ed. Thornton, p. 195.

105. Adams, Autobiography, *Works*, 2:405–6; Ramsay, *History of the American Revolution*, 1:234.

106. Proclamation for a Public Thanksgiving, November 4, 1775, quoted in *Pulpit of the American Revolution*, ed. Thornton, p. 264.

107. *Independent Reflector*, vol. 4 (December 21, 1752), and vol. 22 (April 26, 1753), in *The Independent Reflector; or, Weekly Essays on Important Subjects . . . by William Livingston and Others*, ed. Milton M. Klein (Cambridge, Mass.: Harvard University Press, Belknap Press, 1963), pp. 78, 209.

108. James Lovell, Boston Massacre Oration, April 2, 1771, in *Principles and Acts*, ed. Niles, p. 4.

109. See, for example, "Liberty's Call" (ca. 1775) in *Songs and Ballads of the American Revolution*, ed. Moore, pp. 83–86. Timothy Dwight's *Columbia: A Song* (1777) (New Haven: Press of Timothy Dwight College in Yale University, 1940) may be considered a variation on the theme. The song was popular with Washington's troops, probably as a broadside, and became the unofficial national anthem until 1814. Bickerstaff's Boston Almanack is described in Lossing, *Pictorial Fieldbook*, 1:486.

110. Ramsay, *History of the American Revolution*, 1:150.

111. Jacob Duché, "The Duty of Standing Fast in Our Spiritual and Temporal Liberties" (July 7, 1775), in *Patriot Preachers*, ed. Moore, p. 80. Duché later had second thoughts and became a Loyalist.

112. John Hurt, "The Love of Country" (1777), in ibid., p. 153.

113. Howard, Election Sermon, p. 390.

114. Boucher, *View of the Causes*, pp. 590–91.

115. James K. Paulding, *A Life of Washington*, 2 vols. (New York: Harper & Brothers, 1835), 1:173–74.

Chapter 3

1. Michael Kammen, *People of Paradox: An Inquiry concerning the Origins of American Civilization* (New York: Alfred A. Knopf, 1972), p. 223. Kammen's bibliographical essay (pp. 301–16) amply documents the references to "contrapuntal" style among those who have observed Americans.

2. Jonathan Mayhew, "The Snare Broken: A Thanksgiving Discourse" (May 23, 1766), in *The Patriot Preachers of the American Revolution*, ed. Frank Moore (New York: Charles T. Evans, 1862), p. 19.

3. *Constitutional Gazette*, December 1775, in *The Diary of the American Revolution: From Newspapers and Original Documents*, comp. Frank Moore, 2 vols. (New York: Charles Scribner, 1860), 1:185.

4. *Pennsylvania Evening Post*, January 6, 1776, in ibid., pp. 181–82.

5. *Pennsylvania Journal*, June 26, 1776, in ibid., p. 252.

6. Elbridge Gerry to Samuel Adams, December 13, 1775, quoted by Benjamin F. Morris, in *Christian Life and Character of the Civil Institutions of the United States* (Philadelphia: George W. Childs, 1864), p. 119.

7. Samuel Adams, Oration on the Steps of the Continental State House, Philadelphia, August 1, 1776, ibid., p. 115.

8. John Witherspoon, "The Dominion of Providence over the Passions of Men" (May 1776), in *The Works of the Rev. John Witherspoon*, 4 vols. (Philadelphia: William W. Woodward, 1802), 3:33; Samuel West, Election Sermon, May 29, 1776, in *The Pulpit of the American Revolution*, ed. John Wingate Thornton (1860; reprint ed., New York: De Capo Press, 1970), p. 303.

9. Circular letter to constituents, September 13, 1779, *Journals of Congress*, 13 vols. (Philadelphia: Folwell's Press, 1800), 5:261.

10. Quoted by David Ramsay, *The History of the American Revolution* (1789), 2 vols. (Lexington, Ky.: Downing and Phillips, 1815), 2:267.

11. The most literal example was William Billings's "Retrospect": "The snare is broken, and we are escaped!/ But praised be the Lord/ But blessed be the Lord!/ The snare is broken, and we are escaped!" See Frank Moore, ed., *Songs and Ballads of the American Revolution* (New York: D. Appleton & Co., 1856), p. 243.

12. Mercy Otis Warren, *History of the Rise, Progress and Termination of the American Revolution, Interspersed with Biographical, Political and Moral Observations*, 3 vols. (Boston: E. Larkin, 1805), 3:25.

13. Ezra Stiles, "The United States Elevated to Glory and Honor" (May 8, 1783), in *Pulpit of the American Revolution*, ed. Thornton, pp. 446–47.

14. David Tappan, "A Discourse Delivered in the Third Parish in Newbury, Massachusetts, on the 1st of May, 1783," in *Patriot Preachers*, ed. Moore, p. 295; Warren, *History of the Rise*, 3:328.

15. Ruth Miller Elson, *Guardians of Tradition: American Schoolbooks of the Nineteenth Century* (Lincoln: University of Nebraska Press, 1964), p. 117.

16. Warren, *History of the Rise*, 1:176.

17. Samuel Davies, "Religion and Patriotism the Constituents of a Good Soldier" (1755), in *Sermons on Important Subjects*, 4 vols. (London: W. Baynes, 1815), 3:398.

18. Benjamin Church, Boston Massacre Oration, March 5, 1773, in *Principles and Acts of the Revolution in America*, ed. Hezekiah Niles (Baltimore: William Ogden Niles, 1822), p. 12.

19. John Adams to Abigail Adams, Philadelphia, September 16, 1774, in *Familiar Letters of John Adams and His Wife Abigail Adams, during the Revolution*, ed. Charles Francis Adams (1875; Boston: Houghton, Mifflin, and Company, 1898), p. 37. On September 7, Adams had written in his diary that the Collect "was most admirably adapted, though this was accidental, or rather providential. A prayer which he gave us of his own composition was as pertinent, as affectionate, as sublime, as devout, as I ever

242 SONS OF THE FATHERS

heard offered up to Heaven. He filled every bosom present" (John Adams, *The Works of John Adams the Second President of the United States*, ed. Charles F. Adams, 10 vols. [Boston: Little, Brown and Company, 1850–56], 2:368).

20. Benjamin Rush to Granville Sharp, Philadelphia, September 20, 1774, in "The Correspondence of Benjamin Rush and Granville Sharp 1773–1809," ed. John A. Woods, *Journal of American Studies* 1, no. 1 (April 1967):12.

21. William Gordon, *Religious and Civil Liberty: A Thanksgiving Discourse* (December 15, 1774) (London: E. and C. Dilly, 1775), p. 35.

22. William Gordon, *The History of the Rise, Progress, and Establishment of the Independence of the United States of America*, 3 vols. (New York: Hodge, Allen, and Campbell, 1789), 2:116–17.

23. West, Election Sermon, p. 309.

24. Joab Trout, "A Sermon Preached on the Eve of the Battle of Brandywine, September 10, 1777", p. 215. Bound as Appendix with [Lydia Minturn Post], *Personal Recollections of the American Revolution*, ed. Sidney Barclay (New York: Rudd & Carleton, 1859).

25. "The American Soldier's Hymn," in *The Literary History of the American Revolution*, by Moses Coit Tyler, 2 vols. (New York: G. P. Putnam's Sons, 1897), 2:179.

26. *Virginia Gazette*, June 24, 1775 and *Pennsylvania Journal*, June 21, 1775, in *Diary of the American Revolution*, comp. Moore, 1:86; *Virginia Gazette*, September 16, 1775, in ibid., p. 125.

27. Letter from Philadelphia, n.d., *Morning Post and Daily Advertiser*, December 1, 1775, in *Letters on the American Revolution, 1774–1776* ed. Margaret W. Willard (1925; Port Washington, N.Y.: Kennikat Press, 1968), p. 217.

28. *Freeman's Journal*, June 1, 1776, quoted by Philip Davidson, *Propaganda and the American Revolution, 1763–1783* (Chapel Hill, N.C.: University of North Carolina Press, 1941), p. 166.

29. Extract of a letter from Morristown, N.J., *Freeman's Journal*, January 28, 1777, in *Diary of the American Revolution*, comp. Moore, 1:373.

30. *Pennsylvania Evening Post*, September 4, 1777, in ibid., p. 481.

31. Draft of "An Address of the Congress to the Inhabitants of the United States of America," May 8, 1778, *Journals of Congress*, 4:193; "To the Inhabitants of the United States of America," May 26, 1779, in ibid., 5:171.

32. Benjamin Church [?], *Liberty and Property Vindicated, and the St–p m–n Burnt*, in *Pamphlets of the American Revolution, 1750–1776*, ed. Bernard Bailyn (Cambridge, Mass.: Harvard University Press, 1965), 1:587–97.

33. Charles Chauncy, "A Discourse on 'The Good News from a Far Country,'" (July 24, 1766), in *Pulpit of the American Revolution*, ed. Thornton, p. 127.

34. Exodus 14:25; *Pennsylvania Evening Post*, March 30, 1776, in *Diary of the American Revolution*, comp. Moore, 1:223.

35. Ramsay, *History of the American Revolution*, 1:390.

36. Letter from Philadelphia, October 5, 1775, *London Evening Post*, November 23–25, 1775, in *Letters on the American Revolution*, ed. Willard, p. 213.

37. Patrick Henry, April 1775, quoted by Morris, in *Christian Life*, pp. 115–16.

38. Warren, *History of the Rise*, 1:353–54.

39. "On the Evacuation of Boston by the British Troops, March 17th, 1776," in *American Broadside Verse from Imprints of the Seventeenth and Eighteenth Centuries* by Ola Elizabeth Winslow (New Haven: Yale University Press, 1930), p. 149.

40. [Post], *Personal Recollections of the American Revolution* (October 1780), p. 140.

41. *Boston Gazette*, September 16, 1765, quoted by Davidson, *Propaganda and the American Revolution*, p. 141.

42. Peter Oliver, *Origin and Progress of the American Rebellion: A Tory View* (1781), ed. Douglass Adair and John A. Schutz (San Marino, Calif.: The Huntington Library, 1961), p. 65.

43. "A Warm Place—Hell"; see Elbridge H. Goss, *The Life of Colonel Paul Revere* (1891), 3 vols., 3d ed. (Boston: H. W. Spurr, 1898), 1:58–61. Appropriate verse was supplied beneath by Benjamin Church.

44. "A True Patriot" [Joseph Warren], *Boston Gazette*, February 29, 1768, quoted by Arthur M. Schlesinger, Jr., *Prelude to Independence: The Newspaper War on Britain, 1764–1776* (New York: Alfred A. Knopf, 1958), p. 96.

45. Peter St. John, "American Taxation," in *Songs and Ballads of the American Revolution*, ed. Moore, p. 3.

46. West, Election Sermon, pp. 316–17.

47. Benjamin Hichborn, Boston Massacre Oration, March 5, 1777, in *Principles and Acts*, ed. Niles, p. 27.

48. Philip Freneau, "George the Third's Soliloquy," *United States Magazine* (1779), in *Songs and Ballads of the American Revolution*, ed. Moore, p. 252.

49. *Pennsylvania Journal*, November 29, 1775, in *Diary of the American Revolution*, comp. Moore, 1:168–69.

50. *New Hampshire Gazette*, August 10, 1779, in ibid., 2:192.

51. John Adams to Abigail Adams, Philadelphia, April 27, 1777, in *Familiar Letters*, p. 266.

52. Letter from Philadelphia, May 18, 1776, *Gazetteer and New Daily Advertiser*, July 13, 1776, in *Letters on the American Revolution*, ed. Willard, p. 317.

53. Warren, *History of the Rise*, 1:338–39.

244

54. Gordon, *History*, 2:179. The image of Hessians as minions of the devil seemed to be imprinted with particular force in American consciousness.

55. Ramsay, *History of the American Revolution*, 1:393.

56. John Witherspoon, "Sermon Delivered at a Public Thanksgiving after Peace " (ca. 1782), in *Works* 3:77.

57. April 18, 1777, *Journals of Congress*, 3:115.

58. Ramsay, *History of the American Revolution*, 2:183.

59. Tyler, *Literary History*, 2:165.

60. *Pennsylvania Packet*, October 3, 1780, in *Diary of the American Revolution*, comp. Moore, 2:327–28.

61. *New Jersey Gazette*, November 1, 1780, in ibid., p. 333; *Pennsylvania Packet*, January 16, 1781, in ibid., pp. 337–38. September 25 was the day on which Arnold's unpatriotic activities occasioned his flight from his command.

62. See Winslow, *American Broadside Verse*, p. 139.

63. Ramsay, *History of the American Revolution*, 1:144; Letter from Boston, November 8, 1774, *London Chronicle*, January 12, 1775, in *Letters on the American Revolution*, ed. Willard, p. 6.

64. John Dickinson, "Liberty Song," *Boston Gazette*, July 18, 1768, quoted by Tyler, in *Literary History*, 1:240–41.

65. A Son of Liberty [Silas Downer], *A Discourse Delivered in Providence . . . at the Dedication of the Tree of Liberty* (Providence, R.I.: John Waterman, 1768), p. 10.

66. Gad Hitchcock, Election Sermon, May 25, 1775, quoted by Joel T. Headley, *The Chaplains and Clergy of the Revolution* (New York: C. Scribner, 1864), p. 29.

67. George Bancroft, *A History of the United States of America from the Discovery of the Continent* (1876–79), abr. and ed. Russel B. Nye (Chicago: University of Chicago Press, Phoenix Books, 1966), pp. 154, 156.

68. From a broadside, "Two Songs on the Brave General Montgomery, and Others, Who Fell within the Walls of Quebec, Dec. 31, 1775," in *American Broadside Verse*, by Winslow, p. 147; Gordon, *Religious and Civil Liberty: A Thanksgiving Discourse*, p. 16.

69. Stiles, "The United States Elevated," p. 401.

70. *New York Journal*, September 6, 1779, in *Diary of the American Revolution*, comp. Moore, 2:201.

71. Oliver, *Origin and Progress*, p. 104.

72. *Freeman's Journal*, June 22, 1776, in *Diary of the American Revolution*, comp. Moore, 1:252; William Gordon, "The Separation of the Jewish Tribes, after the Death of Solomon" (July 9, 1777), in *Patriot Preachers*, ed. Moore, pp. 179–80.

73. June 1777, in *Diary of the American Revolution*, comp. Moore, 1:444–45. Moore gives the source as Carver, p. 113.

74. Ramsay, *History of the American Revolution*, 1:277.

75. Witherspoon, "Dominion of Providence," 3:34.

76. Letter of Hezekiah Hayden, July 4, 1776, quoted by Davidson, *Propaganda and the American Revolution*, p. 341.

77. Letter from Philadelphia, May 6, 1775, *Lloyd's Evening Post and British Chronicle*, June 28–30, 1775, in *Letters on the American Revolution*, ed. Willard, p. 102. Perry Miller discussed the "errand into the wilderness" and its nature in *Errand into the Wilderness* (New York: Harper & Row, 1964), pp. 2–15.

78. John Adams to Abigail Adams, Philadelphia, May 29, 1775, in *Familiar Letters*, p. 59; Abigail Adams to John Adams, March 2, 1776, in ibid., p. 138.

79. Letter from Philadelphia, July 4, 1775, *Lloyd's Evening Post and British Chronicle*, August 16–18, 1775, in *Letters on the American Revolution*, ed. Willard, p. 162.

80. Headley, *Chaplains and Clergy*, pp. 112–14.

81. Ibid., p. 123.

82. Quoted in ibid., p. 255.

83. Ibid., pp. 290–91; Thornton, ed., *Pulpit of the American Revolution*, p. xxxvi.

84. Quoted by Headley, *Chaplains and Clergy*, p. 93.

85. Ramsay, *History of the American Revolution*, 2:267.

86. George Duffield, Sermon, March 17, 1776, in *Christian Life*, by Morris, p. 353.

87. Headley, *Chaplains and Clergy*, pp. 164–70, 382–87.

88. Letter from Eleazar Wheelock to the Committees of Safety of the Connecticut Valley, Dartmouth College, July 15, 1777, in *A History of Dartmouth College and the Town of Hanover, New Hampshire* (1891), by Frederick Chase, ed. John K. Lord, 2 vols., 2d ed. (Brattleboro, Vt.: Vermont Printing Co., 1913–1928), 1:379. (Emphasis mine.)

89. Ramsay, *History of the American Revolution*, 2:319.

90. "A Freeman," *New England Chronicle*, November 23, 1775, in *Diary of the American Revolution*, comp. Moore, 1:173.

91. John Adams to Abigail Adams, Philadelphia, April 19, 1777, in *Familiar Letters*, pp. 260–61; Abigail Adams to John Adams, Braintree, September 20, 1777, in ibid., p. 310.

92. Broadside, "The Address of the Congress," ca. May 23, 1778, in "Early American Broadsides, 1680–1800," by Nathaniel Paine, *Proceedings of the American Antiquarian Society*, n.s. 11 (April 1896–April 1897): 499; *New Hampshire Gazette*, July 27, 1779, in *Diary of the American Revolution*, comp. Moore, 2:195.

93. "Timothy Standfast," *Virginia Gazette*, December 30, 1780, in *Diary of the American Revolution*, comp. Moore, 2:359.

94. *New Jersey Gazette*, February 21, 1781, in ibid., pp. 375–76.

95. Simeon Baldwin, *An Oration Pronounced before the Citizens of New-Haven, July 4, 1788* (New Haven: Meigs, 1788), p. 8.

96. Warren, *History of the Rise* 1:85.

97. Orders issued by General Washington to the Army, Headquarters, April 18, 1783, in [Thomas Condie], *Biographical Memoirs of Gen. George Washington, First President of the United States* (1798) (Lexington, Ky.: Downing and Phillips, 1815), p. 410. (Bound with Ramsay, *History of the American Revolution*, vol. 2.)

98. Ramsay, *History of the American Revolution*; Gordon, *History*; John Marshall, *The Life of George Washington, Commander in Chief of the American Forces, during the War Which Established the Independence of His Country, and First President of the United States*, 5 vols. (Philadelphia: C. P. Wayne, 1804–7); Warren, *History of the Rise*; Jedidiah Morse, *Annals of the American Revolution; or, A Record of Their Causes and Events* (Hartford, Conn.: Oliver D. Cooke & Sons, 1824); Elson, *Guardians of Tradition*, pp. 112, 145.

99. Joseph Warren, Boston Massacre Oration, March 5, 1775, in *Principles and Acts*, ed. Niles, p. 4.

100. Letter from Boston, April 22, 1775, *London Evening Post*, June 15–17, 1775, in *Letters on the American Revolution*, ed. Willard, p. 86.

101. John Adams to John Quincy Adams, Philadelphia, July 27, 1777, in *Familiar Letters*, p. 284.

102. Charles Peirce, *The Arts and Sciences Abridged with a Selection of Pieces from Celebrated Modern Authors* (1806), quoted by Elson, *Guardians of Tradition*, p. 233.

103. Ibid., p. 128; F. W. P. Greenwood and G. B. Emerson, *The Classical Reader* (1826), quoted in ibid., p. 330.

104. Daniel Webster, "The Bunker Hill Monument" (June 17, 1825), in *The Works of Daniel Webster*, 6 vols. (Boston: Charles C. Little and James Brown, 1851), 1:72–73, 78; "Completion of the Bunker Hill Monument" (June 17, 1843), in ibid., pp. 87, 89; "The Bunker Hill Monument," in ibid., p. 61.

105. Herbert Richardson, "Civil Religion in Theological Perspective," in *American Civil Religion*, ed. Russell E. Richey and Donald G. Jones (New York: Harper & Row, 1974), p. 174.

106. Warren, *History of the Rise*, 3:401, 336–37.

107. Ibid., 1:140–41.

108. *New Jersey Gazette*, December 8, 1779, in *Diary of the American Revolution*, comp. Moore, 2:246; Hector St. John Crèvecoeur, *Letters from an American Farmer* (1782) (Gloucester, Mass.: Peter Smith, 1968), p. 7.

109. Elias Boudinot, *Journal; or, Historical Recollections of American Events during the Revolutionary War* (Philadelphia: Frederick Bourquin, 1894), p. 3.

110. Tappan, "Discourse," pp. 300–301.

111. Stiles, "The United States Elevated," pp. 438–39.

112. George Duffield, "A Sermon Preached in the Third Presbyterian Church in the City of Philadelphia, on December 11th, 1783, on the Restoration of Peace," in *Patriot Preachers*, ed. Moore, pp. 348–49.

113. The Reverend Dr. Ladd, "An Oration Delivered before His Excellency the Governor of South Carolina" (July 4, 1785), in *Principles and Acts*, ed. Niles, p. 399.

114. Joel Barlow, *The Columbiad* (Washington City: Joseph Milligan, Georgetown, 1825), 1:725–36, in *The Works of Joel Barlow*, 2 vols. (Gainesville, Fla.: Scholars' Facsimiles & Reprints, 1970), vol. 2.

Chapter 4

1. John Adams, *The Works of John Adams the Second President of the United States*, ed. Charles F. Adams, 10 vols. (Boston: Little, Brown and Company, 1850–56), 2:370–71.

2. Jonathan Mayhew, *A Discourse concerning Unlimited Submission and Non-Resistance to the Higher Powers* (Boston, 1750), in *Pamphlets of the American Revolution, 1750–1776*, ed. Bernard Bailyn (Cambridge, Mass.: Harvard University Press, 1965), 1:235.

3. James Otis, *The Rights of the British Colonies Asserted and Proved* (Boston, 1764), in ibid., p. 424.

4. See Nathaniel Paine, "Early American Broadsides, 1680–1800," *Proceedings of the American Antiquarian Society*, n.s. 11 (April 1896–April 1897): 481.

5. For a study treating the qualities which enamored a "ruler" to the citizens in eighteenth-century New England, see Timothy H. Breen, *The Character of the Good Ruler: A Study in Puritan Political Ideas in New England, 1630–1730* (New Haven: Yale University Press, 1970). After the Glorious Revolution, for Breen, the political ideas in election sermons exhibited a marked departure from the past, a departure which led in part in the direction which I am suggesting here.

6. Herbert M. Morais, *Deism in Eighteenth Century America* (New York: Columbia University Press, 1934). The introductory chapters are particularly illuminating on this point. So too is G. Adolf Koch, *Republican Religion: The American Revolution and the Cult of Reason* (1933; Gloucester, Mass.: Peter Smith, 1964); republished in 1968, with a new foreword, as *Religion of the American Enlightenment* (New York: Thomas Y. Crowell Company). "The history of the eighteenth century with respect to deism," Koch wrote, "is the story of its gradual filtration from the philosopher to the common man" (*Religion of the American Enlightenment*, p. 16).

7. *Gaines' New York Gazette*, January 9, 1775, in *The Diary of the American Revolution: From Newspapers and Original Documents*, comp. Frank Moore, 2 vols. (New York: Charles Scribner, 1860), 1:11.

8. Morais, *Deism in Eighteenth Century America*, pp. 98–99. Morais himself discounts these sources and sees the growth of anticlericalism after 1783 as responsible for the spread of deism. This thesis, of course, would not account for the earlier deism of the first phases of the Revolution.

9. Sidney E. Mead, *The Lively Experiment: The Shaping of Christianity in America* (New York: Harper & Row, 1963), pp. 65–66. For a discussion of the evolution of Unitarianism, see Conrad Wright, *The Beginnings of Unitarianism in America* (Boston: Starr King Press, 1955).

10. Ezra Stiles, "The United States Elevated to Glory and Honor" (May 8, 1783), in *The Pulpit of the American Revolution*, ed. John Wingate Thornton (1860; reprint ed., New York: Da Capo Press, 1970), p. 490; David Ramsay, *The History of the American Revolution* (1789), 2 vols. (Lexington, Ky.: Downing and Phillips, 1815), 2:328.

11. Quoted by Koch, *Religion of the American Enlightenment*, p. 50.

12. Isaac Backus, *A Fish Caught in His Own Net* (Boston, 1768), in *Isaac Backus on Church, State, and Calvinism: Pamphlets, 1754–1789*, ed. William G. McLaughlin (Cambridge, Mass.: Harvard University Press, Belknap Press, 1968), p. 279.

13. Daniel J. Boorstin, *The Lost World of Thomas Jefferson* (Boston: Beacon Press, 1948), p. 254, n. 3.

14. "The American Patriot's Prayer," in *Common Sense*, by Thomas Paine, 3d ed. (Philadelphia: Robert Bell, February 1776); quoted by Moses Coit Tyler, in *The Literary History of the American Revolution*, 2 vols. (New York: G. P. Putnam's Sons, 1897), 2:178.

15. October 21, 1774, *Journals of Congress*, 13 vols. (Philadelphia: Folwell's Press, 1800), 1:43; "Dec'aration of the Causes and Necessity for Taking Up Arms", July 6, 1775, in ibid., 1:134, 138.

16. Otis, *Rights of the British Colonies* 1:423.

17. Carl L. Becker, *The Declaration of Independence* (1942; reprint ed., New York: Vintage Books, 1958), p. 60. Becker originally published *The Declaration of Independence* in 1922.

18. George Washington to Sir Edward Newenham, Mt. Vernon, August 29, 1788, quoted by Paul Boller, *George Washington and Religion* (Dallas: Southern Methodist University Press, 1963), p. 106.

19. Ethan Allen, *Reason the Only Orac'e of Man* (1784) (New York: Burt Franklin, 1972).

20. Ibid., pp. 47, 107–8, 30, 55, 57, 80–81, 275.

21. John Wise, *The Vindication of the Government of the New England Churches* (1717) (Gainesville, Fla.: Scholars' Facsimiles and Reprints, 1958), pp. 32, 36–37.

22. As attorney general, Edward Coke enunciated this view in *Dr. Bonham's Case* (1610) at the British Court of Common Pleas. Coke held that the London College of Physicians could not, as it had under an Act of Parliament, inflict penalties on Bonham for performing the duties of a physician without a required license: "the common law will controul acts of parliament, and sometimes adjudge them to be utterly void." Here was precedent for the later practice of disallowing statutes which conflicted with the Constitution in America. Moreover, in applying the test of "reasonableness," Coke was justifying his decision by reference in some sense to a

"higher law." It was unfair, Coke had argued, for the College of Physicians to be the judge in their own case, since, according to law, they should receive half of Dr. Bonham's fine. For a good discussion, see Edward S. Corwin, *The "Higher Law" Background of American Constitutional Law* (1929; Ithaca, N.Y.: Cornell University Press, 1965), pp. 40–57, from which the present remarks have been derived.

23. Otis, *Rights of the British Colonies,* passim; Samuel Adams [?], *A Statement of the Rights of the Colonists (1772),* in *Tracts of the American Revolution, 1763–1776,* ed. Merrill Jensen (Indianapolis: Bobbs-Merrill Company, 1967), p. 238 et passim.

24. Charles Chauncy, "A Discourse on 'the Good News from a Far Country'" (July 24, 1766), in *Pulpit of the American Revolution,* ed. Thornton, p. 119.

25. Samuel Cooke, Election Sermon, May 30, 1770, in ibid., p. 162.

26. Samuel West, Election Sermon, May 29, 1776, in ibid., p. 270.

27. Phillips Payson, Election Sermon, May 27, 1778, in ibid., p. 347.

28. Declaration and Resolves of the First Continental Congress, October 14, 1774, in *Sources and Documents Illustrating the American Revolution, 1764–1788,* ed. Samuel E. Morison, 2d ed. (New York: Oxford University Press, 1965), p. 119.

29. "A Ballad" (1776), in *Songs and Ballads of the American Revolution,* ed. Frank Moore (New York: D. Appleton & Co., 1856), p. 148.

30. Jesse Hopkins, *The Patriot's Manual* (1828), quoted by Ruth Miller Elson, *Guardians of Tradition: American Schoolbooks of the Nineteenth Century* (Lincoln: University of Nebraska Press, 1964), p. 39. Daniel Boorstin has discussed the Jeffersonian relationship to nature in *The Lost World of Thomas Jefferson,* pp. 186–88. It was Martin E. Marty whom I first heard characterize this interaction as a "covenant with nature" in a lecture in 1972.

31. See, for example, Mayhew, *A Discourse Concerning Unlimited Submission and Non-Resistance to the Higher Powers,* in *Pamphlets of the American Revolution,* ed. Bailyn, 1:242; *Independent Reflector,* vol. 37 (August 9, 1753) and vol. 30 (June 21, 1753), in *The Independent Reflector; or, Weekly Essays on Important Subjects . . . by William Livingston and Others,* ed. Milton M. Klein (Cambridge, Mass.: Harvard University Press, Belknap Press, 1963), pp. 314, 265.

32. Jonathan Mayhew, "The Snare Broken: A Thanksgiving Discourse" (May 23, 1766), in *The Patriot Preachers of the American Revolution,* ed. Frank Moore (New York: Charles T. Evans, 1862), p. 29.

33. Chauncy, "A Discourse On 'the Good News,'" p. 140.

34. June 12, 1775, *Journals of Congress,* 1:109–10.

35. In Morison, ed., *Sources and Documents Illustrating the American Revolution,* p. 166.

36. John Adams to Abigail Adams, Philadelphia, February 11, 1776, in *Familiar Letters of John Adams and His Wife Abigail Adams, during the*

Revolution, ed. Charles Francis Adams (1875; Boston: Houghton, Mifflin, and Company, 1898), p. 133; General Orders, Headquarters, Valley Forge, May 5, 1778, quoted by Boller, *George Washington and Religion*, p. 55.

37. "Impartial," *New Jersey Gazette*, January 10, 1781, in *Diary of the American Revolution*, comp. Moore, 2:363; Letter from Philadelphia, February 6, 1775, *Gazetteer and New Daily Advertiser*, April 4, 1775, in *Letters on the American Revolution, 1774–1776*, ed. Margaret W. Willard (1925; Port Washington, N.Y.: Kennikat Press, 1968), p. 63.

38. William Gordon, *The History of the Rise, Progress, and Establishment of the Independence of the United States of America*, 3 vols. (New York: Hodge, Allen, and Campbell, 1789), 3:352. The Articles of Confederation of July 9, 1778, were affirmed by Congress as follows: "And whereas it hath pleased the Great Governor of the world to incline the hearts of the legislatures, we respectively represent in Congress, to approve of, and to authorize us to ratify the said articles of confederation and perpetual union" (March 1, 1781, *Journals of Congress*, 7:43).

39. Allen, *Reason the Only Oracle of Man*, pp. 272–73.

40. George Bancroft, *A History of the United States of America from the Discovery of the Continent* (1876–79), abr. and ed. Russel B. Nye (Chicago: University of Chicago Press, Phoenix Books, 1966), p. 377.

41. Boorstin, *Lost World of Thomas Jefferson*, p. 29.

42. Allen, *Reason the Only Oracle of Man*, p. 238.

43. Isaac Backus, Draft for a Bill of Rights for the Massachusetts Constitution, 1779, in *Isaac Backus*, ed. McLoughlin, p. 487.

44. Mead, *Lively Experiment*, p. 61.

45. "The Correspondent" [John Trumbull], "A New System of Logic," *The Connecticut Journal and New Haven Post-Boy*, 1770, quoted by Tyler, in *Literary History*, 1:205.

46. Mayhew, *A Discourse concerning Unlimited Submission*, 1:238. (Emphasis mine.)

47. Fred Somkin, *Unquiet Eagle: Memory and Desire in the Idea of American Freedom, 1815–1860* (Ithaca, N.Y.: Cornell University Press, 1967), p. 57. Somkin's understanding of the American relationship to the land is also germane to this study. See *Unquiet Eagle*, pp. 91 ff.

48. Otis, *Rights of the British Colonies*, 1:444.

49. Circular Letter of the Province of Massachusetts Bay, February 11, 1768, in *History of the Rise, Progress and Termination of the American Revolution, Interspersed with Biographical, Political and Moral Observations*, by Mercy Otis Warren, 3 vols. (Boston: E. Larkin, 1805), 1:417–18.

50. [Alexander Hamilton], *The Farmer Refuted* (New York, 1775), in *Pamphlets of the American Revolution*, ed. Bailyn, 1:108.

51. Address to the States, April 24, 1783, *Journals of Congress*, 8:150.

52. Bernard Faÿ, *Revolution and Freemasonry, 1680–1800* (Boston: Little, Brown and Company, 1935), p. 231.

53. Ibid., pp. 229–30.

54. Ibid., pp. 315, 241–42; Philip Davidson, *Propaganda and the American Revolution, 1763–1783* (Chapel Hill, N.C.: University of North Carolina Press, 1941), p. 101.

55. Quoted in Faÿ, *Revolution and Freemasonry*, p. 239.

56. Ibid., pp. 245–46; *Pennsylvania Packet*, January 2, 1779, in *Diary of the American Revolution*, comp. Moore, 2:113–15.

57. Thomas Paine, "Origins of Freemasonry," in *The Life and Works of Thomas Paine*, ed. William M. Van der Weyde, 10 vols. (New Rochelle, N.Y.: Thomas Paine National Historical Association, 1925), 9:171–72.

58. I am indebted for this discussion of the symbolism of Freemasonry to Karen S. Campbell, whose manuscript "Freemasonry and the American Civil Religion," has been very helpful.

59. Mircea Eliade, *The Forge and the Crucible: The Origins and Structures of Alchemy* (1956; New York: Harper & Row, 1971), pp. 160 ff. The best short discussion of alchemy by Carl Jung is contained in *The Psychology of the Transference* (1946), printed in *The Collected Works of C. G. Jung*, 2d ed. (Princeton, N.J.: Princeton University Press, 1966), vol. 16, *The Practice of Psychotherapy*, pp. 163–323.

60. Fay, *Revolution and Freemasonry*, p. 317.

61. Allen, *Reason the Only Oracle of Man*, p. 473; George Washington, Farewell Address (1796), in *The Story of the Constitution*, by Sol Bloom (Washington, D.C.: U.S. Constitution Sesquicentennial Commission, 1937), p. 142.

62. Claude Lévi-Strauss, *Totemism* (Boston: Beacon Press, 1963), p. 89 et passim.

63. Boorstin, *Lost World of Thomas Jefferson*, p. 216.

64. Ibid., p. 237.

65. Arthur M. Schlesinger, Jr., *The Birth of the Nation: A Portrait of the American People on the Eve of Independence* (New York: Alfred A. Knopf, 1968), p. 39.

66. Thomas Jefferson to John Adams, Monticello, April 11, 1823, in *The Adams-Jefferson Letters: The Complete Correspondence between Thomas Jefferson and Abigail and John Adams*, ed. Lester J. Cappon, 2 vols. (Chapel Hill, N.C.: University of North Carolina Press, 1959), 2:594.

67. Benjamin Rush to John Adams, Philadelphia, July 21, 1789, in *Letters of Benjamin Rush*, ed. L. H. Butterfield, 2 vols. (Princeton: Princeton University Press, 1951), 1:524.

68. Elson, *Guardians of Tradition*, pp. 222–42.

69. Letter from Boston, November 15, 1774, *Bristol Gazette*, January 12, 1774, in *Letters on the American Revolution*, ed. Willard, pp. 9–10.

70. Joseph Barrell to ———, Salem, May 24, 1775, in *Boston in 1775: Letters from General Washington, Captain John Chester, Lieutenant Samuel B. Webb, and Joseph Barrell*, ed. Worthington C. Ford (Brooklyn, N.Y.: Historical Printing Club, 1892), p. 7.

71. Judge William Henry Drayton's Charge, Court of General Sessions

of the Peace, April 23, 1776, Charleston, S.C., in *Principles and Acts of the Revolution in America*, ed. Hezekiah Niles (Baltimore: William Ogden Niles, 1822), pp. 74, 79.

72. The Declaration of Independence, in *The Revolution in America, 1754–1788: Documents and Commentaries*, ed. J. R. Pole (Stanford, Calif.: Stanford University Press, 1970), pp. 36, 39.

73. Draft of a circular letter to accompany the Articles of Confederation, November 17, 1777, *Journals of Congress*, 3:404.

74. My formulation here follows that of Raffaele Pettazzoni, who wrote that the Judaeo-Christian God represented the convergence of two religious tendencies so that the attributes of the two were "concentrated in the person of a single Supreme Being who is the eternal and impassible Creator and at the same time omniscient, watchful, and avenging" (*The All-Knowing God: Researches into Early Religion and Culture* [London: Methuen & Co., Ltd., 1956], p. 25). See also, Raffaele Pettrazzoni, "The Supreme Being: Phenomenological Structure and Historical Development," in *The History of Religions: Essays in Methodology*, ed. Mircea Eliade and Joseph M. Kitagawa (Chicago: The University of Chicago Press, 1959), pp. 59–66, and Catherine Albanese, "Requiem for Memorial Day: Dissent in the Redeemer Nation," *American Quarterly* 26, no. 4 (October 1974):393–94.

Chapter 5

1. I am extending Lévi-Strauss's understanding of the meaning of totemism (*Totemism* [Boston: Beacon Press, 1963]) to include the feeling function. It was Lucien Lévy-Bruhl who, in *The "Soul" of the Primitive* (1923), delineated an understanding of *participation mystique* which made mystical identification of subject with object a touchstone of the "pre-logical mind" (Chicago: Henry Regnery Company, Gateway, 1966). My own usage modifies *participation mystique* in the direction of Emile Durkheim's sense of the projective identification between community and symbolic center or totem (*The Elementary Forms of the Religious Life* [1915] [New York: The Free Press, 1965], pp. 121–272). The union is more than casual but less than mystical.

2. Peter Brown, "The Rise and Function of the Holy Man in Late Antiquity," *Journal of Roman Studies* 61 (1971):81. My interpretation of the place and significance of George Washington owes much to the Peter Brown article which fits the American situation surprisingly well. Perhaps this is a confirmation of how intuitively right the patriots were in selecting Hellenistic models to guide them in their endeavor.

3. Mason L. Weems, *The Life of Washington* (9th ed., 1809), ed. Marcus Cunliffe (Cambridge, Mass.: Harvard University Press, 1962), p. 35.

4. Marcus Cunliffe, *George Washington: Man and Monument* (Boston: Little, Brown and Company, 1958), p. 213.

5. John Adams to the Continental Congress, February 19, 1777, in *George Washington*, ed. Morton Borden (Englewood Cliffs, N.J.: Prentice-Hall, 1969), p. 75.

6. John Adams to Benjamin Rush, Braintree, February 8, 1778, in *Old Family Letters: Copied from the Originals for Alexander Biddle*, series A (Philadelphia: M. B. Lippincott, 1892), 1:11; John Adams to Benjamin Rush, New York, April 4, 1790, in ibid., p. 55.

7. Benjamin Rush to William Marshall, Philadelphia, September 15, 1798, in *Letters of Benjamin Rush*, ed. L. H. Butterfield, 2 vols. (Princeton: Princeton University Press, 1951), 2:807.

8. Quoted by Caroline M. Kirkland, *Memoirs of Washington* (New York: D. Appleton & Co., 1857), p. 336.

9. Journal of a chaplain in the American army, July 4, 1775, quoted by Benjamin F. Morris, in *Christian Life and Character of the Civil Institutions of the United States* (Philadelphia: George W. Childs, 1864), p. 285.

10. Abigail Adams to John Adams, Braintree, July 16, 1775, in *Familiar Letters of John Adams and His Wife Abigail Adams, during the Revolution*, ed. Charles Francis Adams (1875; Boston: Houghton, Mifflin, and Company, 1898), p. 79.

11. Letter from Philadelphia, n.d., *Morning Post and Daily Advertiser*, January 16, 1776, in *Letters on the American Revolution, 1774–1776*, ed. Margaret W. Willard (1925; Port Washington, N.Y.: Kennikat Press, 1968), p. 228.

12. [Lydia Minturn Post], *Personal Recollections of the American Revolution* (November 27, 1776), ed. Sidney Barclay (New York: Rudd & Carleton, 1859), p. 54.

13. For a discussion of the Parke drama, see William A. Bryan, *George Washington in American Literature, 1775–1865* (New York: Columbia University Press, 1952), p. 173; Isaac Weld, February 22, 1796, in *George Washington*, ed. Borden, p. 98.

14. George Washington Parke Custis, *Recollections and Private Memoirs of Washington* (New York: Derby & Jackson, 1860), p. 172.

15. Bryan, *George Washington in American Literature*, pp. 83–84.

16. *Pennsylvania Journal*, September 10, 1777, in *The Diary of the American Revolution: From Newspapers and Original Documents*, comp. Frank Moore, 2 vols. (New York: Charles Scribner, 1860), 1:492; *New Jersey Journal*, October 31, 1781, in ibid., 2:528.

17. "A New Song to the Tune of 'The British Grenadiers'" (1775), quoted by Moses Coit Tyler, in *The Literary History of the American Revolution*, 2 vols. (New York: G. P. Putnam's Sons, 1897), 2:412–13; Peter St. John, "American Taxation," in *Songs and Ballads of the American Revolution*, ed. Frank Moore (New York: D. Appleton & Co., 1856), p. 12; Francis Hopkinson, "Camp Ballad" (1777), quoted by Tyler, in *Literary History*, 2:142–43.

18. David Ramsay, *The History of the American Revolution* (1789), 2 vols. (Lexington, Ky.: Downing and Phillips, 1815), 1:264.

19. Ibid., pp. 269, 322.

20. Weems, *Life of Washington*, p. 133. The Weems description essentially agreed with the more sober account by David Ramsay in *The Life of George Washington*, 3d ed. (Baltimore: J. Cushing, 1814), pp. 173–81. The first edition was published in 1807.

21. Ramsay, *Life of George Washington*, pp. 174–75.

22. Elias Boudinot, *Journal; or, Historical Recollections of American Events during the Revolutionary War* (Philadelphia: Frederick Bourquin, 1894), pp. 93–95.

23. Personal recollection of William A. Duer, president of Columbia College, quoted by Washington Irving, *Life of George Washington*, 5 vols. (New York: G. P. Putnam & Co., 1856–59), 5:254.

24. William S. Baker's *Bibliotheca Washingtoniana: A Descriptive List of the Biographies and Biographical Sketches of George Washington* (Philadelphia: Robert M. Lindsay, 1889) has listed this many separate accounts (pp. 1–7). The German almanac was the *Nord Americanische Calender* [sic], for which David Rittenhouse furnished the material. See Baker, *Bibliotheca Washingtoniana*, p. 6.

25. See Bryan, *George Washington in American Literature*, p. 53.

26. Ramsay, *History of the American Revolution*, 2:340. Ramsay repeated himself in *Life of George Washington*, pp. 153–54.

27. Abner Alden, *The Speaker* (1810), quoted by Ruth Miller Elson. *Guardians of Tradition: American Schoolbooks of the Nineteenth Century* (Lincoln: University of Nebraska Press, 1964), p. 33.

28. The Society of the Cincinnati was an organization formed in 1783 when the Continental Army was disbanding. It was envisioned as a hereditary association of the exsoldiers and their eldest male heirs. George Washington agreed to become its first president after the Society had come into being and seemed to acquiesce to its various ceremonial and liturgical trappings, such as the wearing of a silver eagle suspended from a blue ribbon as a distinctive mode of identification and annual meetings on the Fourth of July. The hereditary and military character of the association occasioned considerable public clamor which finally resulted in the alteration of the former. For good contemporary discussions, see William Gordon, *The History of the Rise, Progress, and Establishment of the Independence of the United States of America*, 3 vols. (New York: Hodge, Allen, and Campbell, 1789), 3:383–86, and Mercy Otis Warren, *History of the Rise, Progress and Termination of the American Revolution, Interspersed with Biographical, Political and Moral Observations*, 3 vols. (Boston: E. Larkin, 1805), 3:281 ff.

29. Timothy Dwight, *The Conquest of Canaan* (1785) (1788; reprint ed., Westport, Conn.: Greenwood Press, 1970); George Duffield, "A Sermon Preached in the Third Presbyterian Church in the City of Philadelphia, on

December 11th, 1783, on the Restoration of Peace," in *The Patriot Preachers of the American Revolution*, ed. Frank Moore (New York: Charles T. Evans, 1862), pp. 361–62; Ezra Stiles, "The United States Elevated to Glory and Honor" (May 8, 1783) in *The Pulpit of the American Revolution*, ed. John Wingate Thornton (1860; reprint ed., New York: Da Capo Press, 1970), p. 442.

30. Kenneth Silverman, *Timothy Dwight* (New York: Twayne Publishers, Inc., 1969), p. 32.

31. Dwight, *Conquest of Canaan*, 2:736–38; 6:599–608.

32. Letter of George Washington, January 23, 1778, as quoted by Gordon, *History*, 2:319.

33. John Marshall, *The Life of George Washington, Commander in Chief of the American Forces, during the War Which Established the Independence of His Country, and First President of the United States*, 5 vols. (Philadelphia: C. P. Wayne, 1804–7), 2:16; 3:338–39; 5:356–57, 409.

34. Jared Sparks, *The Life of George Washington* (Boston: Ferdinand Andrews, 1839), pp. 75–76, 465. Sparks's *Life* first appeared in 1837.

35. Irving, *Life of George Washington*, 1:183; 3:340–41; 5:203, 301.

36. Arthur Tappan, quoted by Dixon Wecter, *The Hero in America: A Chronicle of Hero-Worship* (Ann Arbor, Mich.: The University of Michigan Press, 1941), p. 129; Phillips Payson, "A Sermon, Delivered at Chelsea, January 14, 1800," quoted by Bryan, *George Washington in American Literature*, p. 59.

37. Quoted by Bryan, *George Washington in American Literature*, p. 62.

38. Paul Suinin (1815), quoted by Cunliffe, *George Washington*, p. 13.

39. T. Erskine, "Recollections of General Washington," in [Post], *Personal Recollections*, pp. 221–22.

40. Warren, *History of the Rise*, 3:317–18.

41. Elson, *Guardians of Tradition*, p. 194.

42. John Hubbard, *The American Reader*, 5th ed. (1811), quoted by Elson, *Guardians of Tradition*, p. 195.

43. Ignatius Thomson, *The Patriots Monitor, for New Hampshire* (1810) in ibid., p. 198.

44. Daniel Staniford, *The Art of Reading* (1806), in ibid., p. 196; Hubbard, *The American Reader*.

45. Joel Barlow, *The Columbiad* (Washington City: Joseph Milligan, Georgetown, 1825), 5:412–15; 7:567–70, in *The Works of Joel Barlow*, 2 vols. (Gainesville, Fla.: Scholars' Facsimiles & Reprints, 1970), vol. 2.

46. Daniel Webster, "A Discourse in Commemoration of the Lives and Services of John Adams and Thomas Jefferson," in *The Works of Daniel Webster*, 6 vols. (Boston: Charles C. Little and James Brown, 1851), 1:148.

47. John Quincy Adams, *The Jubilee of the Constitution: A Discourse Delivered at the Request of the New York Historical Society* (New York: Samuel Colman, 1839), pp. 6–7.

48. Francis C. Gray, *Oration Delivered before the Legislature of Massachusetts . . . on the Hundredth Anniversary of the Birth of George Washington* (Boston: Dutton and Wentworth, 1832), pp. 72–73.

49. James K. Paulding, *A Life of Washington*, 2 vols. (New York: Harper & Brothers, 1835), 2:230–31.

50. Abraham Lincoln, February 22, 1842, in *George Washington*, ed. Borden, p. 147.

51. [Horatio Hastings Weld], *Pictorial Life of George Washington* (Philadelphia: Lindsay and Blakiston, 1845), pp. iii–iv; Nathaniel Hawthorne (1858), quoted by Borden, ed., *George Washington*, p. 1.

52. Ramsay, *Life of George Washington* (1814 edition), frontispiece.

53. Appended to Gray, *Oration*, p. 80.

54. [Catharine Maria Sedgwick], "The Linwoods; or, 'Sixty-Years Since' in America" (1835), quoted by Bryan, *George Washington in American Literature*, p. 207; Kirkland, *Memoirs of Washington*, p. 234.

55. The best account of the legends of Washington the pietist is contained in Paul Boller's *George Washington and Religion* (Dallas: Southern Methodist University Press, 1963), pp. 14 ff. Early sources include [Weld], *Pictorial Life of George Washington* (see especially pp. 37–38, 89, 154), and Kirkland, *Memoirs of Washington*, pp. 473–81. See also Morris, *Christian Life*, pp. 500–501.

56. Custis, *Recollections*, pp. 413–14.

57. Paulding, *Life of Washington*, 2:283; Gray, *Oration*, p. 68.

58. Weems, *Life of Washington*, pp. 20, 187–214 and passim. See also [Thomas Condie], *Biographical Memoirs of Gen. George Washington, First President of the United States* (1798) (Lexington, Ky.: Downing and Phillips, 1815), pp. 439–40; Weld, *Pictorial Life of George Washington*, pp. 34, 146; Custis, *Recollections*, pp. 421–22, 163.

59. George Washington, Farewell Address (1796), in *Life of George Washington*, by Irving, 5:334.

60. Daniel Webster, "The Character of Washington" (February 22, 1832), in *Works*, 1:227, 229.

61. John Quincy Adams, *Jubilee of the Constitution*, p. 51.

62. Gray, *Oration*, p. 53.

63. William A. Bryan, "George Washington: Symbolic Guardian of the Republic," *William and Mary Quarterly*, 3d ser. 7 (January 1950):63.

64. Marshall, *Life of George Washington*, 2:19–20.

65. Ramsay, *Life of George Washington*, p. 236.

66. Paulding, *Life of Washington*, 1:216–20.

67. Kirkland, *Memoirs of Washington*, pp. 55–56.

68. Irving, *Life of George Washington*, 3:iii.

69. See Bryan, *George Washington in American Literature*, p. 108.

70. Custis, *Recollections*, pp. 127–28.

71. Daniel J. Boorstin, *The Americans: The National Experience* (New York: Vintage Books, 1965), p. 349.

72. [Weld], *Pictorial Life of George Washington*, pp. 219–20.

73. (Washington, D.C., 1858), cited by Baker, *Bibliotheca Washingtoniana*, p. 127.

74. Joseph Campbell, *The Hero with a Thousand Faces* (1949; Princeton, N.J.: Princeton University Press, 1972), p. 347. Fred Somkin quotes Campbell in his account of "The Greatest Man in the World" (*Unquiet Eagle: Memory and Desire in the Idea of American Freedom, 1815–1860* [Ithaca, N.Y.: Cornell University Press, 1967], p. 172). My own discussion follows Somkin's.

75. Somkin, *Unquiet Eagle*, pp. 169, 168.

76. Rufus Wilmot Griswold, *The Republican Court; or, American Society in the Days of Washington* (1855), quoted by Cunliffe, ed., in *Life of Washington*, by Weems, p. xl.

77. Weems, *Life of Washington*, p. 27.

78. Sparks, *Life of George Washington*, p. 9; Benson J. Lossing, *Pictorial Fieldbook on the American Revolution*, 2 vols. (New York: Harper & Brothers, 1860), 2:221.

79. *Essex Gazette*, January 18, 1776, in *Diary of the American Revolution*, comp. Moore, 1:192. The child was Martha Dandridge Bancroft of Dunstable, Massachusetts.

80. Ramsay, *History of the American Revolution*, 2:339–40.

81. Kirkland, *Memoirs of Washington*, p. 442.

82. Weems, *Life of Washington*, pp. 53–54.

83. Elson, *Guardians of Tradition*, p. 202.

84. Bryan, *George Washington in American Literature*, p. 118.

85. Sparks, *Life of George Washington*, p. vi.

86. Irving, *Life of George Washington*, 1:vi.

87. For a good discussion of the *theios aner* in the literary context of areta'ogy, see Morton Smith, "Prolegomena to a Discussion of Aretalogies, Divine Men, the Gospels and Jesus," *Journal of Biblical Literature*, 90 (1971): 174–99, especially 174–88. Paul J. Achtemeier's "Gospel Miracle Tradition and the Divine Man" (*Interpretation* 26 [1972]:174–97) is also helpful. My understanding of the "divine man" throughout the chapter has been colored by these treatments of a Hellenistic model. The paradigmatic structure of lives of divine men has been alluded to briefly in these articles, and both Gerardus van der Leeuw and Joachim Wach have discussed a paradigm of the holy founder, respectively in *Religion in Essence and Manifestation*, 2 vols. (1933; New York: Harper & Row, 1963), 2:650–54, and *Sociology of Religion* (1944; Chicago: University of Chicago Press, Phoenix Books, 1962), pp. 341–44. By far the most formative element in my conceptualization of the paradigmatic structure of the life of Washington has come from a manuscript by Alan L. Miller, "Formalist Analysis of Selected Japanese Buddhist Saints' Lives." Miller constructs a model of the lives of holy men in which birth and leaving the family are the manifestation of potentiality; initiation, ascetic practices, study, and meditation represent a period of with-

drawal and struggle; accomplishment occurs in an encounter with the sacred which transforms the candidate into a true holy man; struggle characterizes his later existence in such incidents as conflict with demons; a return to the world engages him in useful and benevolent endeavor; and finally his existence is crowned by a departure in which he again and ultimately encounters the sacred. I, of course, have modified the schema in light of the horizontal character of the American materials.

88. Weems, *Life of Washington*, pp. 55–57.

89. Ibid., pp. 10, 21, 20, 12, 19, 22.

90. Ibid., pp. 30, 42.

91. Sparks, *Life of George Washington*, p. 66; Custis, *Recollections*, pp. 303–4.

92. Samuel Davies, "Religion and Patriotism the Constituents of a Good Soldier" (1755), in *Sermons on Important Subjects*, 4 vols. (London: W. Baynes, 1815), 3:382 n. Davies was cited by Weems in *Life of Washington*, p. 42, and [Weld] in *Pictorial Life of George Washington*, pp. 28–29.

93. Weems, *Life of Washington*, pp. 53, 57–58.

94. Ibid., p. 102. This theme became a favorite in nineteenth-century schoolbooks. See Elson, *Guardians of Tradition*, p. 208.

95. Weems, *Life of Washington*, pp. 119–20.

96. Ibid., pp. 131, 166.

97. Ibid., pp. 167, 168.

98. [Condie], *Biographical Memoirs of Gen. George Washington, First President of the United States*, p. 480; Kirkland, *Memoirs of Washington*, p. 457.

99. Weems, *Life of Washington*, pp. 122, 123, 166.

Chapter 6

1. Sol Bloom, *The Story of the Constitution* (Washington, D.C.: U.S. Constitution Sesquicentennial Commission, 1937), p. 166.

2. John Adams to Abigail Adams, Philadelphia, July 3, 1776, in *Familiar Letters of John Adams and His Wife Abigail Adams, during the Revolution*, ed. Charles Francis Adams (1875; Boston: Houghton, Mifflin, and Company, 1898), p. 193.

3. Margaret W. Willard, ed., *Letters on the American Revolution, 1774–1776* (1925; Port Washington, N.Y.: Kennikat Press, 1968), pp. xvi–xvii.

4. Thomas Paine, *Common Sense*, in *Tracts of the American Revolution, 1763–1776*, ed. Merrill Jensen (Indianapolis: Bobbs-Merrill Company, 1967), p. 434. My formulation in what follows owes much to Hannah Arendt's *On Revolution* (New York: The Viking Press, 1965). Arendt's argument in this book rested on an understanding of the God of the patriots as an inactive ground to supply the mental function of the absolute kings of Europe in the thought world of the men of the Revolution. But the real

absolute, for Arendt, expressed itself more and more concretely in patriotic action in the *novus ordo saeclorum*. See Arendt, *On Revolution*, pp. 179–215. My debt to Arendt has been pervasive in the present work.

5. Michael Kammen, *People of Paradox: An Inquiry Concerning the Origins of American Civilization* (New York: Alfred A. Knopf, 1972), p. 232; Carl L. Becker, *The Declaration of Independence* (1942; reprint ed., New York: Vintage Books, 1958), pp. 277–78.

6. John Adams (1822), *The Works of John Adams the Second President of the United States*, ed. Charles F. Adams, 10 vols. (Boston: Little, Brown and Company, 1850–56), 2:512; John Adams to Abigail Adams, Philadelphia, July 3, 1776, in *Familiar Letters*, p. 191; John Adams to Abigail Adams, Philadelphia, July 3, 1776, in ibid., p. 194. (Two letters dated July 3 were sent by John Adams to his wife, Abigail.)

7. John Adams to Samuel Chase, Philadelphia, July 9, 1776, in *Works*, 9:420.

8. *Constitutional Gazette*, July 17, 1776, in *The Diary of the American Revolution, From Newspapers and Original Documents*, comp. Frank Moore, 2 vols. (New York: Charles Scribner, 1860), 1:269.

9. *Pennsylvania Journal*, July 17, 1776, in ibid., p. 271; *Universal Intelligencer, and Pennsylvania Evening Post*, October 8, 1776, in ibid., pp. 283–84.

10. Major Barber to Mr. Caldwell, July 17, 1776, quoted by John H. Hazelton, *The Declaration of Independence: Its History* (1906; reprint ed., New York: Da Capo Press, 1970), p. 245.

11. Benjamin Rush to Charles Lee, Philadelphia, July 23, 1776, in *Letters of Benjamin Rush*, ed. L. H. Butterfield, 2 vols. (Princeton: Princeton University Press, 1951), 1:103.

12. Abigail Adams to John Adams, Boston, August 14, 1776, in *Familiar Letters*, p. 212.

13. John Quincy Adams, secretary of state, to the Senate of the United States, January 2, 1824, quoted by Hazelton, *Declaration of Independence*, p. 289. There are also good accounts of the history of the Declaration of Independence in John C. Fitzpatrick, *The Spirit of Revolution: New Light from Some of the Original Sources of American History* (Boston: Houghton Mifflin Company, 1924) and Dumas Malone, *The Story of the Declaration of Independence* (New York: Oxford University Press, 1954).

14. Malone, *Story of the Declaration of Independence*, p. 264.

15. David Ramsay, *The History of the American Revolution* (1789), 2 vols. (Lexington, Ky.: Downing and Phillips, 1815), 1:416.

16. Mercy Otis Warren, *History of the Rise, Progress and Termination of the American Revolution, Interspersed with Biographical, Political and Moral Observations*, 3 vols. (Boston: E. Larkin, 1805), 3:308.

17. George Bancroft, quoted by Hazelton, *Declaration of Independence*, p. 239.

18. Ruth Miller Elson, *Guardians of Tradition: American Schoolbooks of*

the Nineteenth Century (Lincoln: University of Nebraska Press, 1964), p. 289.

19. Moses Coit Tyler, *The Literary History of the American Revolution,* 2 vols. (New York: G. P. Putnam's Sons, 1897), 1:521.

20. The term is borrowed from David W. Noble's classic idea and work concerning American antihistorical historians, *Historians against History: The Frontier Thesis and the National Covenant in American Historical Writing since 1830* (Minneapolis: University of Minnesota Press, 1965).

21. John Adams to Abigail Adams, Philadelphia, July 3, 1776, in *Familiar Letters,* p. 194.

22. *Pennsylvania Gazette,* July 9, 1777, quoted by Hazelton, *Declaration of Independence,* pp. 282–83.

23. June 24, 1779, *Journals of Congress,* 13 vols. (Philadelphia: Folwell's Press, 1800), 5:204.

24. Ramsay, *History of the American Revolution,* 1:410.

25. Daniel Webster, "The Addition to the Capitol" (July 4, 1851), in *The Works of Daniel Webster,* 6 vols. (Boston: Charles C. Little and James Brown, 1851), 2:599, 618, 619.

26. Webster, "A Discourse in Commemoration of the Lives and Services of John Adams and Thomas Jefferson," in ibid., 1:125, 113.

27. John Quincy Adams, *An Oration delivered before the Inhabitants of the Town of Newburyport . . . July 4, 1837,* quoted by Fred Somkin, *Unquiet Eagle: Memory and Desire in the Idea of American Freedom, 1815–1860* (Ithaca, N.Y.: Cornell University Press, 1967), p. 204.

28. *Rivington's Gazetteer,* May 11, 1775, in *Diary of the American Revolution,* comp. Moore, 1:75.

29. *Virginia Gazette,* May 27, 1775, in ibid., p. 77.

30. Postscript to *Pennsylvania Packet,* June 19, 1775, in ibid., pp. 88–89.

31. Edward F. Humphrey, *Nationalism and Religion in America, 1774–1789* (Boston: Chipman Law Publishing Company, 1924), pp. 407–8. (Emphasis mine.)

32. September 6, 1774, *Journals of Congress,* 1:11.

33. This formula was used on the death of William H. Drayton, the delegate from South Carolina, September 4, 1779, *Journals of Congress,* 5:255. A nearly identical resolution had been passed the year before on the death of Philip Livingston of New York, June 12, 1778, *Journals of Congress,* 4:247.

34. Congressional committee report, September 11, 1777, quoted by Benjamin F. Morris, in *Christian Life and Character of the Civil Institutions of the United States* (Philadelphia: George W. Childs, 1864), p. 216.

35. Resolution of Congress, September 1782, in ibid., p. 217.

36. A broadside announced the resolves of the Massachusetts House of Representatives on February 20, 1768. See Nathaniel Paine, "Early American Broadsides, 1680–1800," *Proceedings of the American Antiquarian Society,* n.s. 11 (April 1896–April 1897):471. The anecdotes regarding Philadelphia

are from Benson J. Lossing, *Pictorial Fieldbook on the American Revolution*, 2 vols. (New York: Harper & Brothers, 1860), 2:52.

37. October 20, 1774, *Journals of Congress*, 1:33, and in Samuel E. Morison, ed., *Sources and Documents Illustrating the American Revolution, 1764–1788*, 2d ed. (New York: Oxford University Press, 1965), p. 124.

38. June 30, 1775, *Journals of Congress*, 1:128–29.

39. *New York Journal*, November 2, 1778, in *Diary of the American Revolution*, comp. Moore, 2:100.

40. Winthrop Hudson, "Fast Days and Civil Religion," in *Theology in Sixteenth and Seventeenth Century England* (Los Angeles: William Andrews Clark Memorial Library, University of California, 1971), especially pp. 14–15, 6.

41. Congressional Fast Day Resolution, June 12, 1775, *Journals of Congress*, 1:110.

42. John Adams to Abigail Adams, Philadelphia, July 23, 1775, in *Familiar Letters*, p. 84.

43. *Holt's Journal*, June 1, 1775, in *Diary of the American Revolution*, comp. Moore, 1:87–88.

44. Eleazar Wheelock, quoted by Frederick Chase, *A History of Dartmouth College and the Town of Hanover, New Hampshire* (1891), ed. John K. Lord, 2 vols., 2d ed. (Brattleboro, Vt.: Vermont Printing Co., 1913–28), 1:349. Wheelock's remarks in 1775 were directed toward the provincial congress at Exeter.

45. George Washington issued only two proclamations for national Days of Thanksgiving during his presidency, one for the Constitution and one for the suppression of the Whiskey Rebellion.

46. John Marshall, *The Life of George Washington, Commander in Chief of the American Forces, during the War Which Established the Independence of His Country, and First President of the United States*, 5 vols. (Philadelphia: C. P. Wayne, 1804–7), 4:451–52. There were similar commemorations of the Count de Rochambeau and the Count de Grasse.

47. George Washington, General Orders, Headquarters at Wentz's, Worcester Township, October 18, 1777, quoted by Paul Boller, *George Washington and Religion* (Dallas: Southern Methodist University Press, 1963), p. 54; *Boston Gazette*, ca. October, 1777, in *Diary of the American Revolution*, comp. Moore, 1:513.

48. *New Jersey Gazette*, February 17, 1779, and March 3, 1779; *Pennsylvania Packet*, March 6, 1779, in ibid., 2:128–29, 130–34; *Pennsylvania Packet*, August 24, 1779, in ibid., p. 213.

49. *Middlesex Journal*, May 2, 1776, in ibid., 1:239.

50. *Pennsylvania Journal*, September 3, 1777, in ibid., pp. 446–47.

51. Quoted by Morris, in *Christian Life*, p. 622. Interestingly Marshall Smelser has declared in his new bicentennial history of the Revolution: "Problably no modern civilized nation has venerated its national emblem as much as Americans. To them it has assumed a moral value transcending the

mundane purposes of national identification. As a tribal totem it satisfies the real and almost universal hunger for a public symbol of spiritual kinship above and invulnerable to the contentions and changes of politics—and for which no other totem is available to the United States" (*The Winning of Independence: The Quadrangle Bicentennial History of the American Revolution* [Chicago: Quadrangle Books, 1972], pp. 179–80).

52. John Adams to Abigail Adams, Philadelphia, August 14, 1776, in *Familiar Letters*, p. 211.

53. Report of the Congressional Committee, May 17, 1780, in *Journals of the Continental Congress, 1774–1789*, ed. Worthington C. Ford, et al., 34 vols. (Washington, D.C.: Government Printing Office, 1904–37), 17:434.

54. June 20, 1782, *Journals of Congress*, 7:301.

55. Quoted by Morris, in *Christian Life*, p. 248.

56. Benjamin Rush to Richard Price, Philadelphia, June 2, 1787, in *Letters*, 1:418–19.

57. Roger Sherman, June 28, 1787, in *Journal of the Federal Convention*, rec. James Madison, and ed. E. H. Scott, 2 vols. (1840; reprint ed., Chicago: Scott, Foresman and Co., 1898), 1:258; John Dickinson, August 13, 1787, in ibid., 2:517.

58. Luther Martin, in *Secret Proceedings and Debates of the Convention: Assembled at Philadelphia in the Year 1787, for the Purpose of Forming the Constitution of the United States of America*, rec. Robert Yates (Albany, N.Y.: Websters and Skinners, 1821), p. 87.

59. Benjamin Franklin, June 28, 1787, in *Journal of the Federal Convention*, 1:259–60; Madison, in ibid., pp. 260–61. (Emphasis mine.)

60. Gouverneur Morris, George Mason, and James Wilson, September 4, 1787, in ibid., 2:657–59; September 13, 1787, in ibid., p. 719.

61. James Madison, June 26, 1787, in *Secret Proceedings and Debates of the Convention*, p. 169.

62. The best treatment of this dynamic is contained in Bernard Bailyn, *The Ideological Origins of the American Revolution* (Cambridge, Mass.: Harvard University Press, Belknap Press, 1967), pp. 55–93.

63. John Dickinson, June 7, 1787, in *Secret Proceedings and Debates of the Convention*, p. 107.

64. Benjamin Franklin, September 17, 1787, in *Journal of the Federal Convention*, 2:763.

65. Benjamin Rush, "Address to the People of the United States" (1787), in *Principles and Acts of the Revolution in America*, ed. Hezekiah Niles (Baltimore: William Ogden Niles, 1822), p. 402.

66. James Madison, "Federalist No. 45," in *The Federalist*, by Alexander Hamilton, James Madison, and John Jay; and ed. Benjamin F. Wright (Cambridge, Mass.: Harvard University Press, 1961), p. 329.

67. Adams, *Works*, 3:478 (The Earl of Clarendon to William Pym, *Boston Gazette*, no. 3 [January 27, 1766]). Bernard Bailyn elucidated the Adams understanding and its representativeness in *The Ideological Origins of the*

American Revolution, pp. 68 ff. For a discussion of the more traditional understanding of a constitution, see ibid., pp. 175–76 ff.

68. James Madison, "Federalist No. 53," in *Federalist,* p. 365. There had been an older British tradition established by the Magna Carta to which the patriots viewed themselves as more nearly analogous. But the real point seemed to be the usage which surrounded the term *constitution.*

69. James Monroe wrote a reasoned discourse *against* the adoption of the Constitution (*Some Observations on the Constitution* [Petersburg: 1788]).

70. Warren, *History of the Rise,* 3:364.

71. Mordecai Myers, in *Memoirs of American Jews: 1775–1865,* ed. Jacob R. Marcus, 3 vols. (Philadelphia: Jewish Publication Society of America, 1955), 1:54.

72. Warren, *History of the Rise,* 3:357.

73. Woodrow Wilson, *Congressional Government: A Study in American Politics* (Boston: Houghton Mifflin and Co., 1885), p. 4.

74. Enos Hitchcock, *An Oration: Delivered July 4, 1788, at the Request of the Inhabitants of the Town of Providence, in Celebration of the Anniversary of American Independence, and of the Accession of Nine States to the Federal Constitution* (Providence, R.I.: Bennett Wheeler, 1788), p. 18.

75. Jonathan Boucher, *A View of the Causes and the Consequences of the American Revolution* (1797) (New York: Russell & Russell, 1967), p. lxix.

76. *Connecticut Gazette,* November 2, 1787, quoted by Frank I. Schechter, "The Early History of the Tradition of the Constitution," *American Political Science Review* 9, no. 4 (November 1915):724.

77. *New York Packet,* October 2, 1787, in ibid., pp. 724–25.

78. These items are listed in Charles Evans, *American Bibliography,* 14 vols. (New York: Peter Smith, 1941–59), 7:213 ff.

79. Aaron Hall, *An Oration . . . to Celebrate the Ratification of the Federal Constitution by the State of New-Hampshire* (June 30, 1788) (Keene, N.H.: James D. Griffith, 1788), pp. 6–7, 11.

80. Simeon Baldwin, *An Oration Pronounced before the Citizens of New-Haven, July 4, 1788* (New Haven: Meigs, 1788), pp. 8–9, 13, 15.

81. Hitchcock, *Oration,* pp. 9, 12, 17.

82. George Bancroft, *History of the Formation of the Constitution,* 3d ed. (New York: D. Appleton, 1885), pp. 392, 406.

83. Myers, in *Memoirs of American Jews,* ed. Marcus, 1:55.

84. Ramsay, *History of the American Revolution,* 2:351.

85. Francis Hopkinson, *Account of the Grand Federal Procession in Philadelphia, July 4, 1788, to Which Are Added Mr. Wilson's Oration, and a Letter on the Stbject* [sic] *of the Procession* (Philadelphia: Carey, 1788), pp. 1–14.

86. Benjamin Rush to Elias Boudinot [?], Philadelphia, July 9, 1788, in *Letters* 1:474. The same letter had appeared anonymously, bound with the Hopkinson pamphlet.

87. Hopkinson, *Account of the Grand Federal Procession*, p. 18.

88. Benjamin Rush to Elias Boudinot[?] in *Letters*, 1:470–71.

89. Ibid., p. 475.

90. Alexander Hamilton, "Federalist No. 85," in *Federalist*, p. 547; James Madison, "Federalist No. 37," in ibid., p. 270; Alexander Hamilton, "Federalist No. 78," in ibid., p. 494.

91. Louis H. Pollak, ed., *The Constitution and the Supreme Court: A Documentary History*, 2 vols. (New York: The World Publishing Company, 1966), 1:164.

92. *Marbury v. Madison* (1803), quoted by Samuel Eliot Morison, *The Oxford History of the American People* (New York: Oxford University Press, 1965), p. 363; *McCulloch v. Maryland* (1815), in Pollak, ed., *The Constitution and the Supreme Court*, 1:215.

93. Daniel J. Boorstin, in *The American Supreme Court*, by Robert McCloskey, The Chicago History of American Civilization (Chicago: University of Chicago Press, 1960), pp. v–vi.

94. Elson, *Guardians of Tradition*, pp. 292–93, recounts these estimations of the Constitution.

95. Joel Barlow, *The Columbiad* (Washington City: Joseph Milligan, Georgetown, 1825), 8:399–401; 9:699–702, in *The Works of Joel Barlow*, 2 vols. (Gainesville, Fla.: Scholars' Facsimiles & Reprints, 1970), vol. 2.

96. Jedidiah Morse, "A View of the Principles of the Constitution and Government of the United States," in *Annals of the American Revolution; Or, A Record of their Causes and Events* by Jedidiah Morse (Hartford, Conn.: Oliver D. Cooke & Sons, 1824), p. 400.

97. John Quincy Adams, *The Jubilee of the Constitution: A Discourse Delivered at the Request of the New York Historical Society* (New York: Samuel Colman, 1839), pp. 11, 40, 119–20. One copy of the Adams speech, in the University of Chicago Library, had been bound with a collection of sermons.

98. Bancroft, *History of the Formation of the Constitution*, pp. 441–42, 438.

99. Here I follow Somkin, *Unquiet Eagle*, p. 112.

Epilogue

1. The language has been suggested by a recent study of the mythic power of violence on the American colonial frontier by Richard Slotkin (*Regeneration through Violence: The Mythology of the American Frontier, 1600–1860* [Middletown, Conn.: Wesleyan University Press, 1973]). Slotkin's pursuit of the theme in frontier experience during a period which includes the time of the Revolution employs categories which evoke those of the history of religions.

2. Mircea Eliade, *Myths, Dreams, and Mysteries: The Encounter between Contemporary Myths and Archaic Realities* (New York: Harper & Row, 1960), p. 235.

3. For a discussion of the relationship between eschatology and cosmogony, see Mircea Eliade, *Myth and Reality* (New York: Harper & Row, 1963), pp. 54–74.

Index

Bland, Richard, 52
Boardman, Reverend, 103
Boorstin, Daniel, 117, 125, 137, 168, 218, 249n30
Boston Committee of Correspondence, 25, 43
Boston Gazette, 73, 90, 91
Boston Massacre, 50, 61–62, 63, 85; orations, 24, 72, 73, 77, 92, 106, 239n86. *See also* Rituals, Boston Massacre
Boston Port Bill, 50, 75–76, 78, 96
Boston Tea Party, 74, 131. *See also* Rituals, Boston Tea Party; Tea Act
Boucher, Jonathan, 12, 13, 53, 78, 209
Boudinot, Elias, 110, 152
Braddock, Edward, 157, 177
Briant, Lemuel, 36
Bridenbaugh, Carl, 6, 19
British as Egyptians. *See* New Israel
British cruelty, 92–93
Broadsides, 11, 31, 67, 73, 75, 89, 91, 96, 104, 113, 186, 238n66
Brown, Peter, 144, 252n2
Bryan, William A., 150
Bunker Hill Monument, 107. *See also* Battle of Bunker Hill
Burgoyne, John, 103
Bute, Lord, 59, 61, 88, 91

Cabal, Conway, 148
Calvin, John, 55
Calvinism, 34, 38, 42, 95, 127, 134
Calvinism, God of. *See* God of Battles
Campbell, Karen S., 251n58
Celebrations. *See* Rituals
Chalmers, George, 21
Charles I, King, 23, 39
Chase, Samuel, 185
Chauncy, Charles, 36, 37, 40, 41, 88, 121, 123, 187
Cherry, Conrad, 6
Chevalier, Michel de, 66
Church, Benjamin, 74, 85
Church, national, 18, 184, 193, 195
Civil celebrations. *See* Rituals
Civil church. *See* Church, national
Civil faith. *See* Civil religion

Civil liberty. *See* Liberty, civil
Civil religion, ix, x, xi, xii, xiii, 4, 5, 6, 7, 15, 16, 44, 45, 58, 100, 108, 129, 193, 197, 202, 204, 216, 218, 220, 223
Clergy, role of, 11, 37–39
Clinton, Henry, 63
Coke, Edward, 121, 248n22
Coleman, Benjamin, 34
Committees of correspondence, 43, 50, 55, 58, 130
Common faith. *See* Civil religion
Common religion. *See* Civil religion
Communitas, 48, 51, 134
Congress, 3, 6, 11, 18, 24, 25, 83, 87, 88, 93, 112, 117, 122, 124, 125, 128, 130, 141, 147, 150, 157, 159, 169, 178, 179, 183, 184, 185, 187, 190, 193–202, 219
Congress Sunday, 197
Connecticut Gazette, 209
Constitution, 9, 16, 53, 68, 161, 164, 165, 176, 182, 183, 184, 188, 193, 194, 203, 205–19, 261n45; as sacrament, 18, 182, 183, 184, 202, 215
Constitution, British, 52, 203, 207
Constitutional Convention, 145, 163, 202–5, 206, 208
Constitutional Gazette, 68, 82, 186
Constitutional Procession, 176
Continental Army, 145, 163, 194, 200
Conversion experience. *See* Revivalism
Cooke, Samuel, 21, 51, 121
Coolidge, Joseph, Jr., 188
Cooper, James Fenimore, 173
Cooper, Samuel, 37
Cornwallis, Charles, 150, 161, 199
Cosmic Tree, 17, 58–60, 237n45
Covenant, xi, 18, 33, 34, 43, 44, 98, 122, 184, 200, 207, 219, 220, 233n68, 249n30; Puritan, 43, 80
Coxe, Daniel, 129
Crane, Millard E., 3
Creator God. *See* Nature, God of
Crèvecoeur, Hector St. John, 110
Cromwell, Oliver, 23
Cunliffe, Marcus, 146
Custis, George Washington Parke, 150, 164, 167, 177

274

Twenty-fifth of September, 95, 244n61. *See also* Rituals, Arnold, Benedict

Tyler, Moses Coit, 94, 189

Unitarianism, 115
University of Pennsylvania, 139
University of Virginia, 139

Virginia Gazette, 87, 105, 193

Warner, William Lloyd, 5
Warren, Joseph, 24, 73, 106, 131
Warren, Mercy Otis, 27, 30–31, 49, 50, 51–52, 54, 55, 69, 75, 76, 84, 89, 93, 105, 106, 109, 131, 159, 188, 207, 208
Washington, George, xii, 3, 8, 16, 18, 79, 88, 106, 130, 131, 142, 143–81, 190, 199, 213, 215, 252n2, 254n28; Ascension, 179, 180; father, 142, 145, 153, 154, 155, 160, 163, 167, 170, 172, 178, 179, 181, 191; founder, 142, 145, 146, 162, 166, 168, 172, 178, 181, 185 (*see also* Paradigm of divine man); hierophany, 162, 167; holy man, 144, 174 (*see also* Paradigm of divine man); relics, 168–70; rituals, *see* Rituals, Washington; statements by, 30, 83, 105–6, 117, 118–19, 124, 136, 165, 261n45; veneration of, 148, 149, 152–54, 159–60, 171, 172, 173, 179. See also *Theios aner* and for biographies see Hardie, James; Irving, Washington; Kirkland, Caroline; McGuire, Edward G.; Marshall, John; Norton, John;

Ramsay, David; Sparks, Jared; Weems, Mason; Weld, Horatio Hastings; Wineberger, J.
Washington, Martha, 169, 171–72
Washington, Mary, 171, 175
Washington Benevolent Societies, 159
Washington legend, 147, 256n55
Webb, Nathan, 28
Weber, Max, x
Webster, Daniel, 68, 107, 161, 165, 191, 192
Weems, Mason, 145, 151, 153, 160, 171, 172, 174, 175, 176, 177, 178, 179, 180, 181
Weld, Horatio Hastings, 162, 168, 177
Weld, Isaac, 149
West, Samuel, 22, 83, 91, 122
Wheelock, Eleazar, 104, 198
Whiskey Rebellion, 147, 158, 261n45
Whitaker, Nathaniel, 31, 72
Whitefield, George, 49, 103
Wilkes, John, 65
Willard, Margaret, 183
Williams, J. Paul, 4
Williams, Robin, x
Wilson, James, 13–14, 204, 215
Wilson, Woodrow, 208
Wineberger, J. A., 169
Winthrop, John, 27, 100
Wise, John, 35, 36, 43, 44, 121
Witherspoon, John, 30, 83, 93, 100
Woodmason, Charles, 51
Writs of Assistance, 121, 217

Yale University, 115, 149